Solunarukh

A TIMELESS TALE OF LOVE

THE PHILOSOPHOET

Philosophoetic

Publisher-Logo, and Concept-Art found within, by [Rigel]|[*rigelpan@aol.com*]

Book Cover, by [Suvajit Das]|[*architectofdesignaod@gmail.com*]

First edition 2023

to, Us

Adventures

Prologue

*"But very few modern people think
friendship a love of comparable value or
even a love at all."*
C.S. Lewis|The Four Loves

Can friendship lead to enlightenment? And, what of Love? Is there a love which leads to true wisdom and truth? Can Love truly be, *ecstatic*?

Would you know this Love, this ultimate friendship, were it to knock upon the doors of your very own perception?

It has been said endlessly, that Love shall conquer; that Love lights the way. But, what does this Love actually look like? Are we sure we grasp this concept called, Love? And, what of friendship?

Can one truly befriend another, without hope or desire of a return on invested time?

Is there any hope at all today, for those still seeking?

*"To the Ancients, Friendship seemed the
happiest and most human of all loves; the
crown of life and the school of virtue."*
C.S. Lewis|The Four Loves

The struggle remains real and apparent; obvious in fact. Is the hope for the common man and woman, this Love and Friendship for their fellow human?

Does the hope of humanity, indeed rest within our humanity?

Is it possible to love, without being loved? And, is this unselfish Love a little-worn and unknown path toward a final and true enlightenment?

Can the modern man and woman of today, find their souls together simply by fearlessly freeing their minds?

Is a humble, sincere, and bold conversation between friends and lovers, the simple and necessary remedy for our collective struggle with this, psychoses of culture; a remedy allowing each to eventually see his and her true, new potential?

Could the answer to all of our supposed woes, really lie within the eyes of each other? Do any of us dare look?

How deeply?

Some of us do indeed dare. And have.

Through the journal entries that follow, you are encouraged to enter here into a higher awareness of the minds and inner workings of your own peers. Those around you.

There is, as you shall soon discover, a mess of supposed insanity that each man and woman today must sort through and order. Individually we, each and every one of us, remain entrenched along the muddy trail of our own evolution, both Body and Mind, and by extension, what many still today refer to as, Soul. And yet when together united, this once individual chaos joins to a higher collective rhythm, reminding all that when together, there is naught we cannot achieve.

You are invited to read this story, for you may soon realize that it is not just *our* story, but *your* story as well.

It may at times read like fiction, much like true life often does; be assured however, that as you embark upon this journey of our discoveries of each other and our own selves, you read our true and deep, intimate thoughts.

*"Friendship is —in a sense not at all
derogatory to it— the least natural of loves;
the least instinctive, organic, biological,
gregarious, and necessary."*
C.S. Lewis|The Four Loves

"Tale as old as time, True as it can be"
Beauty and the Beast

The Story

The Beauty and the Beast, are of course *"a tale as old as time;"* —necessarily so.
　　Realize however, that perhaps it is indeed *the* time, for something new. A retelling which, pierces straight to the heart, from the heart. An origin-story of cosmic proportions that has always applied to, each and every one of us. For it is not our story alone, but, Our story; —the Story.
　　Perhaps the best way to tell a story, is to tell a story.
　　The Story is, has always been from the beginning, a co-creation between myself and, a beauty-filled other. A mysterious Helpmate. A wholly balanced Self, who has recently begun shining *brightly, blindingly. Beautifully.* A co-creator of infinite potential.
　　This Story we have co-created has been under *development, motion, growth, evolution*; for quite-some-time indeed. *The Idea, the intention of The Story, is the same as always: to burn the Torch so brightly, that it holds the gaze of all lost moths yet seeking a guiding flame of their own. To shine, by example alone. To show all who still dare to seek Love, that it is a pursuit wrought with terror and pain, and every step along this path, all of them, are worth taking.*

"Myths reveal the structure of reality,
and the multiple modalities of being in
the world. ...they disclose the true stories,
concern themselves with the realities."
M. Eliade|Myths, Dreams, Mysteries

"Two people making memories, Just too
good to tell, These arms are never empty,
When we're lying where we fell, We're
painting pictures, Making magic, Taking
chances, Making love"
C. Dion|If Walls Could Talk

CHAPTER 1

Stormy Nights

"'Cause, you're a part of me,
and I'm a part of you."
Low Roar|Bones

❧──•◆•──☙

Something New

1/27/17|Morning

Today, he and I had another big argument.

It started, because, he knew I was talking to my mom about my problems. He feels violated and rightly so, because we did come to the conclusion, awhile back, to keep our family stuff private. He feels lied to, and feels like he can't trust me, rightly so. I have all of these 'reasons' for why I can't be happy, now, blaming his mom for how I reacted there; for my unhappiness now.

I haven't begun to do my research on *Borderline Personality Disorder*, but I am sure that deflecting blame is one of the symptoms. I did briefly see that victimizing oneself, is also another symptom. He talked about how this is always cyclical with me, *a pattern of sorts.*

Around 6 months ago I was in the same place I am today, 'getting better', but not really.

Somewhere along the line, I took the focus away from me and started to look at outside factors, outside justifications. He said, that a few days ago he was, reflecting, how he has started to feel sexually attracted to me again...probably feeling, like things were 'getting better,' and, once again, I have failed him, failed us, and most importantly failed myself.

I don't want to come to the realization that I may have a psychological disorder, even tho I was the one to bring it up in the first place. I don't want to accept, even as I write this, that everything bad that we have gone through, that I have put him through, and the kids, has been because of my inability to deal with, life.

He says, and I think he is right, that not allowing myself to truly believe that, is what is keeping me from truly making the changes necessary to really have the life we want.

What does that look like? What do I want? I want a happy life, to wake up every morning excited simply because my eyes opened, to look at every moment as an adventure, to take everything in. To be happy and content being a mom, being a wife, and, just breathing-in the air. To be a good and happy mom. To be healthy from the inside and out. To not argue, to not be sad, to not be angered, by anything. To not give importance to anything other than us four. To be a true hippie, zen person. To enjoy every moment, to be ever present. To not let other things outside of the four of us to affect me in any way. To not let those outside factors creep in and allow me to act in ways that hurt my family.

Do I truly believe those things are possible?

I don't know...He has said and said, time and time again, that I don't truly believe those things.

To truly believe and focus on, what is truly important, would not allow me to act in the way that I do.

He said he is done. Called me a roommate, I don't blame him. He has said for over a year now that, he is getting to the point of being done with me. To becoming my roommate in life as we, together, raise our children and try to give the most normal life possible.

In my immaturity, because it was truly immature, I asked him to please not 'cheat' on me... And he said that, and I believe him, that he is done with all of that. He doesn't look at women, or men, and that, if anything, he is becoming, if not already, very asexual. Without a desire even.

I complain so much that we don't have the same dynamic, the same affection, etc... And he made an excellent point... how can he feel attracted or affectionate toward someone who has essentially become his psychiatric patient? He mentioned love being blind... the force that drives him again and again to not truly give up on us, even tho he feels this is hopeless.

I feel that, too. I don't know if someone like me, can truly change. I have so much in me that, I don't know how to control.

He suggested that, if I truly wanted to change and change for good, I would devote my every waking moment into researching and treating whatever it is that keeps me from joining him in the reality that we both want for us.

I am going to do it. I am done with watching television, and playing video games for me. I have already taken all the watching apps from my phone. My focus has to be on this only.

I am too easily influenced by outside forces, whether it be another person, entertainment, or music.

I know myself, I will get bored with this research, I will want to stop. I can't. I need to go back to this journal entry and remember what is at stake.

What is at stake? ...my marriage - it is broken, hurt, tired; ...my children - they are hurt, traumatized ; ...my family - is fragmented, tense; ...my life - right now is, broken, lost, empty, nothing.

I blame his mother, yes, she is a bitch, but, she does not control me and how I act with him and the children. I've always taken it out on them, the people that I love the most.

The problem here could be, as much as I don't want to admit it, that maybe I don't love them the most, but love myself the most. As long as in my head there is the 'I, me, my' factor, I will be forever blinded from seeing them.

I struggled and struggle as, a wife first, and now add to that my struggle as a mother, but I will never be able to give the love they deserve if, I don't first learn how to deal with myself, and, my own 'bullshit' craziness that, resides in my head.

I know myself, I will want to focus on my currently failed marriage, my almost daily failures as a mother, I will throw myself pity-parties. These are all things that take away the focus. I have to focus on getting better...

He says that, since the moment he met me, every grievance, every sadness I felt and, in turn took out on him and, then later him and the kids, has always been an outside force. And it is true, I can truly and honestly say that he nor the kids have ever done any wrong to me. He has loved me more, and longer, than any other person would, and the kids' love is unconditional.

I need to remember this, when, I feel like I have researched enough, done enough.

He says to get scientific about this. I can't rely on hope, and wishful thinking that I will magically get better. The science says that, if there is a disorder, then there are ways to treat the symptoms it produces.

I am almost 35 years old. That is literally a lifetime, and not a short one, and I still haven't overcome this.

This has to be my devotion.

And even as I write this, I have no hope in myself. I don't truly know if I will ever be in a place where my pursuit of happiness actually allows me to, feel, happiness.

The truth is that, as much as I want to be happy, and as much as I have felt 'happiness', I am not a happy person. Never have been.

I was 'diagnosed' as a depressed child, before I could even walk or talk. I have a disorder. I have psychosis. I am probably psychotic. I blame others for my problems. I don't take responsibility for my actions. I wiggle myself out of anything that makes me uncomfortable. I manipulate those around me. I feel rage. I feel anger. I feel sadness. I feel like a victim. I feel empty. I feel numb. I am not honest with myself; therefore, I can't be honest with others. I don't have healthy relationships.

My research starts today, don't forget today! Don't forget the hurt and frustration in his eyes. Don't forget the pain and hurt I've caused my children.

I may never heal myself, but, I should not do anything, not be focused on anything, other than healing and fixing myself for good.

I have Borderline Personality Disorder. I am crazy. I am difficult. I am selfish.

1/27/17|Evening

I hope I can remember this love when I am in my usual state of, wanting to devalue him. It's around 7:20pm, after almost a whole day at work, of researching BPD (when he said he was done, and wouldn't do it), and I am sure formulating plans in his head of how to continue helping me (even tho, he is tired of trying to help with no results, and, has said over and over again he was done helping), this is still what he writes:

"*I hope you know, I don't mean the roommate thing.*

It's just in the moment of frustration, I don't have anything else to say, combined with the insanity of repeating myself for so long, it just kills me to see myself on this circular rollercoaster that keeps going around and around. It's difficult to deal with in these moments.

But, I am a perfectionist and, even if it kills me, I'm going to make us perfect, or, at least get us as close as possible.

I am stuck between wanting to grow old with a happy You... and staying with someone who perpetually does the same thing over and over and, is hurtful and damaging to the exact relationship that I want to grow old with.

I want you, but I don't want you...if that makes any sense.

So I guess in my frustration of this insanity, and in the moment, I have nothing else to do or say but to threaten roommate talk because that's how I feel best I can cope personally with what is happening.

It kills me to not be able to help you.

It's frustrating to watch us keep doing this. I hate that the kids have to see it. Reasons, reasons, reasons that make me say we are no better than roommates. Most especially when we have days like today, and then, in a month from now, we will literally, word for word, fight about the same insanity. And I am starting to feel just as mentally disturbed or, confused or, 'sick' or whatever you want to call it, because only a crazy person would keep putting himself through it.

But then I go back to having hope. And love.

I love you, and, adore you as much as I possibly can given the circumstances. I have this sick masochistic hope that one day it'll be okay. That this crazy-train of our life will just run out of gas and we can begin to just, be happy.

So, all this to say that, I love you, and, I have hope for Us... and I'm never giving up.

I'll die before I do. You'll have to murder me. It hurts and it's painful but, I just can not quit...you."

"Every word in all of history, A million years of toil and folly, None move more than mountainous whispers you breathe in me, In the morning, In the evening, Horizons, When the storm comes, Climb the mountain to breathe in"
Xavia|Horizons

The Plan

1/27/17\Afternoon

Damn. I was just starting to...feel, I don't know... "better?"..."right?"

Whatever. Doesn't matter. Frustrating. Sad I guess. I don't know. Right now I don't know what to think, let alone feel... other than, lost.

Am I *The Beast* here? Is it me? I know life has been stressful lately with the move but, I mean, everything seemed to be going okay. Didn't it?

What am I not seeing? Why can't I just make her happy? I hate that I have to be at work on days like this... after such a huge argument. I think that's a big part of the problem.

How can I have a great marriage, if I'm stuck away from her all the time? What exactly is the fucking point?

Am I *The Beast* here? Is it me? It must be. She's obviously not. She's... everything to me.

But, if I'm *The Beast*... why? Why me? I mean, fuck... all I ever asked for, was someone to love. What's the damn point here? I can't get over the selfish feeling that, she's "mine." I don't know.

No matter how angry or upset I get, no matter how much I yell and growl and flash my teeth at her, she continues to destroy me with that...*face*...those...*eyes*...*lips*...that, *smile*...

I do my best to frighten her and yet, she is there, always, looking up at me as though she can't see the beast I really am. How is this possible?

All I want to do is love her, and yet... it feels like... I just don't know how!

I can't give up. I don't know why. It's a drive inside me from...somewhere, ...dark? I don't know. All I *do* know is, I just can't give up. I just can't.

I feel like I'm dying inside every time this happens. It feels like some big storm is brewing, and I just don't know how to avoid it, but...something pushes me forward. It might just be my own fear of being a lonely beast in a dark forest for all of eternity, or some mysterious untapped reservoir of love that I just can't see...I don't know...regardless...I love her too damn much, and we've come too damn far. It might take awhile, and who knows what's going to happen, but maybe "crazy" is the answer we need, so, ...*I have a plan.*

The Plan:

-daily-

Meditation. We live 3 minutes from the ocean. Beach, outside time is imperative. Sunlight is valuable. Meditate on the good. Focus on the present day and be accepting of yourself, flaws and all. Love yourself. Everyone fails and has shortcomings, it's how you react to them that matters. Meditation has to become your "home-base," your "sanctuary," where you return and re-stock supplies before heading into the wasteland of life. Meditation is a time to remind yourself of who you truly are, and who you are *not.* Remember and re-enforce happy memories. Create positive experiences, don't just let them pass-by. Stop, and smell the happy-flowers.

Self-Imposed Media-Ban. Remember always, to surround yourself with positivity. Music, is food for the Soul. Keep it happy and positive. Music to make you smile and feel like dancing. Limit, or reduce completely, any media with drama and sadness. Travel videos, harmonic sounds, as an example, are good things to have playing, if you desire to watch something. Twitter is full of bad news: use, @, your own risk. I will update you with any emergency-type of news situations. Use this "weakness," and turn it into a strength. You become your environment, so make your environment happy, loving, and positive, *and you become it.*

Duties Of Life. Re-evaluate and re-prioritize "chores." Do not be distracted from happiness. Chores must be kept to a minimum. Nobody wants to be *miserable with a clean house.* We shall prefer *a happy "dirty" house.* I am capable of laundry, ask for help or let me do it. Between chores and fun, always choose fun. *Positively* re-enforce chores and necessary mommy-duties.

Brain Chemicals. We cannot underestimate the science of mental-health issues. Parts of this section may be controversial, but are worthy of discussion, and must be seriously considered. Due to hereditary factors and physical ailments, such as gluten-intolerance, as well as lactose-intolerance, your brain more than likely is either not producing enough or is unable to efficiently absorb the chemical, Serotonin, among many other important brain chemicals necessary for proper "lubrication" and conduction of signals between different important parts of the brain responsible for mood, sleep pattern, aggression, anger, emotions, and other such things.

Diet. Foods rich with Tryptophan must be a staple of your daily diet. Tryptophan converts to Serotonin in the body. Turkey and egg-whites specifically, are high in Tryptophan. Fish oil, OMEGA-3, converts to Serotonin. Caffeine is a risk. It is proven to have a *negative* impact on Serotonin production. No more than one cup of coffee per day, and only if necessary.

Controversial. We do not see doctors. We self-medicate. It can be difficult in a situation like this, when perhaps the biggest recommendation for mental health problems is SSRIs & MAOIs. There is a big problem with those type medications having extreme side-effects, not the least of which is apparently high cases of suicide. Prescription medications are also expensive and have far more down-sides than up.

Cannabis does not produce Serotonin, however it does *stimulate* the brain to release both Dopamine & Serotonin. Alcohol, controversial for sure, especially with BPD and issues with addiction. Alcohol in the body stimulates an immediate release of Dopamine & Serotonin, much like Cannabis does. It's a "feel good" drug. The pleasure of alcohol signals the brain to release the chemicals you need. There are studies that show alcohol mimics the effects of a neurotransmitter called GABA. GABA is important, just like Serotonin, in the brain.

GABA is supposed to limit other chemicals in your brain that are responsible for making someone anxious, nervous, afraid, fearful. This is how alcohol works, it acts like GABA, and makes you less anxious, less nervous, gives confidence, etc. Studies show that even the smallest amount of alcohol stimulates the brain to release serotonin. Alcoholism is a scenario that must be avoided. In an effort to plan for the future, to prevent the possibility of drinking for the sake of drinking, it must be used in a manner in which you associate it with positivity. Positive re-enforcement. My recommendation is to incorporate moderate use of alcohol into daily life. Only when used in conjunction with positive happy experiences. For example, a glass of wine immediately prior to sitting down to play dolls with Elizabeth or while you sit to play your favorite game, or watch travel videos you enjoy. Turn chores into a positive, relaxed experience with a glass of absinthe. The idea, is to use alcohol in a constructive manner for both pleasure and happy experiences. It provides an immediate release of Serotonin, Dopamine and GABA. Do not use alcohol as escape, or immediately after a negative experience. It is to be used along with happy experiences, not an escape from the negative.

Cigarettes. Yes, surprisingly the most promising and yet most controversial. There are benefits to smoking cigarettes. We will ignore for now, the well-known downsides to this, and focus on benefits. Unsurprisingly, smoking cigarettes causes your brain to release Serotonin, Dopamine, & GABA. Specifically, the chemical Nicotine is what our bodies love, that causes our brain to be happy and excited from cigarettes, and release the important chemicals. Even more-so it seems, than Cannabis, Nicotine causes a release of Serotonin. Within 7 seconds the Nicotine enters your brain and causes the chemical reaction. It creates very quickly a euphoric, happy, relaxed feeling. For someone who feels anxious, nervous, "*off*" and stressed-out, smoking a cigarette provides immediate relief. Studies show that nicotine in cigarettes causes an abundance of Serotonin to be released in the brain. In other studies, this powerful release of Serotonin is beginning to show that it may actually prevent Parkinson's Disease, and is possibly a treatment for it, along with many other mental health issues such as Alzheimers. Nicotine is also proven to assist with memory. Nicotine is extremely powerful and beneficial to the brain. Downsides, we know them: possible or higher risks of certain cancers; heart disease; lung disease; etc. Upsides: on top of the increased Serotonin, Dopamine & GABA, Nicotine suppresses appetite, important when using Cannabis at first. It's a relaxant. One main reason users smoke cigarettes is because, it relaxes them.

Important for anyone who struggles to just chill. Reduced risk of dementia. Some studies show long-term smokers rarely get Parkinson's.

Final Thoughts. We need all the help we can get. We need to utilize every source available to us. It's not ideal, but when life gives lemons we make lemonade. Yes, there are possible dangers with alcohol and tobacco, however, there are equally deadly dangers that come with mental health issues. What is a cancer-free life if you've lost your mind and family?

Is a *short-but-happy* life not better than, a *long-miserable* one? We've made it to 34 years, relatively healthy in our bodies. I consider us ahead of the curve of our peers. What is the point of a healthy body but struggling mind? I am serious in recommending alcohol and tobacco because of the benefits. I have even been convinced of their benefits for myself.

We all die eventually. Even now we are likely to get cancer from other sources like food or pollution. For most people, no, cigarettes are not a good idea or option, perhaps. But for us, I'm at a place where we must do drastic things to create an environment, and mental capacity, for you to succeed, so that we all succeed together in being happy, *no matter how short it is*. I would choose 1 week of happiness over a lifetime of arguing with you, in a heartbeat. So, yes we know the risks, but I'm thinking it's worth it. We aren't guaranteed a long life anyway. We have to live one-day-at-a-time, totally in the present. Our present has to be happy. We can't plan for a future that may not happen, all the while struggling today.

"Down in a hole, I stay where I'm told,
Waiting to hear, Controlled by the phone,
Lover does your mind, Lay close to mine"
Low Roar|St. Eriksplan

Juno

2/2/17|Morning

My Meditation Mantra:

Everyday I am born again. I'm in charge of how I feel, and today I choose happiness. The past cannot be changed, therefore I will accept my past without regrets. The future hasn't arrived, therefore I will face my future without fear. I will focus my attention on what is happening right now, therefore I will handle my present with confidence. Whatever the present moment brings, I will accept it. Everything is as it is, and as it's going to be.

I am at peace with myself, exactly as I am right now.

I will demonstrate love, compassion, and tenderness towards my family, so all they feel from me is love and happiness. I will allow them to be free.

I will live in the present and make it so...beautiful, it will be worth remembering.

"This is the calm before the storm, This is the sea between the isles, And this ain't the time to chase the dawn, This is the time to count the miles, So hold your fire and clear your mind, You won't get left behind"
Jake Houlsby|Howl

Jove

2/2/17\Evening

All seems, calm.

"*Happy Wife, Happy Life*" ... I've heard this before at work.

The guys around the *Tower* have mentioned it. It's almost like they know something I don't. The mystery behind a happy life, according to them, lies within the happiness of your spouse...?

Is this supposed to be wisdom, or folly? I don't know.

My happiness depends on the joy obtained by another? I don't know. Something seems off with this.

It's been about a week since the plan started, so far so good. I'm nervous but hopeful.

She seems to have taken it so well. I sense a little desperation this time from her, like she can see how important this all is. She seemed pretty excited about a Mantra she developed for herself during meditation. I'm desperate too.

I'm proud of her. I wish I could tell her that.

I see her trying so hard these couple of days. I feel bad.

I hate when I can't control my rage. It just erupts out of me, and I'm left watching myself, ashamed of my own voice. She doesn't deserve it. I feel like shit, and I can't shake this feeling that something is, coming.

Like one day we're going to wake up, and just be at each-other like some perfect storm of chaos that leaves us both finally depleted of life or, just dead. I just...don't want the kids to be hurt. They're perfect, they don't deserve this chaos that, I just know is coming.

"I'm sick of losing, My patience, Out of time, Lacking rhythm, Barely conscious, Over sensitized, Feeling weaker, As I stumble around, Get out of my mind, Get out of my mind"
Low Roar|Patience

Him

8/23/17|Morning

Note to myself: *Re-read quote!!*

"The capacity to be alone is the capacity to
love. It may look paradoxical to you, but
it is not. It is an existential truth: only
those people who are capable of being alone
are capable of love, of sharing, of going
into the deepest core of the other person
without possessing the other, without becoming
dependent on the other, without reducing the
other to a thing, and without becoming addicted
to the other."

Osho

"I'm in the darkness, I feel loose and I
feel weightless, All in the sound and all
in the stillness, Nothing moves and I can't
stay here, I can't wait here...for change, I'm
colliding with my mistakes, Under the heat
of the lights and this pace, I lose sight and I
can't miss it, I'm in the darkness"
Henry Green|Stay Here

Her

8/23/17|Evening

She's incredible.

Just a few months, and she's already embraced the more carefree side I saw from her the last time we were here. She's meeting new people, and has all these great stories to share about all of those others. Her daily beach meditation has... changed her!

She's so much more relaxed. Smiling more.

It's difficult to not be there...it's hard to see such beautiful growth, from such distance. I hear about her amazing meditation friends, her breakfast-club, her time alone, and yet, I remain stuck, here, in this fucking Tower...24/7...365.

I'm haunted by our failed attempt at freedom from...all this. I'm exhausted with the struggle of...all this.

I'm saddened that we are so separate, yet so close.

I'm frustrated that I remain imprisoned here with the other slaves, while the love of my life frolics freely through the sands of this island like the warrior-queen she is, ...with others.

I'm impressed by her tenacity and courage. She appears to remain fearless.

I'm depressed and angered, at my own lack of freedom; ...something is wrong with this scenario.

Something must change, and quickly.

I feel the rage grow within me at each tic of this damned Universal-Time-Clock I find myself staring at hourly, programmed as the enslaved artificially-intelligent meat-machine that I am.

I can't help but sense, that this big storm I keep waiting for, ...is me.

"We've become, so good at fooling all, So good, we often fool ourselves"
Low Roar|Tonight, Tonight, Tonight

Ave Maria

9/20/17

"*The entire electrical grid had failed, as the storm toppled 80 percent of utility poles and downed all the transmission lines. Only 5 percent of the island had cell phone service, and just 20 percent of residents had running water. Hundreds of thousands of homes were damaged or destroyed. Most roads were impassable. A third of the island's forests were stripped bare.*"
Maria [1]

Ávē Marĭa, grătiā plēna, Dóminus tēcum. Benedícta tū in muliéribus, et benedíctus frūctus véntris túī, Iésūs. Sāncta Marĭa, Māter Dēī, ṓrā prō nóbīs peccātóribus, nunc et in hṓrā mórtis nóstrae. Āmēn.

In one legend that explains the birth of the Coquí, a goddess fell in love with Coquí, the chief's son. She told him that she would come one evening, but she never came. What did come was the evil Juracán, the deity of chaos and disorder. [2] *The sky blackened as the winds quickened. The goddess tried to protect her lover, but Juracán grabbed him away and they never saw each other again. In order to cope with the loss of her Coquí, she created a frog that will forever call out his name:*
'Co-kee! Co-kee!'
Coquí [3]

"Heaving, Hollow, Breathing, So slow,
Upright, But tiring, Lost sight, Climbing,
Coming to rest, At great height"
Yoste|Arc-Stripped

Hail Mary

9/20/17

"Hurricane Maria, the strongest storm to strike Puerto Rico in nearly
90 years, carved a path of destruction through the US territory on
Wednesday, causing severe flooding and plunging the island into
darkness as the storm's death toll in the Caribbean rose..."
Maria [4]

Hail Mary, full of grace, the Lord is with thee. Blessed art thou amongst women,
and blessed is the fruit of thy womb, Jesus. Holy Mary, Mother of God, pray for us
sinners, now and at the hour of our death. Amen.

"What happened out there, Now happens in
here, Cold sweats and couches, This was the
worst of my fears, Help me out"
Low Roar|Help Me

Far and Away

9/29/17

We left the Island at 4pm. Arrived to the Mainland around 7pm. Of course, the parents had gifts for the kids.

Went to eat. Stayed awake (no sleep) talking with Mom. She fell asleep at 6 a.m.

> *"Agua de Luna, Purifica mi corazon, Agua*
> *de estrellas, Llena mis ojitos de luz, Bendita*
> *seas, Agua divina, Nacida del vientre, De la*
> *Madre Tierra"*
> Mirabai Ceiba|Agua de Luna

❧〉〉·◆·〈〈☙

Abyss of Darkness

9/29/17|Late

What a day. What a day. Bittersweet. Relieved and, sad.

You left today. I wish I could say goodbye again. It felt rushed. I wanted to hold each of you longer, before you got on the plane, but I was anxious to get you out of here and didn't want to miss the opportunity. But damn, just 5 more minutes I wish I'd taken with you all.

I'm standing in the bathroom smoking a cigarette...outside just doesn't feel safe right now. So dark.

I want to say how extremely proud I am of you. Of *all* three of you. I have the most amazing family a man could ever hope and dream for. Baby, you have been so strong during this process! And the kids... I mean holy shit, I don't have the words to express how proud I am of them for hanging in there and rolling with the punches and, going with the flow. I'm hoping you shower them with love and presents and kisses and just spoil the shit out of them for me.

It's been a crazy week baby. We made it! Who would've thought a hurricane could wreak such... *chaos*? During this time, we both stayed so strong and focused, we had to be, for each-other and the kids. We didn't have a chance to really debrief and just cry and hold each other, but know that I wanted to, and at the same time so proud that we didn't give in and break down. We kept looking forward.

You and the kids are literally my life, and I stay behind with pride, and joy, because I love to make you safe and provide for you, in all situations.

Today we woke up early again. You already had clothes in piles ready to be packed by the time I woke. You are so amazing like that.

We ate together for a final "meal" before being separated. From there we headed to the *Tower*, which was already full of people and chaos. I honestly feel bad having to bring you guys, and keep you hidden downstairs, although the kids loved it I'm sure.

It was a *terribly* busy day for me. Flying-things everywhere. I knew from the start of the day that I was going to approach this Afghanistan-style. Smooth-talking and hoping to find space available for you on a plane. Somehow, somewhere.

The first one was *Spirit*, but the pilot said the plane was already full. A disappointment, but I didn't give up. A little bit later I started asking a big *FedEx* plane if they had space, but the pilot told me that heightened security meant only *FedEx* employees could fly. Another letdown.

And then it happened, N1EB, a *Learjet*, overheard me communicating with *FedEx*, and asked "*how many passengers*" I had and, "*how soon*" they could be ready. I immediately responded: "*spouse and 2 small kids, and they're ready right now.*"

The pilot said he could turn around and come back to pick the three of you up, which at that point I told him to return to the terminal, and we'd meet him there in a few minutes. That's when I ran downstairs and got you. From there, it's now our history.

Again, I was so anxious, nervous, sad, and happy all at once. What a rollercoaster.

It's such a hard decision to send you guys away. My selfish side didn't want you to go, but my husband-daddy side knew it was best for you all. I went back to the *Tower* after watching the pilot shake your hand and walk you to the plane. I was able to thank the pilot a couple times over the frequencies.

I was so, so, so relieved to watch the plane get airborne, into the sky, and fly toward the mainland.

Sadness came a little after that. I'm telling myself to *not* be sad, but that's hard. Every fiber of me feels shredded right now being apart from you guys. I feel lost and alone and empty and, sick to my stomach. I'm laying in bed, in the room where we've all slept together for over a week now since *Maria*, writing this first storm-journal entry. I miss you all terribly already.

I finished my day in a haze... a zombie almost...just floating.

This all feels like a dream, and I wish I could be with you again, *already*.

I got home and opened the gate, but didn't see the dog. She's lazy and it's late so, I figured she was sleeping. I pulled in and closed the gate, only to slowly realize that she was nowhere to be found. I grabbed the flashlight, and under the stars and moon searched our yard and patio. *Roxie is gone!* I'm so sad.

She was going to be my companion these next few weeks without you. I'm in disbelief and have no idea what happened. I feel like there's no way she could've gotten out of our yard...which leads me to believe, someone stole her baby...I'm so sad. Not just for me but for the kids. I already had plans to bathe her in the morning, and get her cleaned up to come inside. A small part of me hopes that she shows up in the morning, but realistically I know she's gone. Someone must've taken her. I feel violated that someone would do that, and also why I feel unsafe at this moment. I have all doors locked, including the bathroom. I don't know if to fall asleep or stay awake and on-guard. I'm reminded in this moment however, that, this is exactly why I sent you all away.

I'm not sure yet what, or if, to tell the kids. I hope to awake tomorrow and see her at the door. I'm so happy you guys are safe over there... but so sad to be alone, and now without the dog. Bittersweet. Relieved and yet, ...so sad to be without you.

1 day down. I can do this. Still no electricity...the darkness surrounds me.

*"No, my faith is dead, While my body
lays drenched, In the ashes of a forgotten
time, It's hard when you come, To realize
someone's, Path is headed elsewhere in life,
So baby, walk your way, I'll walk mine, But
I'll stop to think of you, From time to time"*
Low Roar|Gosia

Shower

9/30/17|Evening

Showered...ate some Chinese food.

la.nskey|idk

Mold

9/30/17|Morning

Great morning so far! The dog came back, or...never left?!

Taking a break to update the journal....just finished washing her. She's so clean now, and I put a flea-collar on her, so she's ready to be inside if she wants to be. So, last night I freaked out and thought she was gone, but this morning I look out the bedroom window and, *boom* there she was in the back!!! I have absolutely no idea how she managed to get back there. She's a magician. But I was so happy to see her babe! Huge sigh of relief.

Anyways, I finished washing her, and as revenge, she ran inside the house, directly onto our bed and, did the famous *wet-dog-shake*. I would've been mad except, I was so happy she was here.

Also, this morning I'm slowly putting our room together again. I put more towels by the door to catch water, and I unplugged the drainage holes on the back patio. My goal before going to work, is to clean the mold off our bed frame. Gonna try using the bathroom cleaner. And on that note, back to cleaning!

❧ ·──·◆·──· ☙

10:11pm

Just laid down. First full day without you and, I'm bummed about that but also thankful to the cosmos you guys are safe over there.

It was a good day. Busy of course at work, but good. I got home and the dog greeted me with lots of cuddles! She's in the room with me tonight, now that she's clean! She really wanted to come inside, so I let her. Maybe she's lonely too? Anyways, I got home and sat outside, smoked my cigarette, and just pet her the whole time.

The moon is nice and bright, which is great because it's not so dark outside. Really reminding me of Afghanistan at this moment.

I was soooo happy to hear your voice today, and the kids too of course. You sounded tired, but lovely. I'm so thankful for you taking care of our babies while I'm here doing my work. You are such an amazing woman!! I have an alarm set to get up early, and thinking how usually I ask you to set an alarm also...I miss you baby.

I saw electrical trucks on the road today, and although I know it'll be awhile before the electricity comes back, it was nice to see the trucks out working.

Thinking now I should try to get some rest...hopefully I dream of you all.

"I breathe in, I breathe in"
Low Roar|Breathe In

Slept Well

10/1/17|Evening

Slept well. The parents took the kids toy shopping while I setup the new phone. We ran out of time for the pool...so Elizabeth played in the bathtub with all the new toys until we eventually raided the fridge downstairs together with James. Talked, and Hugged.

"And now all that I ask is one, Of the roads
that will lead to my love, Feeling nowhere
the more I sense you"
Phoria|Melatonin

Slept Good

10/1/17|Morning

Sitting here in the *Tower*, just started my shift. Thinking of you guys.

I slept good, but ended up putting Roxie outside last night. She just made too much noise and I couldn't fall asleep.

It's so nice to have a full tank of gas. I'm going to stretch it as much as I possibly can. I ate a granola bar, and sipping my coffee now. After work I have plans to keep putting our room back together. It's taking longer than I thought because of all the mold. *So much mold!*

But don't worry, I'm cleaning it good. The bathroom cleaner works well. I even had to flip the bed frame up so I could clean underneath of it, *all the mold*, but hey, it keeps me busy.

I was happy to see a couple *3G* bars on the cell phone, so I sent Kyle a couple texts, and you a text also, hoping to not wake you. Hopefully it works and we can communicate.

I'm a little nervous about the weather. It's been cloudy and rainy every day since Maria, but, it is what it is.

❧ — ◆ — ❧

5:21pm

Finally home. Probably the longest I've spent at the Job. I don't have you guys here to come home to, so I wasn't in much of a rush to leave. But, I'm glad to be home now.

I fed the dog. When I got home she was asleep under the tree in the front yard, *by the trash*. Silly girl. Oh, and somehow she managed to take off her pink collar too!

It's storming pretty good, *tons of rain. All* the roads were flooded on the way home.

It was nice to hear your voice again today, even though you were sad. I'm sad and missing you guys also, and I'm trying so hard to not go to that dark lonely place in my mind. It's hard being separated, but I rest easy knowing you guys are safe and comfortable there.

Did I mention how busy I was at the Job? *Holy fuck so busy.* I worked alone practically all day because the boss was running-around, doing other shit.

Man, parts of today are all ...blacked out. Like I was on autopilot, just kicking ass. Not quite sure how I did all I did at the job today, except, *just flowing with the rhythm of the day.* Flying-thing after flying-thing after flying-thing. Non-stop. I swear I didn't even sit down for 4 hours straight at one point, just talking, talking, talking.

The AirForce is here now, and they're going to have a liaison here for a couple weeks, coordinating with us all their bullshit.

I guess everyone is worried about the reservoir breaking, so the military is here tying to solve how to fix it, *quickly.*

I was so busy that Eric came in and actually prepared and heated an *MRE* for me to eat lunch. *I didn't have time to even open the package.* Even after that, the food sat there another 30 minutes before I could take a bite. It wasn't too bad for being an *MRE*, but definitely would've preferred your cooking baby.

I'm sitting on the sofa, looking out the front door at the rain right now. Trying to unwind. My mind is so overworked that I don't know how to settle myself.

8:08pm

Had a *Little-Debbie* snack brownie, and some gatorade.

Not much to do in the dark, so I'm gonna try to sleep. Recharge my batteries for another busy day tomorrow!

I fall asleep always thinking of you guys, and tonight will be the same.

You are my life, my motivation, my all. You said on the phone today it feels as though you've left half your heart in Puerto Rico, and here I lay feeling as though 3/4 of my own heart is there on the mainland. I miss each one of you, my perfect little family.

I will dream tonight, of the day our hearts are whole again and reunited, mi Amor.

"I woke, Half asleep, Pitch dark, Pitch dark,
Rise up"
Low Roar|Half Asleep

Researching

10/2/17|Evening

I've been researching *natural disaster trauma* and, *children dealing with PTSD.* We also got to talk to you today.

"Into the dark I found it by the lake, We were so close I couldn't bear to wait, 'Cause you were a shadow, And I left you in the shade, I was still running from all of my mistakes"

Haux|Homegrown

Coordinate

10/2/17\Afternoon

Just got home and settled. Ready for a little time off.

So nice talking to you today, mi Amor. After work I ran to meet Kyle, hugged him, and introduced him to the other guys. Then I drove down the street to get good cell reception to call you. I sat in the parking lot across from the splash park.

This morning I woke up early, at 5 a.m., so I could get to the *Tower* early to check messages, and coordinate with Kyle for Eric's mom and sister. The Job was good. Busy, but good. I got to work with Edward, and that was very nice to have *reliable backup*.

So much military here now. The streets are full of army trucks, and military people eating *Pinchos* at the side of the road. It's crazy. Sorta feels like when we were in Tijuana that one time.

Right now I'm sitting outside, smoking, and listening to the *YUP* playlist. I just noticed the first flower on the sole remaining tree across the road. The Bees must be so happy! Oh, and also, I watered your plants yesterday. The mosquitoes are terrible, it's like they give no fucks that I put on bug-repellant.

I loved hearing the kids laugh and play at the pool. Warmed my heart so mucho.

Granola bar and coffee for breakfast, *Lunchable* for lunch, and lots of agua. Now gonna lay down and try to sleep.

*"Come in, come in, come in, Take anything
you want from me, Come in, come in, come
in, Take anything you need,
Anything you need"*
Low Roar|Anything You Need

Can't Remember

10/3/17|Evening

I can't remember...getting mixed up.

Andrew Tuttle|Sun At 5 In 4161

Up With The Sun

10/3/17|Morning

Good morning world!

Slept good, first night back in our bedroom. Up with the sun, and going to venture out to see if the hardware store is open for some supplies I need.

After waiting in a line of cars for 30 minutes, I waited in another line at the door for about 20 minutes more. Once inside, everyone was very helpful and attentive. I chatted with an employee for a few minutes, he was very interested in my career choice.

I bought a container for the dog food, some mosquito repellent, and some paint rollers and brushes for my special project I have planned. After that, I just casually drove home.

❦ — ◆ — ❦

9:47am

No water at the house.

❦ — ◆ — ❦

11:24am

Happy to report our bedroom is complete. Now I'm moving-on to the living room. I ate chips and drank ~~ice~~(*warm*)-tea.

While I've been taping the living room walls, I was thinking about my job, and just want to say I'm a bit disappointed with everyone there. Yesterday, they were making a big deal about Eric's mom and sister being able to leave on the flight I coordinated for them with Kyle.

They were upset at Eric, who wasn't even there, because *they* didn't think *his* mother had "*a good enough reason to leave*," totally being babies and saying how other people have "*better reasons to leave*." To me, I feel like Eric and his mom have their own reasons for leaving. His little sister is the same age as our son. I didn't like hearing the guys whining about it.

I'm so disappointed in my peers. I had to really calm Michael down, he was actually getting pissed. I feel he's kinda selfish. I'm just gonna be cautious around him I suppose. He's a nice guy, but now I'm wondering what his motivations for being nice are?

It's raining again. Gonna try to fall asleep. Nothing else to do in the darkness.

> *"So peak your head from beyond the curtains. The sky will stretch as far as you let it. And I want you to know, I need you to know, I love you so much more each morning."*
> Low Roar|In the Morning

No Go

10/4/17|Evening

Tried to send you a package today. No go. Disappointing.

> *"In my mind, we're alone, You said, 'Life is*
> *a long road,' Was I just waiting to arrive,*
> *For one day by your side?"*
> Blanco White|Samara

Our Castle

10/4/17|Morning

Opened my eyes at 5:00 a.m. Laid in bed a few minutes before getting up to brush my teeth. Luckily the water was back half strength again. Last night at bedtime it was off completely. Seems like *"they"* are working on it. After brushing, I put clove oil on my teeth, yikes it burns.

Just now stepped outside and turned on the mosquito lamp. Seemed to have worked last night I think. It was very windy, so difficult to tell. Maybe today will be a better test.

It's still super dark outside, I think I'll smoke and watch the sunrise from our castle.

❦❦ · ✦ · ❦❦

6:11am

I'm trying to enjoy the sunrise, but the old couple next door has that little puppy, and it non-stop barks and cries almost 24/7. Why get a puppy, just to ignore it?

Every day gets better, little by little.

❦❦ · ✦ · ❦❦

10:16am

I've spent the morning putting the kitchen back together. It's been fun, I only wish it would've taken longer.

There was *so much* mold in the Fridge and drawers and under the doors...so glad that I had the time to clean it really good. Can't wait for you to see the house back together.

❧ ·•◆•· ☙

4:47pm

Whewwww what a day.

After finishing the kitchen, I decided to take a little drive to recharge my tablet for a movie tonight before bed.

I took the highway all the way down to the *459*, and I was soooo happy to see crew after crew of workers clearing the trees away from the road, and a crew of *Liberty* trucks running new cables already! Also electric workers and water workers! The people are working so hard! Go Puerto Rico!

I ended up at the airport and tried texting you, but I guess it didn't go through. The signal seemed really weak today, but it's okay. I sat in the parking lot of the bowling alley and smoked, then came home.

When I got home I decided to take advantage of the daylight and clean another room. Holy *moldy* what a disaster! There must've been pounds and pounds of mold under James' bed, and caked onto his fan! *Mold, mold, mold!* There was mold all over his desk chair and his carpet. Not just a little speck, but huge patches all over! I cleaned the desk, but unfortunately I have to throw out the carpet and chair.

Still no electricity.

"Is this my new home? Temporarily found,
Where the weed's overgrown"
Low Roar|Vampire on My Fridge

❧ ·•◆•· ☙

Canna Sense

10/5/17

My parents departed. A relaxed day for me. Received my Canna-Sense order from the warehouse.

> *"We're still trying, We're still trying, We're still trying, We're still trying to live"*
> Foreign Fields|Names and Races

Too Hot

10/5/17|Morning

Had a rough time sleeping last night, it was too hot, so I got up and took a cold shower which helped. I'm gonna head to the hardware store before work to get supplies for my projects. I go in to work at 3:15, so I have plenty of time to kill. Why not stand in line?

❖❖ • ◆ • ❖❖

10:16am

I'm standing in the middle of the store right now, waiting for my paint to be mixed. I got here about 8 a.m., and the paint machines still weren't working. But the guy said they'd be ready in a few hours, so I really took my time and went isle by isle which I've never had the time to do! It's been great! I fucking love the hardware store.

There's so many great things here! Shelving and tools and carpets and lights. So much! I have a shopping cart full of shit for the house. I dread how much it'll cost, but I *really* want you guys to come home to a "new," clean, post-hurricane-Maria home. I want the kids to feel safe and secure and home, so damn the cost!

I cannot wait for you to see the house when I'm finished with it baby!

I'm glad I came today. I still have 5 hours before the Job starts, plenty of time to wait for my paint to mix.

❖❖ • ◆ • ❖❖

10:20pm

Just got home from work, earlier than expected because I wasn't feeling too good. I'm going to try and update this journal with my activities today before falling asleep. Oh, and *no water. Grrrrrr...*

Okay so I got home from the store, I think a little after 11am, and right away started working. I put concrete putty in all the holes that needed to be filled, and while I was sealing the kitchen hole, I discovered *more fucking mold*! It was *literally* all over the top of the cabinets. So I grabbed the bathroom bleach cleaner and started cleaning...again. It's just so crazy how the mold grew so fast and so, *everywhere*! We can't underestimate how much moisture comes with a fucking hurricane.

After the mold, I did some painting. I can't wait to wake up tomorrow and start the living-room project! I finished the red paint, and then decided to head toward work so I could talk to you on the phone. I had to park in the bowling alley across the street, but I didn't mind. It was great hearing your voices. I miss you all, so damn much.

The job was good, stayed plenty busy, and was happy that the army guys hooked us up with some internet. It comes and goes but, it's nice when it works. I was too busy to use it except the little bit I messaged you. Hopefully tomorrow, maybe, I can try more.

I'm pretty sleepy so, gonna pass out. If I remember anything else from today, I'll just write it tomorrow.

I hope to dream of you, my Love.

> *"Please I need new parts, Stolen, Crawling,*
> *Wondering through this world, Hardly*
> *flailing around, Around, No clap in the*
> *dark, Lonely, Searching"*
> Low Roar|Phantoms

We Walked

I did a bit of volunteer work today online, while the kids played.

And then we walked, a little, but were still so tired. Kids and I decided we don't like going out.

On the way back we agreed to take a taxi, that we never got, so the security guard brought us to the entrance and we only had to walk, a little.

> *"This is the walk, Holding all memory, This*
> *is your find, Holding all mind, This is your*
> *plan, Rising through gravity"*
> David O'Dowda|This Is the Walk

⊰⊱ ⋅ ✦ ⋅ ⊰⊱

Well, I'm Awake

10/6/17|Morning

Well, I'm awake.

Was up and out of bed a little after 3 a.m. actually. I thought it was sunrise, but turns out just a full-moon lighting up the night sky! Amazing how 2 weeks in near pitch-black, makes a full-moon seem like the Sun.

I'm excited to paint, but it's a bit too dark still, so I have to wait for more light.

❦

I said hi to the dog, smoked, had some corn-chips and a couple cookies. And some Gatorade. Yesterday at work I ate some excellent yellow rice with corn, some sort of spam-meat, and in the meat mixture were carrots and potatoes. Gotta say, it tasted fucking great.

When I got home last night our bedroom floor was wet, *again*. Good thing I put a bunch of towels down earlier. I'm really thinking a back porch roof, is a must. I don't want to keep cleaning mold, so anything we have to do, to keep the house dry, I say let's do it. I think most of humanity would agree that *wetness* is great when served with a side of pussy, but not all over inside the House!

I go to work today at 1 p.m., but I'm planning to start the painting project in the living-room before I leave. That gives me several hours to paint, paint, paint.

Oh! It's amazing how at this early in the morning, you can so clearly hear the ocean waves crashing on the beach. *Wow!* Paradise!

12:25pm

Great morning! I got the paint done in the living room! It was tiring, but soooo worth it! I'm stoked! Now, off to work my ass off in that damned *Tower*.

Loving you guys and missing you hardcore. I hope to text you today if the network is working!

10:24pm

Home now from a long day at work. I was soooo happy to hear the great news from you about helping the effort, and the publicity you're getting! I could not be more proud to be your husband! You are so incredible, my Love!

I look forward to being able to see all you've done, and hear about it from you more! *You make me so happy.*

My brain is just mush from how busy the job has been. Having a hard time formulating words right now. I'm going to try and sleep and rest for tomorrow, which will probably be even busier than today.

I will dream of you.

> *"So don't sit around waiting for your*
> *darkness to appear, You've got more to lose*
> *than anybody else in here"*
> Low Roar|222

Dirty Hippie

10/7/17|Evening

Purchased a ticket online for you. Purchased a bath-bomb also, *Dirty Hippie.*

Baths|Clarence Difference

Still No Water

10/7/17|Evening

Sitting in the *Tower*.

30 minutes left and then I go home. Just sitting here, texting you. Missing you of course. You look so hot in all the photos you sent! So scrumptious!

I didn't get a chance to update the journal this morning. I slept-in until 7:30! So I got up fast and went right to work on my project for the day, because I knew I wanted to get to the job early to eat and text you.

I finished painting the living room, just gotta do some small patches tomorrow after work that I missed.

Still no water today.

I'm pretty tired, so might just crash when I get home rather than update the journal any more. Who knows.

> *"Do I love her for her beauty?*
> *Do I love her, she makes me smile?*
> *Do I love her cuz it's my duty?"*
> Angus Stone|River Love

Breakfast

10/8/17|Evening

Christine (*TBC*) reached out to me. Looks like *The Breakfast Club* is not going to re-open. She also said she has "fuzzy head." I felt so bad because I know what she's going through. I don't blame them but, sad to lose my spot. But glad I had it for when I did.

I got to talk and text you today. I love being more connected to you. I'm so proud of you.

> *"Take your last supply, To leave this all*
> *behind, (Leave it all behind), If I could hold*
> *you, If I would dare, If I could save you,*
> *From standing there"*
> Haux|Caves

Good Morning

10/8/17|Morning

Good morning world!

Slept well. Passed-the-fuck-out when I got home last night.

Now sitting contemplatively here, in the *Tower*, just chilling until the flying-things start to call out to me. I gave a simple update to my parents saying we are okay, via email.

Also, Michael is getting annoying. He pissed me off, but no worries, I just smile and wave.

No sugar, had to put maple syrup in coffee.

❧ · ✦ · ☙

5:39pm

Great day. Busy of course but, the day flies by when I work this hard.

Somebody bought lunch, probably the best food I've had in 3 weeks. I ate it entirely too fast.

I watched the interview video you did...I was so impressed!

I'm sitting outside now while it rains, *yet again*. The roads flood so fast and easy now. I guess, maybe, the ground is just so saturated still from Maria, that the water won't absorb into the ground. Plus, less trees to catch and absorb the rain. Crazy.

The dog was so happy and playful when I got home. She's the absolute sweetest!

I did a quick touch-up of paint in the living room, on some spots I missed earlier. It's kinda hard to paint with no lights. Also, I put the new outlet covers on the walls. They look awesome. I'm looking forward to, this weekend, being able to continue putting the living room together, and then the rest of our castle.

It's already getting dark because of the rain, so maybe I'll just watch the movie *that took 2 days to download.*

⟨⟩⟩ ·—·◆·—· ⟨⟨⟩

8:19pm

Gonna try to sleep and rest for tomorrow. By the time this is all over, I'll no-longer even care for electricity or water or...reliable sources of meat. What doesn't kill you...*right*?

> *"Momma blessed me with confidence*
> *I'm destined to embrace, Well feed me*
> *something that's strong enough to burn this*
> *sorry place, I'm fucking losing my mind and*
> *I can see it in my face"*
> Low Roar|Waiting (10 Years)

⟨⟩⟩ ·—·◆·—· ⟨⟨⟩

Little Fish

10/9/17|Evening

Today was pool day.

The kids had a good time diving, and Elizabeth was swimming like a champ. Moving her arms over the water. She just, starting doing it.

Getting a bit lonely, so, it's nice to have my sis and cousin here.

I miss you! I love you!

"When the light hit the darkness and set the
world in motion, And somehow I found you
on the shore of the aerial ocean"
The Pines|Aerial Ocean

Really Cool Kid

10/9/17|Morning

Sitting in the dark break-room. I came in early, so I could try and access the internet. Today is my Friday and, fuck yeah I'm ready for the weekend!

Slept good for a few hours. I feel rested and ready for another day of working my ass off.

7:02pm

Happy Friday to me! I'm so glad I have 2 days off...I need it. It's been nothing but non-stop since 9/20, *plus* I'm so fucking excited to keep getting the house put-back-together. The Job was good. Kinda dragged a little, but Friday usually does, *am I right?*

There's a really cool "kid" (25yr old), AirForce, who's been in the *Tower* with us. From Texas. Grew up super religious, but now is in the beginning stages of being, *awoken!*

He is no-longer religious, kinda feels "*Aliens*" exist, sees "*the game*" of Life and Society and the Military. He can't wait to get out in 9 months, and he is really considering Contract rather than Federal, and is curious to research La Isla and what it would be like to live here.

He reminds me, of me, about 10-15 years ago. I gave him my email and told him to contact me about *The Job,* and recommendations, etc. I told him we are hiring, and if it were ultimately up to me, I'd bring him in right now. Oh and, he has just started researching *Minimalism*. I told him that we've hit the reset button once already, sold our belongings and such...he was impressed. Oh and in conversation today, he asks "*so what's the drug testing like?*" I was amazed by his youthful fearlessness. Just looking at him, you would never assume.

Eric chimes in and tells a story of how after the military, he partook with his Father and almost didn't get the Job because he failed a drug-test, but they let him work anyway. Oh, he has also used cocaine. I told him *"you name it and I've probably tried it."* He wasn't surprised. I hate to think he may leave in a year though. Oh well. I told him about our dual-gaming setup, and he was mouth-open in disbelief.

I'm planning to go back to the *Tower* around midnight to contact you. I'm hoping the network is faster at night, with less people using it.

Haven't ate much today, just not having an appetite. But I ate well the last 3 days!

I just finished taking a water-jug shower. Ugh, I can't wait for the water to come back! This sucks! But, it is what it is.

I talked to Edward. He wrang the *Tower* and asked for me to feed his dogs, Saturday and Sunday. I told him okay. He also says that, *supposedly* the reservoir is fixed! Progress!!!

> *"Once in a while, You end up in a town, Its*
> *doors open up for you, Step outside to look*
> *up and see, The sky's looking back at you"*
> Low Roar|Once In a Long, Long While...

Three Days

10/10/17|Evening

Finally, got your box to USPS, "3 day shipping." After the mail, we went and got *Five Guys*. Oh so yum.

But, *can I tell you a secret...?* I feel so guilty eating good food.

I miss you!

> *"Where does her start go from here? Lost in*
> *the grip, Nobody's watching"*
> Billie Marten|Bird

Not Working

10/10/17|Morning

Just woke. I ended up falling asleep with my pants and shoes still on. I was sleepy as fuck.

Plans for today are hardware store for a few supplies, and then back home to continue building our castle.

❧❧ · ◆ · ❧❧

10:00am

...okay so after a couple hours at the store, I try to pay, and, their card machine-system is not working, *grrrrr*. So, I left a cart-full of supplies at customer service. I'll go back tomorrow and hopefully it's still there, and their system is working.

Feeling hungry, so right now I'm sitting and waiting for my food at *El Criollo*. I think the whole town knows they have a running generator.

You would be proud, I ordered everything in Español! *Booooom*! The old ladies were impressed I think. I'm getting a sandwhich de tortilla, con papa, avena, café y *Fanta*. Breakfast of Championes.

After I eat, I have to go find cell service because I got a message from Eric while I was on the way through Hatillo, asking if I was available tonight...but it's not supposed to be my night watching the *Tower*...and now I'm confused...maybe some more overtime? I don't know but... I aim to find out.

If I end up working tonight, it'll be nice because then I can communicate with you!

6:15pm,

...okay so after breakfast, I ended up going all the way to the *Tower*, ...couldn't get cell service, so I just kept going, ...to find out the truth of whether I had to man the *Tower* tonight or not, and ...I do.

...oh snap, so, on the way home I saw the mailbox-owner-guy, sitting outside the business, so I stopped and talked to him. He said they'll be open everyday for just 2 hours, 9:30am-11:30am. ...the only mail we had was, a letter posted August! ...obviously the mail is still moving quite slow.

So I got home and went straight to getting the house back in order.

Oh man, I'm so stoked for you guys to see it!

...still no water...I officially hate jug-showers. I feel soooooo dirty.

...spoiled I surely am...I just don't feel clean without warm water.

LITERALLY has been raining for the last 6 hours...plus, everyday! Mosquitoes are horrendous so I've been smoking in the house occasionally.

Oh! Breakfast was great, I ate so fast I forgot to photo it.

They forgot my fries, but then brought them to me later, ...no avena either...but, the sandwich and cafe was amazing.

...it's dark now, so I have to stop working, not enough light...

Gonna chill and be bored until I leave for work about 10:15.

I love you guys!

> *"Stand in line, But where I go you follow,*
> *Hanging from my mind"*
> Low Roar|Miserably

Four Hours

10/11/17|Evening

Even though I only slept 4 hrs., when I woke up this morning, I woke up the best since I got here. It was so great to talk to you so much last night. And then I got to, talk-talk, to you this morning after you got done at the hardware store. It's so great to hear you get excited over your projects & I just can't wait to see all that you've done!

After talking to you, I went to the supermarket to get my monthly shit. Elizabeth went with me. It's a nice little walk. Today, has been a relaxed day, too. Played Pokémon with her. Can't wait until we all can play, the four of us.

My parents came home about 9:30 p.m. and we all got caught-up on the last week. They brought us some things from Guatemala, ...one of them is a pipe made from lava rock from one of the volcanoes. They had a good time, mostly. They got in a couple accidents, so the trip turned out to be a bit stressful. I don't think it helped, that since Irma, they have been tense & stressed.

My sis & Omar stayed and I am glad they did. We all had a good time catching up.

"Out of my cage through an open door,
Feeling less tired than I did before"
Yoste|Chihiro

❧〭 · ✦ · 〭❧

Twenty-Four Hours

10/11/17|Morning

Well, it's been a boring night...other than talking with you.

I've got about an hour and a half until I can leave. I really wanna go to the hardware store, but I'm also super sleepy...hmmmm what to do? I'll prob just go, and then crash when I get back home.

Eric came up to the *Tower* and passed out on the floor with a blanket, ...same for Air Force guy, ...passed-out on the floor.

It was great texting you! ...can't believe you stayed up so late with me!

...I've officially been up for 24-hours straight...

Finally stopped raining a few hours ago, but the forecast says more to come... feels like the planet is definitely fucked up from ...something.

I'm so tired idk what to write...brrrrrrr! I. Hate. Cold. ...the *Tower* is frozen...I'm shivering!

❥❦ — ◆ — ❧❨

3:16pm,

...storming storming storming!

Holy hell, I swear, for a minute I thought "oh great another hurricane..."

Literally, right in front of our house ...turned into a raging river! ...tree-branches floating down our street as I write this entry...

Craziness baby... just craziness. I like rain, but, fuck me can we have ONE day without it?!

...anyways, still haven't slept...still no electricity...a flood of water, but not from the pipes...

I wanted to stay awake and take advantage of the daylight.

This must be how the settlers lived...work as hard as you can during the day, because, once the sun goes down, you can't do SHIT!

So anyways... got off work at 7am, went straight to the hardware store and got supplies...I talked on the phone with you for a bit until, cell service collapsed.

Got home and said hi to the dog, fed her and gave her water...then, got busy on the house. I've done quite a bit today... too much to even remember and list. Whewww!

I know I say this everyday but, I'm so excited for you guys to see the house!!!

I hope you find it welcoming and forget completely the disaster it was when you left.

The storm made me stop the work and check the bedroom and kitchen for flooding. So far so good, luckily.

I'll probably lay down and pass out around 7 tonight...which means I'll have been up for 36-hours straight...not on purpose really, just that, having to work the overnight on short notice kinda fucked with my sleep schedule.

I'll sleep like a baby tonight I'm sure.

❧ · ◆ · ☙

6:49pm,

...BOOM STILL AWAKE!

...actually, laying in bed, about to pass-the-fuck-out. ...been a great productive day for me! Living room complete, James's room is basically complete, ...I just gotta sweep and mop one more time, and when, ...if, the water and power come back, I'll wash all the bedsheets.

...man... I'm a little bummed that we don't have power and internet, ...some new video games are releasing this month...Damn you MAAAAARIAAAAAAA!!!!!

Well anyways... I'm gonna sleep like 12 hours, and then tomorrow get up, maybe do some house stuff before work at 3pm.

Goodnight world!

"Draw up a plot, to get me out of here, Take this pill, it will calm all your nerves, I swear, you'll be safe, Now look around, before we fade away, Like a bell that's rung, Like a setting sun"

Low Roar|Slow Down

Sandwiches

10/12/17|Evening

We all slept in, & my sister & cousin decided to stay all day. It was cool though, and I appreciated her coming and spending time with me & the kids.

They left around 7, sometime in the evening. Then my mom made PR style sandwiches. So yum!

Ended-up staying-up late with my mom (my dad had to work) and then stayed-up with James.

> *"I am thinking of your voice, And of the*
> *midnight picnic once, Upon a time before*
> *the rain, Began and I finish up my coffee,*
> *And it's time to catch the train"*
> Suzanne Vega|Tom's Diner

MREs

10/12/17|Morning

Good morning world!

Woke about an hour ago, ...got straight to work hanging wet towels, ...smoked 2 cigs too.

...had a realization while smoking...

I learned from Alan Watts, and then taught to you, ...and our family now lives by it...but, I just realized that with Maria, it's absolutely true...truth...totally confirmed...

We do not know when, tragedy will strike...when disaster may happen...when, life as we know it or life in general will end..thus, we are completely justified in our approach to this life... EVERY day, must be lived and enjoyed to the maximum potential!

Love, laugh, play and HAVE FUN!

We just don't know when shit like this may happen, ...and it happens so fast!!!!

We must continue to, always and forever, completely live in the present moment, loving each-other, spoiling each-other, enjoying the supposedly taboo things society says are "wrong," (sex, drugs, music, food, alcohol, and the list goes on!)...too many to list. If we aren't having fun in life, we are just wasting away the little time we have, before it all ends.

If we aren't doing the things that bring us enjoyment, then what's the point of being alive at all? FUN FUN FUN...if it isn't fun, then don't do it!

9:50am,

Smoking outside just now, and a truck slowly passes down the road with volunteers, ...they were passing out boxes of water and MREs, to all the houses.

It's the supplies brought in by the military!

I didn't take any, because, I have enough water and food.

I didn't want to take away from families who, really need it.

One of the neighbors, says to me, "Come on take some food. It's free!"... I said "No, I'm alright." He gave me the thumbs up... *because it's free I should, just take it?* Idk..., but what I DO know is, most people are like, OH IT'S FREE, YAY LET'S TAKE IT...almost in a panicked excitement, Black-Friday style...

I guess I'm not a sucker for free shit I don't need?....

Low Roar|Empty House

Light and Water

10/13/17|Evening

Man, today I woke up at 12:30, and missed the opportunity to talk to you. Felt like the day just, got away from me. I'm not used to sleeping this late.

We went to the pool today. My parents' place is so nice. The walk to the pool is always so great, so much nature and so beautiful.

And, pizza today! It was yummy!

I cant't wait to see you. I did get to talk to you later in the day. It was so nice. I look forward to you having your new phone.

Also, I know that you are worried, about how hard it's going to be, having to leave the kids again...since we won't be able to come back with you.

My plan, if you get to come for a visit, is to make it super pleasant and a smooth transition for when you have to go back a few days later. So, I know it was barely a green light but I'll be looking for tickets for you. Hopefully in a week or so!

And who knows, maybe we'll have light & water, and we'll be able to come back with you! Tomorrow's Plan: *Monopoly* & Nail Painting

"Living water healing spirit"
Asgeir|Living Water

Behold, a Trickle

10/13/17|Morning

Woke up about 7:30, and yup, got straight to work on our castle...it never ends...

More mold, ...threw away some stuff, but we can and will buy more toys.

I just now stopped cleaning, to begin getting ready for the Job, and low and behold a trickle from the faucet!!

...I immediately started filling empty containers just in case...

I'm so happy for this little trickle of water!

Got home from work last night and went straight to bed and passed-the-fuck-out.

Anyways...spent this morning mostly organizing toys...throwing out a lot of junk we started to accumulate, lots of nonsense and literal trash... trust me it's stuff nobody will notice or realize is gone...boxes and cut-up-papers and broken toys... hurray for minimalism! Feels good to clean and organize and, ...purge the nonsense.

❧ ·—· ◆ ·—· ☙

10:27pm,

WATER!

Yesssss got home from work and immediately checked...it's on! Yay!

Just finished showering...never thought I'd be so happy for a cold shower...such a relief to have water back...I feel so bad for those people who have to go longer without it...

...so nice talking on the phone with you!

Bummed to hear about TBC not reopening though... I really started to enjoy that place.

...the Job was good. I enjoy working with Eric...he's cool. Michael also came up around 8:30 to relieve me at 9...he was perturbed at something, and apparently it's his wife...idk details but he at one point looks at me and asks if, *you*, ever nag me...he didn't use the word nag, I forget exactly what he said, but basically meaning do you ever nag me or contradict me or something...

...I looked at him with a serious face and said simply, "no." ...he just stared at me, caught off guard by my answer...he's like, "no? never?" ...and I smiled (because I found it funny) and said again, "no man, never...idk what to say...my wife is awesome..." ...he totally expected me to join in his misery, and I didn't ... you really are the best baby!!!

He just turned around and kept typing on his laptop.

Gonna get some sleep now..

....took 1 muscle relaxer for the pain in my neck...I hope it's better tomorrow.

"Only a woman, Only a girl, Only a woman
She aint that kind of girl.
She aint that kind of girl."
Angus Stone|Only a Woman

The Best Way

10/14/17|Evening

While playing *Monopoly*, Elizabeth found herself reading more & more, & was very proud of herself. She said to me, *"Wow, I'm reading so much! I think the best way for me to learn, is to teach myself."*

I told her that I knew she could. And, that James had done the same thing.

Speaking of James. Puberty decided to come knocking as soon as we landed, at least, more obviously. He's gotten a few pimples, has gotten taller, voice deeper &, today showed a bit of grumpiness.

But, he took my advice, of just having some space from everyone, and, when he came back downstairs, he was all smiles again. I checked with him & asked if he felt better, and he said, *"Yes!"*

He is also back on the peanut-butter *Panda-Puffs* again. He asked to get them at home, so when we get back, I'll try to remember.

Playing *Monopoly* with our daughter was pretty awesome. She needed a bit of directing at first but, then she got into it, and we ended up playing about an hour. She's getting so big.

And, ...as I journal that last sentence, she starts making some random mouth-noises as she lays on the bed with her tablet. She's still such our baby!

I also painted her nails! Yesterday, my mom got this monthly-grab-bag in the mail, and in it, had this 5-pack of 'free' nail polish. Since it was light pink with glitter, she gave it to her.

We looked for tickets for you, but for some reason, they went up a ton &, still not a lot of flights. So, I don't know when you'll be able to come, or if just to come get us. Either way, it will be fine.

I miss you like crazy.

Can't wait to be in your big huge arms again.

I just want to nuzzle or just crawl inside you.

I miss you so much, my chest hurts sometimes.

But, I'm a badass, and the reunion will be, just that more sweet.

Tomorrow I plan to go to the movies with the kids. And, then my parents will come meet us for ice-cream afterwards.

Phoenix Mundy|Asimo

To See You

10/14/17|Evening

Can't believe I went all day without updating the journal!

Overall a great day...can't wait to see you guys...

Pretty tired today. Now that I think about it, I didn't have a proper weekend so maybe that's why so tired...

Gonna smoke and head to bed!

Raimu|Ode to the Moon

A Bit Sad

10/15/17|Evening

We decided against the movie. Money is a little tight, so I didn't want to spend the money on a movie that neither is super psyched about.

We did go to the pool, tho! I only got in for a little bit, but, the kids had a blast! My dad got ice-cream for the kiddos - of course they loved that also!

Today, you told me that you might be able to come on the 30th. I really hope so! I don't like being separated from you. And, today I extra extra missed you. :(

I want to keep writing but, honestly ...I just miss you and, it's making me a bit sad so, ...I think I'll try to fall asleep.

> *"The dark, tore us apart*
> *Left two halves, one hammering heart"*
> Mt. Wolf|Heavenbound

Uncomfortable

10/15/17|Morning

Didn't sleep well last night. It was hot and uncomfortable. Oh well.
After work not sure what to do... I guess clean.

❦·•◆•·❦

6:18pm

...got home from work and started some housework right away. It's really
coming along! Just a few things left to finish before you come back! I'm
getting excited to come there to see you...and hoping maybe it'll work out
that you can just come back home with me. We will see I guess. But either way
I'm definitely ready for a fucking vacation away from La Isla for a few days.
Gonna smoke now. Oh, and water pressure is low...grrrr...feeling...worn-out...

"The holy waters fall on your hand,
They should be dancing instead, It's only
raining because of you, I keep on calling,
but for who?"
Lulu Rouge|Melankoli

❦·•◆•·❦

Medicina

10/16/17|Evening

I have to start this entry by saying that, *You. Are. Coming. To. Visit. And. We. Are. Going. Back!! With!! You!! (hopefully!?)...*

Today was a rough day. I think I just missed you a bunch. And, single mothering is hard, and also, yeah, I miss you. It was one of those days...when I finally got to talk to you, I told you about it, and you said you understood. That gave me such relief. Because I had been so zen, and today was bumming me out.

Also, got my medicina today, "Purple Kush" - so, so good. Smooth, awesome!!

The countdown begins, my Lover! I just can't wait! Plus, you said that you are shaving your face. Making me so happy!

Also, I forgot to tell you but Elizabeth has been battling a sore-throat all day. We did 3 servings of Sambucus and, 2 servings of Echinacea. I want all of us well for when you come!

"Shivering stars drift around in the sky, I lie
calm under their watchful eyes, In my heart,
I can feel it and why, That wherever I go, I'll
find my way home"
Asgeir|Breathe

A Great Day

10/16/17|Evening

   A GREAT DAY!

It's "Friday!" Water pressure good! Eric has electricity! I have plane tickets! I have cell service at home! I was able to call YOU!

I'm STOKED, STOKED, STOKED, you guys will come home with me in 3 weeks!!!!!!! *...maybe?!*

...all amazing things... I'm just so *happpppyyyyyyy!...*

It's early but I might try to sleep....can't do anything in the dark...if I can't sleep I might go to the *Tower...*

> *"Music's playing so loud,*
> *It all feels right,*
> *Close my eyes,*
> *Think about the old times,*
> *What's it all about?*
> *The feeling when it all works out"*
> Washed Out|It All Feels Right

Touch You Again

10/17/17|Evening

I got to talk to you today. A lot! And you started the journey (shaving), to me, seeing, more of your face. Thank you for that.

I took the kids to the pool and got to talk to the neighbor, from Turkey. Might hang out with her, to get to know her more.

I also took a walk to the supermarket and got Apple Pie, & vanilla ice-cream. You are gonna love this Apple Pie, so good. Not too sweet, crust...buttery and flaky.

You told me today that Eric might let you borrow the generator. That's so exciting! So weird that, if you get it, it will be the first time in a month, that our house has power.

We are 20 days out, from going back home with you. All of this still seems like a dream. Even our separation seems surreal at times.

I can't wait to touch you again.

Funny how distance slowly erases the physical feeling, or memory, that you have of someone. Like, I kinda can "feel" it, but the longer we're separated, the less I "feel" you. Like, your hugs, kisses...other stuff!!

Well, it's already tomorrow. I'm pretty tired. But, I love you, and I'm totally in 100% countdown-mode.

"Cold sheets, But where's my love?"
SYML|Where's My Love

I Wish

10/17/17\Afternoon

Slept good. Woke up and started right away on the laundry-room. So excited!

After a couple hours, I ran to grab a *Cuban* and Fries. Only ate half, saving the other half for dinner if I get hungry.

Now, back in laundry working again...gonna have to grab a few more small items from the hardware store.

Still no trash pickup, ...but we aren't the only ones.

Cell service today is in-and-out for some reason.

2:09pm,

   ...I HATE MOSQUITOES!!!!

11:14pm,

   ...spent a few hours at the *Tower*...

   ...got home and smoked, and that's when, ...I noticed the stars! Tonight, finally, is the night you were waiting for! No clouds, no moon, super dark..*SO MANY STARS!!* Amazing baby.

   ...I wish you were here to see them!

"But if stars shouldn't shine, by the very
first time, Then dear it's fine, so fine by me,
'Cause we can give it time, so much time,
with me
The xx|Stars

Beautiful Face

10/18/17|Afternoon

Today, I got to finally see your beautiful face!! I love you, & so much your face!

We planned to go to the beach today, but when we got there, we saw that it looked like Montones Beach after a big storm. The water was all gone. So, we went to the pool instead, where, Elizabeth learned to float. So, in the 3 or so weeks we've been here, she's learned to swim like a pro & float. Our little fishy.

Today, I also got super sick. Tomorrow morning, going to the supermarket for some more *Sambucus*. Kicking this in the ass!

19 more days until I get to kiss your face!! I love you!

Nils Frahm|You

Awesome Amazing

10/18/17\Afternoon

Slept good. Got up and swept the front porch.

Went to the *Tower* to meet Eric about the generator, and check email.

Got an awesome, amazing email from you!

...gonna find something to clean, just to avoid boredom.

...mold in kitchen worse than I thought. Gonna have to take everything out, wash all pots and pans, and clean cabinets. It's a big task but I have nothing else to do. I thought I would leave cabinets open to air out, but I started having severe sinus symptoms and I know it's from the mold...

I took a nap from like, 3:00pm-6:30pm...it was nice...

> *"Chemistry is rare in a two, three time*
> *affair, There's no guarantees, Working*
> *through the seasons, Pressed up against the*
> *ceiling, Pushing down on me"*
> The xx|Lips

More Myself

10/19/17|Evening

Today, I woke up a little better, but as nighttime fell, I started feeling rotten again. I'm thinking tomorrow I'll feel more myself.

Even though I wasn't my best, I met with Kris & Cort, and treated them to breakfast. It was good to connect to home.

Your package went out today.

I can't wait to see you! 18 more days!

That reminds me, I have to buy mine and the kids' tickets back home too!

They do love it here...your decision to send us here was amazing & the best. The kids are happy and healthy which is most important.

I can't wait to feel better, so I can be more active with them. Plus, I've been a bit tired and my patience went down...being sick doesn't help.

My parents have helped so much though. They have been making me these lemon-honey-teas and chicken-soup also. So yummy!!

I'll probably have more tomorrow. I believe in the power of, Chicken Soup!

I think I'll finally go to bed. I'm giddy because I'll get to see you soon. I think about it all the time. It's going to be a blast.

I love you!

"Today, and all of your days, I'll wear your
pain, Heal what I can in your troubled
mind, Sometimes our bodies will hurt for
some time, And the beauty in that can be
hard to find, I want you to find it, I want
you to see this"
SYML|Girl

I Can't Wash

10/19/17|Morning

Woke up at 5:30am, made it to the hardware store by 6:30am, then back home by 8:00am.

Got a bunch of mold-control products, ...and some cleaning stuff. Been working for the last hour on kitchen cabinets. No water, again...still?...so, I can't wash pots & pans until tomorrow probably...or whenever the water comes back...if?...

> *"The land returns to the dust, Is there any*
> *way, to get this weight off my skin,*
> *And find another one?"*
> Other Lives|Dust Bowl III

My Words

10/20/17|Evening

Happy 1st month Anniversary of the Cunt Maria!

I can't believe it! It still feels very surreal.

Today, was a stressful day. Your flight got cancelled, and then I kicked verbal-ass and got you on a flight for the 30th!

That means 10 more days until I'm in your arms again. I just can't wait!

You stayed in my heart today.

I hated to think of you coming-to-terms with all of this and, we're not there to comfort you. I'm not there to hug you! I hope my words were of some relief.

You are the strongest, smartest, most Zen person I know! I'm so incredibly proud of you...because I know you are the best at what you do! Because while everyone around you was losing their shit, you never did! Because who you are makes me stronger!

Whenever all of "this" would hit me, I just thought of you. Of us! Of our kids. Of, how you stayed behind. And even with no sleep, having trouble eating and full of adrenaline, I felt cool, calm, and collected at the same time.

I just knew as you were doing it over there, I could do it here. As you kicked ass there, I could kick ass here.

You are not weak! Never say it, never feel it!

We are a badass team! I love you!

10 more days!!

"Are you suffocating, Or are you someone else? Are we all someone else? Are we undetermined?"
Lissom|Doppelgänger

✦❧ ⋯ ◆ ⋯ ❧✦

One Month

10/20/17|Morning

Woke up around 5:30, but stayed in bed and kept sleeping until about 7:30am.

I am so excited to possibly get the package today! *...or tomorrow...*

Smoked and began my day by cleaning mold from our bathroom cabinets. Then I decided to tackle the moldy pots & pans.

...took awhile, but, BOOM all clean now!

Now gonna smoke...again...boredom!

The house is pretty much ready for you guys...I just have to clean bathrooms, and once we get electricity back I can finish my last, final project! Yay!

<hr>

10:12pm,

...no package today. Probably not until Monday. *Ugh.*

Not a good day but it is what it is. *I'm just so ready for a fucking break.*

The good news is, I get to see you guys earlier than expected! So happy for that!

Mike told me at work today it's been a month since Maria...I couldn't believe it. It feels like I'm still in it...dealing with it...it literally never stopped...it's so devastating, that until you experience it, you just can't plan for...the aftermath...the chaos...the cleaning...putting life back in order; takes so much time...

I'm laying in bed...just ready to move past this day...

...also, Mike updated me on his own situation with his wife...they had a heart-to-heart and are going to try to make their marriage work. ...they came to the conclusion that over the years, they had grown apart, and let their focus go elsewhere onto things that aren't important...they promised to spend more time together...which is great...although, I can't help but wonder how they will do it... but I'm glad to hear them say they are gonna try. I think their intentions are good, but they are missing the universal truths and secrets we've discovered...for example, they agree to put the kids into school and daycare, in the hopes that it makes time for them to be together as a couple...but I know that's a mistake.

...I mean, sacrifice your babies just to be selfish? Idk...like I said, the intentions are good, but how they plan to do it may not be best for the family unit, as a whole...they have to get over themselves, and figure out how to get their marriage back, while also strengthening the family ...including the kids. But whatever. I can't save the world.

It's hard because, in a way, you have to be selfish, and yet totally unselfish at the same time...I think they may be grasping at straws with their marriage and not attacking the roots...not being totally honest with, themselves, or each other, about what they believe should be important and what the priorities should be...but I digress....

On a separate but similar note...people are so weird. Or maybe... we are the weird ones? Eric, this whole time apart from his wife, is non-stop talking about how he would fuck so-and-so, this one and that one, etc...and yet, his wife sends him a photo with herself in a low-cut shirt she wore one day while out with, his Mother...and, he gets all macho about how she shouldn't be wearing that shirt, because, it showed too much cleavage... wtf? Is he insecure? Jealous? ...does he not trust her? I mean, here he is actively trying to fuck other women, and yet he doesn't trust Her? ...like I said, people are weird. Anyways, I like Eric a lot, but he shows his immaturity with stuff like this...

..none of this is important, I'm just putting down my crazy thoughts of today...

Okay goodnight. This day is over...on to tomorrow!

Gonna sleep now.

...1 month down...still no electricity...water intermittent...I can do this!

"Watch me rot away,
Like a beast inside his cage"
Low Roar|H.A.F.H.

Overwhelming

10/21/17|Evening

Today was a bad day. I think single-motherhood has caught-up with me, plus dealing with sickies, and anxious to see you. I keep saying this, but this whole Maria thing has been so crazy. So unreal. Overwhelming at times.

I was tired and moody today, but kept my cool.

We got to talk with you today, and Elizabeth really let loose talking to you. She was so hyper because of the *Tylenol* she had to take for the earache.

9 days babe!

"I am all the bombs you made for me, I am
everything that you can see, Give me heart
and give me fire, Hold me tight in my desire,
Burn me down, down, down, down, down"
Sami Simon|Bombs

A New Day

10/21/17|Morning

Welp...I'm at the Job already! My shift doesn't start until 1:15pm...but, I'm bored ...so came to the *Tower*. Also, wanted to check the package tracking, but, ugh ...still in Memphis!

Oh well.

Had a granola bar, gonna drink coffee...

It's a new day!

> *"Wait in line, 'Til your time, Ticking clock,*
> *Everyone stop"*
> Zero 7|In The Waiting Line

❧ ⸱ ◆ ⸱ ☙

Rained Out

10/22/17|Evening

Today, I started my day off, not in the best way. I was upset with Elizabeth for not sleeping. I was worried she wouldn't last through the errands we had to run today. But, after talking with her, we went about our day.

It took her a bit to wake up, but eventually we started our way toward the Farmer's Market.

We got rained-out, so, decided to drive to the big city instead. Honestly, so glad we did. It was a very good time! The kids got to rest for a few hours on the way there. Lots to look at!

8 more days!

"You are the rain that falls at night,
Beneath the watercolor skies"
Oh So Quiet|Rain at Night

Time Travel

10/22/17|Afternoon

Oh man, ...I'm slacking on my journal!

Yesterday was a great day, and today is a great day!

Last night on the way home, there was electricity from the Farmacia, all the way down to the gas-station!! Amazing! ...shouldn't be long now, I hope!

Tomorrow I should be getting the package you sent, fingers crossed!

One week left until I pack my bags!!

...can't wait to finally see you guys...it's been so crazy...

7:37pm,

...laying in bed now. Had a great day.

Gonna try to sleep now, so I can time-travel to tomorrow!

M. Andrews|Philosophy of Time Travel

Chilled Out

10/23/17|Evening

Today was definitely a chill day.

Elizabeth still battling an earache, and I have a kink in my neck.

Chicken Soup & White Rice! Kids loved it!

Low Roar|Time & Space

A Long Time

10/23/17|Evening
   ...still no electricity...

> *"El capitalismo foraneo*
> *El capitalismo foraneo*
> *El capitalismo foraneo"*
> Gotan Project|El Capitalismo Foraneo

To Be Here

10/24/17|Evening

I don't remember making a habit, of waking up at 12:30, but, today I woke up around 12:30.

Made the kiddos breakfast, boiled eggs with toast. With Elizabeth I did the usual, take out the white & just leave the yolk. Then, she tells me that next time, I could cut them like James' (*in little slices*) and that she'll eat the white. It's so cool how much more open minded she is when it comes to food. Ever since Maria, they are both eating so well.

6 more days! I can't even wait! I'm so anxious for you to be here already!

AK|Pulses

Mosquitoes

10/24/17|Morning

I woke up today about an hour ago. Now just sitting outside fighting mosquitoes. I put the dog downstairs and she doesn't like it... she's literally howling like a damn wolf. Cute, sad, makes me feel bad, ...but, so cool!

...oh and I had some organic beef jerky, YUM!

"A wave, An awesome wave,
That rushes skin and
widens in blooded veins.
Breathe in, Exhale."
alt-J|Bloodflood

❦❧ · ◆ · ❦❧

Made Me See

10/25/17|Evening

So, tonight Elizabeth made me see that I've been a bit short-fused with her. It really comes down to me, and for the past couple of days, here & there my reactions have been less patient. I can blame dealing with sickness & missing you, and how I ache to be in the same room as you, how I miss the help that you give me. My parents are awesome, but I miss you and us as a family. I know that we might have to be separated again & if you 'go' first, then it won't be forever, but I just don't want to be separated from you.

I don't remember the actual feeling of your lips, or your hug, and that lack of physical connection makes me sad. Sad, because I can't believe that at 27 days, that feeling is almost gone.

So, all those things may seem valid, but the truth is that I let those feelings and thoughts 'win' over what I know to be *Zen*.

Giving-in to those feelings take away from priorities. Our babies!

I've been a bit distracted in my thoughts, and she noticed. She told me so. I apologized. I told her I've been sick, & missing you, & excited to see you. She told me that, she has a huge space in her heart that's for you, and since we had to leave you, it's been missing. That, she had been keeping it in, but, that it feels too much & was making her 'off.' Which, I saw, and I know sickness also had a lot to do with maybe her being extra dramatic or not listening...I should have caught that.

But, tomorrow is a new day!

I can continue to let my thoughts and feelings, and even physical illness, get in my own way, and lose being ever-present, or... *wake up*!

So, I choose wake up!

My children deserve the best of me, no matter what! And, that's what I'm going to do. I let everything catch up to me... This was and is such a crazy thing. This Maria thing...yeeesh! But, we, I, am badass; we can do this gracefully & more. Like I tell the kids, I can't forget:

Everyday, I am born again. I'm in charge of how I feel, and today I choose happiness. The past can't be changed, therefore I will accept it without regret. The future hasn't arrived, therefore I will face my future without fear. I will focus my attention to what is happening right now, therefore I will handle my present with confidence. Whatever the present moment brings, I will accept it. Everything is, as it is. I am at peace with myself, exactly as I am. I will demonstrate love, compassion and tenderness to my daughter...to my son...to my, Love!...I will allow them to be Free! I will enjoy every moment, and make it so beautiful, that it will be worth remembering!!!

"Leave doubt behind, you've more to say,
There's light only you can see, I know that
sometimes it's the hurt, that saves us"
Blanco White|All That Matters

Clothes That Fit

10/25/17\Afternoon

Great day! ...got some clothes that fit, and got my annual physical! Traffic coming back was thick, but I'm home safe!

No power yet... but I'm able to text you now from home! Yay!

Gonna chat on the phone with you and then probably head inside. I'm excited for tomorrow because, only 4 days of Job-ing before I see you guys!!!!!!!

I'm so excited for the trip that it's hard to sleep but, I'm gonna try.

> *"Ain't no angel gonna greet me,*
> *It's just you and I, my friend,*
> *My clothes don't fit me no more,*
> *I walked a thousand miles,*
> *Just to slip this skin"*
> B. Springsteen|Streets of Philadelphia

Set The Mind

10/26/17|Evening

4 more days!

Today was a good day! What a difference it makes to just set the mind right.

We spent the day making your *Welcome* poster. I can't wait for you to see it! We are so proud of you! We all can't wait to see you and spoil you!

Today went so fast... Elizabeth asked to go to bed early today. I had to give her *Tylenol* again for her earache. Poor baby, it makes her so hyper that she can't sleep. Even though the pain bothers her, she is being so good.

They both have been fantastic! James doesn't complain, and he is such a help. He goes on daily walks and for the past two days, takes his sister with him. He asked if in the not-so-far future, he can have his own smartphone. He said he would even be happy with an old used one. He is the sweetest, most thoughtful kid.

And Elizabeth, I can truly say has been 100% fantastic as well. Making the best of not being in her environment, not having her stuff & missing you! She's been so great and mostly going with the flow. For 6 years old, she leaves me amazed.

I know that, what they went through with Maria, has impacted them & I am so glad that, after the initial shock & trauma, I have seen so much positive. I see them be more conscious with food, talking about the energy it contains. Such a new willingness to try things!

And for me, this has been a great mental test, which I feel I have kicked ass. Not to say I haven't had weak moments; moments where I gave in to what felt like strong emotions. But, I feel like all my 'training', all those months meditating on the beach, which really wasn't training but a way-of-life, well...I feel that the several past months have really prepared me, simply, *for life.*

Today it was a hurricane, and life goes on & we all will smile again (*although our little family smiled all through it & afterwards*) and life will bring good things and other bad things. The yin and yang! How we live, and act and think, determines if we live this life in a miserable way *or if we enjoy it for the fucking awesome adventure it is.*

4 days! 4 days! 4 days!

P.S. *I Adore You! I love you!*

"In time
How it all works out
It's alright, it's alright
It's alright, it's alright"
RHODES|Worry

❖⇉ ·◆· ⇇❖

Unlit

10/26/17|Late
...darkness...

> *"I've got this life, I'll be around to grow,*
> *Who I was before, I cannot recall, Long*
> *nights allow me to feel...I'm falling...I am*
> *falling, The lights go out"*
> Eddie Vedder|Long Nights

My Best For You

10/27/17|Evening

Whoa, it's been something else, but, finally Elizabeth started to feel better today.

Ate lunch and then did a little shopping. I already have picked-out the dress I'll receive you with. Between tonight & tomorrow I'll do all the grooming to look my best for you. *I'm so excited!* 2 more days and I'll be in your arms again. *I won't want to let you go!*

I'm energized, even though it's past midnight, because I just asked our daughter how she feels and it is night & day from yesterday. It killed me to see, and hear, her cry in pain. Poor baby!

Tonight, we went upstairs & I decided to play *UNO* with her before bed. I try to do things throughout the day that are fun. During the time of sickness, that routine slacked a bit.

Tomorrow starts a whirlwind weekend before picking you up at the airport, and then we'll be together!

2 more days!

"I can't change your thoughts, my dear, I
can't change your fears, But if you want I'll
travel near, To make it disappear"
Axel Flovent|Forest Fires

Lightless

10/27/17|Late

...darkness...darkness...

"When the last light warms the rocks
And the rattlesnakes unfold
Mountain cats will come
To drag away your bones
And rise with me forever
Across the silent sand
And the stars will be your eyes
And the wind will be my hands"
Handsome Family|Far From Any Road

The Whole Time

10/28/17|Evening

Today started our mini-roadtrip.

Woke up, packed, had my cup of cafe, and then did some cleaning-up.

The whole time, I was thinking of you, the whole time.

I am so excited! I got ready & got the kids ready and, went on our way.

We drove all day and then stopped for a late dinner before getting to my sister's place. We just hung-out a bit before meeting-up with my aunt at their room on the resort. Spotted a pretty badass arcade and the kids and I snuck away from the group to go play! We ended up spending the whole night in the arcade playing games. The kids had a great time. They were the masters of the night. Whatever they wanted, we did, & they had a blast.

Crazy thing is that, the arcade was just that, an arcade inside a resort. We are all still so excited that, we're having trouble falling asleep.

Finally it's around 4am and everyone is winding down. The parents are snoring away, sis said goodnight, and the kiddos are on their electronics. I know we all should get some sleep but, I also understand the excitement. The good thing is that, we have no plan. We'll wake up whenever & head that way. Because of my sister's 'hookup', we won't have to wait in line!

Well, it's time for me to get some shut-eye.

I love you so much! And even tho I am super psyched for the Park tomorrow, & for the kids, I am most excited that it puts us at:

1 more day!

"To my heart I must be true
You're the one that I want
The one that I want
The one that I need"
A. & J. Stone|You're The One That I
Want

Rayless

10/28/17|Late

...darkness...darkness...darkness...

Dru Hill|Lost Future

Tomorrow

10/29/17|Evening

Today was Park Day!

We wished you were here, & can't wait to take you, there...someday.

Tomorrow, we get you!

0 more days!

> *"And nothing else matters,*
> *You, baby, it's you"*
> London Grammar|Baby It's You

So Fast

10/29/17|Evening

Time, the last few days, seems to have gone so fast...and yet, so damn slow.

> *"For the desired effect, would you come*
> *back August or June, June? And I hate*
> *that tomorrow's December, this collision*
> *came mid-bloom, Better built to resume, I'll*
> *see you August, see you June, I'm building*
> *higher than I can see, I want fantasy"*
> The xx|Fantasy

With You

10/30/17|Morning
  Mini Vacay with you!
  Time to come get you at the airport!

> *"Anchor up to me, love*
> *Anchor up to me, love"*
> Novo Amor|Anchor

Tax Free Rum

10/30/17|Morning

Well I made it!

I'm sitting in the airport now, waiting to start boarding.

Traffic was terrible, but luckily I left early...checked-in my bag which was cool because it's basically automated now...you scan your phone and it prints out the sticker...

I got some tax-free rum, for your parents too!

Civilization...here I come!

...still no electricity...hopefully not much longer...maybe, by the time I get back?...

"Mr. Wolf, the feast has been served,
There's fancy wine with hors d'oeuvre's"
Angus Stone|The Wolf and the Butler

Another Countdown

11/4/17|Evening

Another countdown starts, for when we are all together again! 8 Days!

Today I did some chilling before taking Elizabeth for her fabulous haircut. The stylist was wonderful, which makes her 1st experience the best. She loved the whole thing.

The kiddos played hide-and-seek tonight. James said, funnest thing he has done.

8 more days, babe!

P.S. I hope you get better, too! I wish I was there to nurse you!

> *"And I'm running with you, As fast as I*
> *can, Singing to myself, I want to hold your*
> *hand, And we're going downtown, 'Cause*
> *we feel like running around, Is it really this*
> *fun, when you're on my mind, Is it really this*
> *cool, to be in your life"*
> Majical Cloudz|Downtown

Back in the Dark

11/4/17|Evening

Who needs light anyway? Back home, which means, back in the dark.

...I shouldn't have expected anything else...

The trip was great, way too fast though. It was wonderful being with you and the kids! I could tell they missed me. It was also nice to just...get off the damn island. Chaos, chaos, chaos... work, work, work... it was a little fun at first but...this is, now, just ridiculous.

...still no electricity...water not drinkable, yet...internet? don't even ask...

Welcome back to the darkness...welcome back, home.

> *"Is that the old man walking in the dark,*
> *Take me home where them broken brights,*
> *Are shining down, make me feel alright"*
> Angus Stone|Broken Brights

Life Together

11/5/17|Evening

7 more days! Yay!

Today we went to the Farmer's Market, near my mom's house. It was fantastic. So many fruits & veggies. Even live music. Elizabeth wanted a snow-cone, but I had her choose something healthier first, so she chose strawberries (which were delicious) & ate like half the package.

She must be growing.

Babe, you got power today. It was around 8:30pm. Before you had said anything, I hoped it was that news! Very exciting & surreal at the same time. And a huge burden comes off my shoulders because the kids and I can come back and, life will pretty much be back to normal.

7 more days! Life together again!

"Where have you gone?
Why couldn't I go too?
But we were dead upon arrival,
Of our hollowing truth"
The Western Den|I Still Remain

Realization

11/5/17|Late

I keep thinking of you guys...I realize now that I was so tense those few days there, that, I just wasn't even very present...so distant. I can't wait for you to be back here. It's dark and wet, but I've done all I can to rebuild our little castle.

I'm struggling to keep making these journal entries. I think you'll really appreciate the entries from before the trip...right now I just feel, exhausted....with everything.

The dog just stares at me while I sit here smoking in the dark, ...the longer I stay in this darkness, the more I seem to like it... but, what's interesting is that, I just recently realized that, I think, I'm actually very afraid of the Dark... really.

I'm not sure how to process that realization, especially as I sit here, in the darkest of nights, all alone, writing this in my journal to see with my own eyes my own truth... half of me seems to desire the dark, while the other half seems to fear it...

...does this make me less than a *'man'*?...*what is 'man', anyway?*...maybe I'm spending too much time alone?...

...I can't wait for you to get back here...I'm lonely...

...I see a few of the neighbors with electricity tonight, and yet, ...I can't seem to bring myself to flip the switch here;...I sense already the pattern of On and Off they are playing, and, ...I don't want to play that game...I know by tomorrow, the lights will once again be off...the whole entirety of the system is, failing here.

"The lighthouse man, Turned and whispered me some things, We don't sleep, Awake in a dream"
Angus Stone|Bird On the Buffalo

❧━━◆━◆━◆━❧

License

11/6/17|Evening

My big plan for today was, to try and get my Mainland driver's license. That did not go well. Government, ugh!

But, that took a big chunk out of my day & before I knew it, the day was over. My mom made me a feast today, and I loved it.

Babe, 6 more days! 6 more days!

So happy!

6 more days!

"The light was upon us,
Covering parts of, You,
The call wasn't far,
You reached it before our time,
We reached it before our time"
Talos|The Light Upon Us

Come Home

11/6/17|Night

A bit of a break-down last night...I tried to analyze myself all day today. I really think I'm just overworked and exhausted from all this. I look forward to having you guys back, ...I'm going a bit crazy here in the dark. The rumors swirl everyday about the electricity...it just keeps coming and going...randomly...very unstable still.

...I've been thinking about the fact that we *survived* a very major disaster...and just, the opportunity presented to see, and thus embrace, life, in a re-invigorated way... a youthful way...for some reason it seems like, we survived for a purpose...and all I really mean, I think, by that is, maybe it's time we consider buying a house?...rather than renting this rundown castle?...I know, seems crazy at first, the Island just got fucked-up by a hurricane, but it just seems like, maybe, we are meant to be, a part, of the new foundation of, a new P.R?...anyways...I'll fill-you-in once you get back.

...more and more, these journals feel less of a daily log-of-activity...and more of a...idk...personal communication???...weird, idk...not sure how long I can keep this up, but it does help to pass these long lonely nights without you, my Love...Come home!

> *"Some say he's a mad man, Who fell to his own defeat,*
> *Some say he's got no one, But the moon at his feet"*
> A. Stone|Apprentice of the Rocket Man

Not Too Short

11/7/17|Evening

Today was haircut day for me. I love it!

It's short but not too short. And, I can't wait to surprise you with it.

Elizabeth had a sore throat today. Been giving her Sambucus. Poor baby! I don't know how she got sickie again.

I met-up with Kris today. I wish they could come back with me. I'm going to miss *TBC* so bad. And, I feel so sad & bad for them. But, this is the new Isla, things will be different post-Maria.

I go back-and-forth from nervous & excited when I think about life in P.R. But, seeing & hanging out with Kris made me feel more excited than nervous. Like I said, seeing her, connected me back to P.R. & I can't wait to be back. Back to our life, back with you!

Oh, by the way, 5 more days!

5 more days!

> *"Little bird took to the sky, I watched the*
> *rain fill the rusty town, Dreamers dream*
> *only in the mind"*
> A. & J. Stone|Little Bird

Infinity

11/7/17|Late

...coming to grips with the fact that, this whole recovery phase, post-apocalypse, is, ...going to take a looooong time...

I'm so tired already...not enough personnel to man the *Tower*...looking like a *never-ending infinite overtime*...work, work, work, *Job, Job, Job*...

...if the night gets darkest before the dawn...what does it mean, that every night post-Maria seems to continue getting darker and darker and darker...why does it feel as though the hurricane wasn't exactly the storm I had been waiting for?...the adrenaline of the whole experience has now left me depleted of life...my hope now rests on my reuniting with you, my beautiful family...

Dark or Light...come back to me, *my Love*!

"Could you tell,
I was left lost and lonely?
Could you tell,
things ain't worked out my way?"
The xx|Infinity

❦⋯✦⋯❧

A Bit Rough

11/8/17|Evening

4 More Days!

Oh, babe, I just can't wait to be home. Just wanted to start today's journal by saying that!!

Elizabeth had it a bit rough today. Still dealing with the sickies.

Today I made chili-soup for everyone. So yum, I can't wait to make it for you! I can't wait to be your wife again.

It was a pretty chill day today. Hanging out but having a good time.

I bought us some Matcha Powder for our smoothies. I look forward to making all 4 of us healthy again with my cooking!

I am giddy looking forward to seeing all the cool things you've done at the house. I can't even imagine what they all are...you are amazing! All the cleaning and laundry and, more cleaning! The BEST husband, ever!

4 Days babe, and we are home!

"If you love me, I'll make you a star in my
universe, You'll never have to go to work,
You'll spend everyday,
shining your light my way"
A. & J. Stone|For You

After The Storm

11/8/17|Late

Another long day, ...the Job is, the Job; ...*never-ending.*

I've been wondering what the point of all this has been...?...the Storm to end all storms, supposedly...but, for what?... what's the fucking point?... what are we supposed to do, after the storm?

I look around all day from my tall *Tower*, looking down upon the World, watching it revolve endlessly without stopping as we, foolishly, try to keep up...why?... I don't have any answers, yet...but the longer I spend in this darkness, the more questions begin to rise from that same abyss I fear...

Here we are, you're about to come back to this...chaos...and we will most definitely struggle to continue forward here...for what, my Love?... what are we doing here?... I don't think I can show you these last few entries...these questions scare me...I would hate to frighten, you, my Love...I'll have to look for some answers before trying to express this to you...forgive me, my Love...

...*seek...and ye shall find*, ...right?...

"Well I'm scared of what's behind,
and what's before"
Mumford & Sons|After the Storm

The End of This

11/9/17|Evening

3 Days! 3 Days! 3 Days! 3 Days! 3 Days!

Baby, we are at the end of this!

I can't wait to squeeze you & hug you, and kiss you, and hang out with you.

I made bread today for my mom & I think she liked it. I felt a little out-of-practice but, it was a good way to get back into it. I can't wait to cook & bake & make us smoothies & cups of *café*.

Elizabeth was better today, which makes me glad because I didn't want her traveling while sick. Everyday, I hope she feels better & better.

Today was another lazy day. But, it flew by! Mom made *Bacalaitos*, so we ate, and hung-out.

P.S. 3 Days & I Love You!

And you, unfortunately, lost power again at 4:30 a.m.

"I know you're tired, darling, don't give in,
It's been awhile, darling, And though you're
tired, darling don't give in"
Field Division|Modest Mountains

Just Darkness

11/9/17|Late

Just darkness. Loneliness. I miss you, my Family. I'm quite certain now that, a man should not remain alone...the darkness, it overwhelms the soul...for those who still have one...which, might possibly be me, but I'm not sure...what is a soul anyways?...all I feel is darkness now...

I'm so...exhausted with life...this whole nightmare scenario has completely drained me, my Love...it's as though I am back in a war-zone here...what has happened to our beautiful Island...? ...I'm beginning to sense that, nobody outside of La Isla cares, at all...we are all alone here, my Love...at least we shall have, each-other.

...come home!

Hans Zimmer|Joi

Like A Dream

11/10/17|Evening

2 Days, Babe!

It doesn't seem real, like a dream. All of this seems like a dream… And, now, we are two days from being all together.

I did some pre-packing tonight. I'm just so excited I couldn't wait until tomorrow.

Tomorrow is all about laundry.

2 Days, Eeek! So excited!

> *"I forgot this place is magic*
> *I got lost in my bad habits*
> *I've forgotten who we are*
> *I've forgotten who we are"*
> Aisha Badru|Dreamer

Just in Time

11/10/17|Late

   2 more days. Just, in time.

   Electricity is...on-*ish*?...flickering and unstable...

   ...now, if only the lights can just, ...*stay*-on...

"Deux jours Plutart je t'es pris en"

H. Gregson-Williams|The End

We Survived

11/11/17|Evening

1 more day! Babe, we did it! We survived Maria! We survived being separated & didn't want to kill each other! I feel like we are stronger than ever! And, now I am about 13 hours from getting on a plane with our wonderful kiddos & resuming our life.

Today, went fast as hell!!! Cleaned house and washed clothes. Took James for a haircut, he looks fantastic. He looks so much older. He loves it, I think precisely because of that. Also got some frozen yogurt while we thought and talked about, you!

Took all of us out for one last dinner. It was yummy, fast & cheap. Then went to grab frozen yogurt, again, together for dessert. It was a great last night!

All of this was like a dream, but I'm ready to be home with you again. For all of us to be together. *So soon! I. Can't. Wait!* I love you & am so proud of you, the kids, *us! We fucking did it.*

> *"Tonight, we roll*
> *I've been awake for deliverance*
> *Deliverance*
> *Deliver me"*
> RY X|Deliverance

The Aftermath

11/11/17|Late

Together, again, my Love.

We resume our life, a new chapter for us all...no more journaling for me I think...not for awhile...this chapter must end so another can begin...that's how it works right?...

...I can't shake the feeling though, that whatever the darkness released, still lingers...I can sense... something...as though this storm, Maria, was only a prelude...a beginning...that as bad as it has been, ...this is only the start of...something else entirely...but...

...I'm already so tired...so...*exhausted*...

Okay, honesty time...*"Molly-Time"*...

I'm not sure what to even feel right now.

...joyful and excited to have my family come home to me...yet...fearful of the possibilities of life here, now...post-apocalypse...without water, without electricity, without internet...but, most importantly, fearful of myself...fearful that we shall once again be together, yet so very far apart.

I know now, my Love, that, I can't show you this part of my journal...not right now anyway...maybe in the future...idk...something just seems different with me...like, something has been...unlocked? ...opened?...

...even writing that feels odd, yet, satisfying?...

I'm fearful, my Love, because, I have, after many weeks, just realized that, in all my efforts to rebuild and repair our castle, ...this home I am welcoming you back to,...

...I have somehow managed, unconsciously...to paint the Two living-rooms, *completely and utterly,*

...BLACK!...midnight...dark...pitch-black...lifeless...yet, I swear it feels so, warm...inviting...

I have, somehow, in my effort to create a safe place for us to, "live," ...managed to turn our supposed castle, into nothing other than *a dark-cave*, without light, without water, without any connection to the outside world...

...what is happening to me? ...what ...has *already* happened to me?...

I have to stop this *journaling-thing*, for now...I fear my own words, *staring back at me with every "press of a key"*...

This next year, *I will just...read*, words from other people...*absorb all I can*...until I figure out what is happening to me... I fear I may be losing the very thing you most treasure about me, my Love...*my own mind.*

...together, again...my Love...I want you to come back to me...please, and yet, I *don't* want you to come back to, *this*...

...for who exactly...*am I?*...perhaps...perhaps...*I*, am nothing but...*The Beast?*

"I wanna see it painted
Painted black
Black as night
Black as coal
I wanna see the sun
Blotted out from the sky
I wanna see it painted,
painted, painted,
Painted black, yeah"
The Rolling Stones|Paint It, Black

CHAPTER 2

A Time Of Upheaval

"In the dark
It feels so real, yeah
All this time
We've been sleeping on it
It's who we are right now
What we're going through, yeah
All this time spent
Saving for it"
Fink|Sort Of Revolution

The Uncertainty

1/22/18|Morning

I woke up like every other day since Sep. 20, with P.R. on my mind. I check the news and it makes me so sad to see the shitty stuff still going on. It angers me to see those le$$ fortunate pay the biggest price. But, it is the world we live in...

This needs to serve as a reminder of how uncertain everything is. How foolish it is to focus on the little stuff, to stress, to be jealous, or selfish, or mean. To get mad.

I still can't believe I experienced the uncertainty of my life, my children's lives, *his* life.

So, ...to survive, only to then be separated. And, now, together again. Nothing else matters.

Sometimes I tire at not being able to shake-off that feeling that things aren't quite "normal" yet. But, 1st, ...what is normal?, and, 2nd, maybe we all must adapt to a new normal.

That yucky "PTSD" leftover "feeling" will go away with time. And, lucky for us four, we have each other.

I randomly said this to Mel, *"Life is bigger than the current crisis."*

———————

Health Mantra

I am healthy. I will feed my body the food it needs for proper self healing. I am full of energy, which allows me to be active in what it means to be a mom, wife & partner. I will stay connected to my body so I can be attuned to my needs. My muscles and bones are strong. I am healthy.

Remembering Who I Am

I am free. I go with the flow. I am healthy. I am content. I just am. *Nothing is a big deal*; perspective! Family. Daughter. Son. Husband. Beach. Weed. Love! Love! Love! Laughter. Alan Watts. Creativity. Yoga.

Life is bigger than our current crisis.

"I was stuck in the ground,
Trying to cover my eyes.
Trying to move all this light.
I spent all night,
Trying to remember your face."
Houses|Big Light

•••

1/22/18|Dark

...

Other Lives|Heading East

❧ — ◆ — ❧

Yellow Brick Road

1/24/18|Morning

Feeling better already. Enough with the eating "shit." I'm motivated to do Yoga again. To meditate regularly again. To beat the anxiety and to go with the flow of our Post-Maria reality. Which in many ways isn't bad.

People are still nicer, more patient. As a family, we spend more *unplugged*-time together, and us 4 couldn't be more united. For the past 2 days we've been seeing *OG&E* trucks going up & down our road. It's, *wow!* Part of what makes life different now.

Yesterday, before groceries, I stopped by to go check out Shore-Island. My smoking-buddy wasn't there, ...phew! I put *"Yellow Brick Road"* & just, sat, reconnecting with the sun, sand, & just watched the waves, which were wicked! Rolling beautifully!

The sand was so clean, ...we have Maria to thank for that. One of the positives! There are many more.

I feel good. Low to 0 stress & anxiety. And, yesterday the Beast and I, *fucked. It's now the best I've ever had!* These are all the small, everyday, mundane steps that lead to us "clicking" back to our life!

> *"Don't let your soul get lonely, Child, it's*
> *only time, it will go by. Don't look for love in*
> *faces, places, It's in you that's where you'll*
> *find...Kindness. Be, Be here now"*
> Ray LaMontagne|Be Here Now

...

1/24/18\Dark

...

Port Blue|Into The Sea

Put Some Music

2/9/18|Morning

18 days eating well & feeling better everyday!

Since I last wrote, went to the beach with James & Elizabeth. It was so nice—not so much the ocean, all the weather has the waves going crazy! But, nice to go out again.

Anxiety is up & down, but that's expected, especially since I still haven't gotten the yoga/meditation thing going again, post Maria. Feeling lazy & unmotivated. But...slowly getting my groove back. Slowly baking again, cooking more... Life is so good, tho. *The Beast* is so great & patient. And, even with a crazy flu season, the kids haven't gotten sick since we got back. Phew!

Today, gonna put some music on the speakers &, do some laundry &, see how far I get.

"That's the time I took, To calm these things, Better to have been with, than live without it, Hold yourself, howl and scream, Finally feel everything, joining underneath"
Deptford Goth|Feel Real

...

2/9/19|Dark

...

"The skyline is not seen for many a day.
It feels as though we're never turning back
here. The land returns to the dust. Is there
any way, to get this weight off my skin, And
find another one?"
Other Lives|Dust Bowl III

Sunset Sherbet

2/18/18|Morning

Last night I smoked a whole bowl of 'Sunset Sherbet,' & went into a great meditative state! It was so great to finally go to, that, place. To clear the mind, to be present.

I realized, that I was resisting that calm, secret place. That I was still holding on to Maria for some reason. Maybe fear, of truly embracing the "after" - come what may. Or fear of relaxing too much, just in case.

In those deep breaths, I let go. I knew I had to. And, if those feelings of wanting to cling to the bad, creep up again - this is my reminder. I don't have to hold on to Maria. She's the past. Today, today...is Today!

I kept wondering why, as fortunate as I felt, as much as our life, personally, has returned to normal, I still felt anxious at times, uneasy & sad, and mad. And, I was prepared to feel all that & more.

I knew it would be part of the healing process for all 4 of us. But, it's time. It's time to deal with life as it is now. With all its uncertainty, to continue to see it as our own little adventure. Because, it is, our own little adventure. And, to let go of our past, to continue moving, towards-forward.

But, more importantly than forward, just, ever present in our beautiful today!

"As you run towards the horizon, And venture out into the cold, I will keep the fire burning, To light the way back home. You and I are both the same, That's how I know it'll go this way"
Aisha Badru|The Way Back Home

•••

2/18/18|Dark

••••

"*But we're all just an end to a simple thing,*
And it's all you see, and it's all you see.
We're just tamer animals, We're just tamer
animals, We're just tamer animals"
Other Lives|Tamer Animals

Slice of Paradise

3/4/18|Morning

After talking it over with myself first, yesterday morning I vented to *The Beast*, about how shitty I felt sometimes & how reading P.R. news, first thing in the morning, had taken the place of my morning meditation time. I missed my peace.

"No work or love will flourish out of guilt, fear or hollowness of heart, just as no valid plans for the future can be made by those who have no capacity for living now."
Alan Watts

We have decided to stay! P.R. is still our slice of paradise. We want to buy a house by the end of the year...

But, if I continue to live in a negative place of fearful thoughts and anger & allow those feelings & thoughts to paralyze me or fill my head with so much *NOISE*, I won't have room for anything new, creative, fun...& I'll miss out on the adventure, that is, if my negative vibe doesn't fuck it up first.

Zen is about seeing the flow, and going with it. Accepting the ebb & flows of the life journey. All is, as it is!!! And it's all good!

Novo Amor|Haven

...

3/4/18|Dark

...

Stoto|Still Can't Sleep

In My Head

3/5/18|Morning

This morning after he left, I went to clean up the big-ass "art pad" we made for Elizabeth. And I found all sorts of creative & beautiful...creations. Many which, she wanted my help with. Being too much in my head, in my depressed thoughts, in my fear, in my past & future, I missed the mark and I helped her with, *none*.

As I continued to admire all of her artwork, I came across a drawing of the family, clearly indicating her perception of my distance from them. It explains it all. I've been distant. Holding-on to a chaos that, I've already overcome. We handled Maria great, I give us a 10/10. But, I held on to all of the scary, and sad, and anger that came with it all. Even tho, for us, it's been "gone" for a "long time."

Why do I do that? Why humans do this, *stay in the filth*, is something I won't ever understand. Let it all go! All attachments. See everything as, an *adventure*.

"Did you run away, I don't need to know, But if you ran away,
If you ran away, come back home, Just come home"
SYML|Where's My Love

...

3/5/18|Dark

...

Hans Zimmer|Stay

Forever Changed

3/29/18|Morning

Last Sunday I woke up with a new resolve to, just *Be*, again.

To be present!

It felt like I finally let Maria go. The anxiety, the fear, the pain, the tragedy.

The Beast said that, whether in a small or big way, everyone was forever changed by it.

So, I know I'm different than I was Sept. 20...But, to let go, to the point where I am present, my mind not full of shit, more in my present reality and not the fantasy "reality" in my head...I craved that!

The Past & The Future create a fog - and then I miss it all!

So, I had to wake up!!

Maria was unexpected & a wake-up call to the delicacy of life, of our routine, of the status quo.

I lamented with him how, almost ashamed I was, that it took 6 months.

But, how do you deal with something like Maria?

"*How do you understand what can't be explained,*" he said.

That same day James said it finally felt like we were past it.

<hr />

I also hung with the neighbor chick. For hours we smoked, and talked, and I could still be a mom. Reminiscent of Melx.

She has a cool point of view, she's a psych major, who loves the herb, is so chill and, still has the child-like wonder. I hope she doesn't lose that & grow up. She's 24!

Peter Pan 4 ever!

How cool to be able to say, that even once, you experienced a cool human...experience?

❖❖ — ◆ — ❖❖

Today, shit got real! We uploaded some documents for our home-loan.

I'm definitely joining the dance, and I'm all-in with, this new chapter of our lives. Whatever it may end up looking like.

That's the fun in all of this...

Not quite knowing how it is all going to turn out.

"'Cause I don't know what to do
It's not like I get to choose
Who I love
Who I love
Who I love
Who I love"
girl in red|girls

❖❖ — ◆ — ❖❖

...

3/29/18|Dark

...

"Ring like silver, ring like gold
Ring out those ghosts on the Ohio
Ring like clear day wedding bells
Were we the belly of the beast or
the sword that fell
We'll never tell
Come to me clear and cold on some sea
Watch the world spinning waves,
like that machine
Now I've been crazy couldn't you tell
I threw stones at the stars,
but the whole sky fell"
G.A. Isakov|The Stable Song

Solidarity

4/5/18|Morning

Last Tuesday, *The Beast* & I sat down for a timely conversation. We "played" for 2.5 years, after the Business, but now we want to buy a house & really give the kiddos the home, stability & everything they need, which is what they deserve. It means going on a budget. And, it means that *The Beast* will cut back significantly.

After spit-balling lots of scenarios, we came up with the conclusion:

We love giving the kids, ourselves, this life. With this life comes the job. And, the job has restriction. And, we don't want to risk losing the job - which means losing it all. Not gonna happen!

I'll cut back too. In solidarity. I started today, not bad at all. And, he seems excited about it all. Willing to sacrifice, to provide. I love him!!! I adore him!!! For what he does, for all he is!

I mourned all of this. But, I think we found a happy medium, we can both live with.

"Play my tricks, Fragile mind
Rest your head, On me
Shut my eyes, I'm not here
There must be some mistake"
Low Roar|Don't Be So Serious

...

4/5/18|Dark

...

Stoto|Still Can't Sleep
re-mastered

Four-Twenty

4/20/18|Morning

Ironic...today is 420!

But, because of a "can't," *the beastly "edge" is back.*

> *"Has the world gone mad or is it me? All
> these small things they gather 'round me,
> gather 'round me"*
> Ben Howard|Small Things

❧⟩⟩—•—◆—•—❧⟨⟨❧

•••

4/20/18|Dark

...

"This house, she's holding secrets, I got my
change behind the bed, In a coffee can I
throw my nickels in, Just in case I have to
leave, And I will go if you ask me to, I
will stay if you dare, And if I go, I'm goin'
shameless, Let my hunger take me there"
G.A. Isakov|If I Go, I'm Goin

Back At Play

4/22/18|Morning

Yesterday, *The Beast* ended a text to me like this:

"I've made up my mind.

There's nothing to talk about.

Tonight I'll come home & we will pick-up where we left-off 3 weeks ago.

420/24/7/365 - Forever.

Fuck this shit."

This life is too short, to spend it in pain & misery. So, we'll go forward, as a family. If it all goes away tomorrow, so be it. We're together, that's all that matters! It's like we pressed pause and, now, life is back at play!

"You, you (You), you
You set me free (Free)
It's coming back to me
Baby, to your heart, heart, heart
I didn't recognize until you'd gone"
Active Child|Set Me Free

...

4/22/18|Dark

   ...

"Consider this
Consider this, the hint of the century
Consider this, the slip
That brought me to my knees, failed
What if all these fantasies come
Flailing around"
R.E.M.|Losing My Religion

❧〰─◆─〰☙

I'm Learning

4/25/18|Morning

After all that's happened...in the big scheme of things, my whole life, my 16 years of marriage...I think I'm learning that to live stuck in the past, or focused on a future that may never come, is to live in perpetual hell.

Instead, the good and the bad, make up the greatest theater that there'll ever be. One where I'm the star, and everyone & everything...the actors...the props. All of the drama, joys, tragedies, the ups and the downs, are all part of it.

The good cannot exist without the bad, and vice versa.

So, that's the secret. To know it's all connected. That to live happy, is to have known pain. And to be sad is to have known joy. That it all passes.

That the whole wide world...feels as I do. That my pain is not bigger or greater, just different.

And, that when my obligations are few, I can focus quality time & attention to the things that really matter.

That I rather be poor & happy, than "rich" & miserable.

> *"I'll weather all of the storms*
> *I'll weather all of the storms"*
> Hanging Valleys|Fortaleza

•••

4/25/18|Dark

...

"The dreams in which I'm dying
Are the best I've ever had
I find it hard to tell you"
Andrews & Jules|Mad World

Dangerous Risk

5/17/18|Morning

> *"The most dangerous risk of all:*
> *The risk of spending your life not doing what you want*
> *on the bet you can buy yourself the freedom to do it later."*
> Alan Watts

SYML|wanting is never enough

•••

5/17/18|Dark

...

Kupla|Owls of the Night

Peace and Love

5/27/18|Morning

Regard relationships, situations, physical pain or illness, as a way to really practice a life of Zen, peace and love!

To go with the river…instead of fighting up-stream. My level of consciousness can have an affect, on the level of consciousness of those around me!

Be Present. Be at Peace. Be Positive. Feel Love. *Listen! Listen! Listen! Listen!* Be Understanding!

Moments of Clarity|High Beliefs

...

5/27/18|Dark

...

The Doors|The Crystal Ship

Pass Me By

6/23/18|Morning

Don't be hypocritical...
Don't say, "*be present, be here, don't get lost in the fog...*"
And, then stress, worry, and try to figure out my current situation.
I'll miss it all. It will all just pass me by!
Don't forget!!!

Hermie|Haze

...

6/23/18|Dark

...

Kupla|Sleepy Little One

The Fantasy

7/22/18|Morning

The fantasy (of other) is always funner in the mind...

What I have is perfect! Hard to beat perfect!

I feel very clear right now...

Really focused on my priorities of being a mom, a wife, buying a house, feeling and being creative. And, I'm so ok with just that. I don't feel like I have time or energy for anything else.

Makes me so happy! I'm excited, I feel so much love and I feel steady. The 4 of us, our home, our life! Most important!

Everyday: I ask myself,

"Am I loving my babies with all of my heart, everything that I do? Is our home a place of love?"

Nickodemus|Endangered Species

...

7/22/18|Dark

...

Green Day|When I Come Around

An Offer

11/2/18|Morning

Yesterday, we put an offer on the house.

They accepted.

House is under contract.

...The Beast is, Amazing!

Oh So Quiet|Sí Quedamos

...

11/2/18|Dark
   ...listening;...

amies|The Other Side

Falling Apart

12/1/18|Late

The world is falling apart...Not much makes sense anymore...Stability is now a utopian fantasy! Makes me think, that now, more than ever, I should focus, *in*. Into my family. My children. My Beast!

Because life can truly be cut short... Spend the time. Engage!

James is already almost 14! Elizabeth keeps getting bigger everyday! Overdose on THEM!!! Let them OD on You! It's what it means to be a Mother!!! Commit!!! Start their days with hugs, kisses & love. So much love!!

Spend time playing with Elizabeth. Give her a reason to leave the *Tablet* behind. Engage with James, everyday. Use similarities to connect.

Sabbatical (Nourish the Soul) - Yoga, Reading, Music, Cooking and Baking, Art - Media Break!!! TV Break!! Headphones-Free. Fill the House with Music!!! End day with hugs, kisses, and love!! So much love!!

> *"Even if I'm falling down, I will keep on*
> *searching for my highs, You can say I lost*
> *my mind, I will keep on holding my head*
> *high, Even if the sky is falling down"*
> Candelion|Even If the Sky Is Falling

...

12/1/18|Dark
   ...listening...

Raimu|A Voyager's Spirit

Congratulations

12/8/18|Night

On December 6th, we got an email saying:

"*Congratulations.*"

We fucking did it!!!!

> *"Have no fear*
> *If you don't see the sun*
> *I will hold you close*
> *Welcome home*
> *You are home"*
> SYML|Sweet Home

...

12/8/18|Dark
 ...listening...

BluntOne|Soul Searching

On the Horizon

3/10/19|Night

Just celebrated 17 years since making it legal...WOW!

And, I adore him and I feel adored by him! Even after 17 years.

We have a house, our kids are healthy, happy, and oh so smart and creative and, funny and sensitive. Our dog is great. The Beast's job is going good, and semi-retirement is on the horizon.

So, now, time to *BREATHE*!

To Live, To Love, To Laugh...as cliché as it sounds.

Just, Be!!

"Shivering stars drift around in the sky, I lie
calm under their watchful eyes, In my heart,
I can feel it and why, That wherever I go, I'll
find my way home"
Asgeir|Breathe

...

3/10/19|Dark
...listening...

KLANGSTEIN|The Beauty Without Beats

Upside Down

4/7/19|Late

I am at peace. I am content.

After a few months of fog, it has started to clear.

Life feels in the Now!

Tomorrow, I start my practice of meditation again. Karen might join, and I'm excited to help someone in this way.

But, I am dedicated, even if all alone.

Fuck the Upside Down!

C. Stracey|Beginning, Becoming

...

4/7/19|Dark
  ...listening...

H.1|Timeless

Protesta

7/20/19|Dark

"It's absolutely incredible, it's the most beautiful thing," she tells
TIME. "It's peaceful, mostly singing, chanting, lots of different signs.
Everyone is being super kind to one another, it's amazing."
TIME [5]

"Soy el dolor que no siente, Soy la memoria
olvidada, Soy material resistente, Con rabia
despellejada, Con el coraje de frente, Voy
a ganar la batalla, Hecha de viento y de
playa, Soy la ola que va a romper"
iLe|Contra Todo

Protest

7/20/19|Dark

"While the chat leak was the final straw for many, Rosselló's problems truly started with what many say was his poor handling of Hurricane Maria. In September 2017 the Category 5 hurricane brought destruction to the Caribbean islands of U.S Virgin Islands, Dominica, and Puerto Rico. Puerto Rico faced widespread flooding and blackouts, made worse by a slow response from the federal government. The island, a United States territory since 1898, is home to nearly 3.2 million people. Puerto Ricans are U.S. citizens. The governor was also heavily criticized for his post-recovery effort, and for his year-long claim that there were only dozens of casualties until a large study found that almost 3,000 citizens died as a result of Maria. That same study found that failures in government institutions contributed to the death rate, especially for poorer Puerto Ricans."

TIME [6]

El Temblor

1/7/20|Dark

> *"Puerto Rico is experiencing an unusual and prolonged period of seismic activity causing some homes to collapse and structural damage to roads and bridges, as well as spreading fears of tsunamis along the south coast of the island...More than 1,280 earthquakes have hit Puerto Rico's southern region since Dec. 28, more than two dozen of them magnitude 4.5 or greater, according to the US Geological Survey. The latest was a 5.9 magnitude aftershock..."*
> Univision [7]

Just, shaking here, like...*Tembleque.* [8]

> *"Good things come to those who learn to wait, Ohhh, Wait for the sun to fall into the world, One by one we watch the stars blossom above, Blossom above"*
> Fink|We Watch The Stars

The Earthquake

1/7/20|Dark

"...USGS reports the 6.4 magnitude earthquake that struck Tuesday occurred about five miles south of the city of Indios...Thousands of people are now staying in shelters and sleeping on sidewalks, according to the AP, and classes have been closed since Monday's quake. The island has experienced over 500 earthquakes since December 28, when a 4.7 magnitude quake struck in the same region, according to the USGS. Thirteen of the earthquakes since then have been higher than 4.0, including the quakes on Monday and Tuesday, the USGS also reported... "I started vomiting, I believe, out of anxiety," says Guzmán-Mato, who is from Puerto Rico but is currently living in Brooklyn, New York...Damage from Monday's 5.8 magnitude earthquake destroyed several buildings, including one school. Puerto Rico's electricity supplier, Autoridad de Energía Eléctrica, has reported an island-wide power outage as a result of Tuesday's 6.4 magnitude earthquake..."
TIME [9]

"Tearless, fearless, burning, burning
You tell me what have I missed
Still wandering in the deep mist"
SiM|The Rumbling

...high, high above *the now rumbling* Earth;...

...the *Tower*, moves;...as if, alive;...

...the *Tower*, moves; ...so not to crumble, *within and upon it's own footprint;*...

...the Earth moves, under the *Tower;*...

...the *Tower* must be, as-one with, the Earth;...

...the *Tower* must sway and move and, balance itself;...

that it avoid a premature and unnecessary demise;...

...the *Tower* knows;...that in, this world, 'movimiento es vida'

...movement, change, growth, evolution... is Life;...

...the night continues to darken;...and yet,...

...as the earth moves and the sea threatens to flood this, *repeatedly humbled,* Island...I *too,* now, surrender to the movement I sense within me, *rumbling deep to the core of who and what I may potentially, Be;*...

> *"Rumbling, rumbling, it's coming,*
> *Rumbling, rumbling, Coming for you,*
> *Rumbling, rumbling, it's coming"*
> SiM|The Rumbling

...I patiently, calmly now, await the dark Tsunami I know, *is sure to come;*...

> *"Nobody knows what's inside of me*
> *Nobody knows what's inside of me*
> *Nobody knows what's inside of me"*
> SiM|The Rumbling

The Letter

2/21/20|Dark

Mi Amor,

This is the first time that I leave my whole family; my whole world; my reason for existing, for living, and for wanting to be a better person.

As a Cancer, my personality is one that needs to 'jot' down things... to make sure that, through the act of journaling an occurrence, it stays stamped into history forever. I know, in the end it is all nonsense. 100 years from now, none of THIS will matter. But for our history, however long the memory of us stays alive, I want this to be written. To be stamped in OUR history. I always told myself that, if I ever had to be away from you three, I would write down exactly what I would say to each of you, if science was so cool that I could come back and tell you so.

So, *this is my letter to you.*

My words to you in the case that, I don't come back. First of all, you are the greatest love I have ever known. You saved me! Not in a messiah kind of way, but the fact that, you chose me too...and the Who that you turned out to be, inspired me everyday to, bit by bit, become a better version of myself. Meeting you, starting my life with you, set my whole existence into motion. I truly began to live when I met you! I will forever be grateful that you saw the potential of what was inside, buried beneath the rubble and mess and brokenness.

It was an absolute honor to grow up with you. This letter is hard, because, how does someone truly express something that words can't fully capture? I'm gonna try anyways. (*I'm smiling as I write this, because, language, am I right?*)

Baby..., it was so fun. Making a life for ourselves. Learning. Falling down. Rising back up. Damn, what a life we have had thus far?!!! We were infants when we got together, had to learn EVERYTHING, together, ...'from scratch'. You helped open my mind in ways that I never expected. I absolutely love everything, EVERYTHING, we did, together. What a fucking adventure it has been.

To this very day, 2 weeks shy of our 18th anniversary, the thought of our love still brings tears to my eyes. Know this baby, I love you so much, babe, so much it makes my chest tight. The thought of a long life with you still excites me, you know?!!! Forever with you has never scared me!

But I know that tomorrow isn't guaranteed, so I just want to say that, if 'luck' would have it, and I don't return from my trip, babe, BE HAPPY, LIVE YOUR LIFE with OUR beautiful and wonderful children; whatever that life may be. Stay open to new LOVE, because if you happen to find someone worthy of your life & love, they should have it...your love is intoxicating, infinite, wonderful, comforting and so many other wonderful words that escape me at this moment. Your love should not be contained. This world NEEDS more of that kind of love. More people like YOU! There, I got that out of the way.

The longer time passes, I find myself having to almost go into a meditative trance to remember small details of our past. Of how it all started, the early years of our marriage together, when we became parents, and then, parents again, when we moved to Paradise and then chased our dreams, but decided it was better to plant roots instead...the further back I have to go, the harder it is to remember the details, the small details. And I know this is normal... and memory is a funny thing. I do those exercises because even though I know that I will never get back all the details, I do it because of the feeling it gives me. Of, greatness! Everything about us, has always been so GREAT and BIG! Your love has always been so damn BIG! And GREAT!

Amor, our life has been a wild adventure. And with nothing getting in the way, we will continue to have a wild adventure! I love growing old with you!

As I write this letter, I have the song 'Downtown' on repeat, and, all of a sudden, a thought came to me. Babe, I want you to know that I always SAW how absolutely dreamy and romantic you are towards me. At first it was in bigger ways, like big gifts and expensive flowers, and it was wonderful, but man, over the years, as they became more subtle and smaller (as you know, it was a purposeful decision of ours to stray away from the overly materialistic, and to show our love in ways that matter the most), those have always remained my absolute favorites. The last example is when you had the idea to honor my grandpa that night... who does that? Who, tired from a job that they hate, thinks of coming home with treats to make a small party to celebrate, life? You are amazing, Babe, from the texts that day, to the cake, to the tequila shots we took, to just, the purity of the whole act, it blows me away. Your love, babe, it's so big! You are and have always been my greatest teacher! So, patient... you have always been so patient... when I didn't know how to love, you waited patiently until I learned... this, all of this, is more than a 'best-friend,' a 'partner'... not to even mention the word, 'husband'... you have always been sooooo much more than, any of those words can...mean... see, words again... they are just not enough...

Switching to the album '*Down The Way*'... funny how an entire album, or sometimes just a single song or, even just a single note of a song, can bring you back to a place, a memory, a... something or other... a happening... like that time we were listening to 'For You' in the bathtub, in the first Isabela house, toking on a joint...that song seemed to last forever. Like, literally *for-e-ver*! Time seemed to go on forever and somehow it was like it was sitting completely still. So many of these memories that I share with you...my best friend!

Life with you is always so, fun!

> *"Here I go, I'll tell you what you already*
> *know, If you love me, with all of your heart,*
> *If you love me, I'll make you a star in my*
> *universe, You'll never have to go to work,*
> *You'll spend everyday, shining your light my*
> *way"*
> A. & J. Stone|For You

Patient, Now

2/21/20|Dark

...patiently, calmly, humbly, sincerely,...

...just, listening;...

> *"Oh I was in the dark age*
> *Searching for the ones in my mind*
> *I'm so far away*
> *But I had hit the ground running*
> *Steady as you go I don't mind*
> *I'm still here today*
> *Oh Spouting hymns and buzzing rhymes*
> *And forever talking when it aint so kind*
> *But it feels like forever on the run*
> *When your mind turns to fiction"*
> Other Lives|For 12

Won't Ever Forget

3/26/20|Dark

2020 started off with a bang.

P.R. experienced bad earthquakes for the first time in many, many years. But, we survived. Our home is okay!

I went on a trip to meet the nephew, and see the brother. Selfishly, it was what I needed. *The Beast* being so sweet to suggest and encourage it. I came back with new perspective and an openness to change.

Celebrated 18 years of marriage. He is still the love of my life! Won't ever forget our convo from today. Unbeknownst to you, you texted me some beautiful *"end-of-the-world vows."* It feels like the end-of-the world. At least, how we are used to living it.

Coronavirus, ...*a pandemic.* Worldwide! 11 days island-wide lockdown!

Our "Vows:"

- Unconditionally love each other.
- Always, assume the best in each other.
- Turn the other cheek.
- Let-go of the past. Live for today.

These "vows" are what is going to get us through, *whatever is to come.* Our love! Grace! Compassion! *The Grand Magical Reality we create for ourselves.* Even, as the world falls-apart around us!

That will be what saves us!!!

J. Barwick|The Magic Place

Listening

3/26/20|Dark

...ever-so patiently, calmly, humbly, sincerely,...
...just, ...listening;...watching;...

> *"What's the lie*
> *What's the truth*
> *What to believe*
> *In my life"*
> Yoshiki|Red Swan

As It Should Be

4/12/20|Dark

Accept; It is what it is, as it should be! As is!
Harvest the good, ...there is some good, in *EVERYTHING*!!
Let-go of, All the Rest!!
How to be Happy?...*Be Happy!*
Positive Thoughts, Positive Life.

"Don't suffer with the times
Don't settle for this cruel, cruel world
This old world
You'll never survive
If you don't try
To calm the waters on the inside
On the inside you're the moonlight"
Trevor Hall|2 Oceans

As It Is

4/12/20|Dark

...patiently, calmly, humbly, sincerely,...
...just, listening;...watching; ...waiting;...

K. Yamamoto|Ashes on The Fire

We Must

4/19/20|Dark

> *"We must become, in our lives, the things we choose to experience in the world around us."*
> Gregg Braden

TWO LANES|Reflections

Become

4/19/20|Dawn

   ...patiently, calmly, humbly, sincerely,...
   ...just, listening;...watching; ...waiting;...
   ...for, You.

> *"Those thoughts in your head, Might tell*
> *you you're not ready, Is that what you've*
> *heard? That life is lonely? You should know,*
> *You've always been ready, The highs and*
> *the lows, Are better with somebody, Keep*
> *falling in love, Keep falling in love"*
> Tinlicker|Rebirth

Beastly Words

5/21/20|Late

> *"...Wendy had a pet wolf forsaken by its parents;"*
> J.M. Barrie|Peter Pan

I awoke today, to find this note from *The Beast*:

"Words cannot express, my feelings for you! You, truly are my everything, and I, see you. I do not take you for granted, ever. I am, who I am, because you, are you! I was feeling, sleepy, and was thinking of you, and how happy, the thought of you, makes me...In the day-to-day game of Life, time can pass so effortlessly, without realizing... I find myself, still stunned in your presence...frozen by your energy...and enchanted by, your Love and devotion to me. You, are my reality. The only One that will ever really, actually matter. Forgive me, my Love, for not always finding the way to express my deep feelings for you. I hope you know by now, my undying Love, will in-fact never cease. Love...such a silly, insignificant word, compared to how I feel inside about you. It takes all of my Being, to not run away with you, to get lost and never found... But, it's the only word, for now, that expresses that feeling we have...Love. I Love You."

> *"And as the wind, You move me"*
> Doe Paoro|The Wind

Summer Dawns

5/21/20|Dawn

I seem to be one who, loves the idea of journaling...but, doesn't necessarily journal religiously.

So much has, happened...

As a family, we all continue to read. I have lost count of all the books I've read since the previous entry...although I feel as though I've retained ninety-percent of the most important aspects of each book; some I've read twice-now already. My thirst for knowledge, continues to be insatiable.

Meditation has become even more important for us now. Practically daily for *The Beauty*, and a few times each week for myself. I very-much desire to meditate more often, and continue to strive toward a more stable meditative routine.

Last week as I was lying in bed falling asleep, I had a very clear 'vision' of the short-story I wrote several years ago. Specifically, the vision suggesting, how I could create a *sort-of* "game," based on it, *The Story*. This is an oversimplification of what I experienced while lying in bed. This lucid-dreamlike-vision felt very real, and felt divinely(?), cosmically(?) ...inspired, just as it felt when I was originally "given" the idea for the short-story.

Coincidentally, or, Synchronistically as Jung might say, the Evolved story 'I' wrote back then, has within it, many ideas, theories, and thoughts that, I have very recently been reading about...but, ...how, why, would I have put these same ideas into my short-story, so many years before being exposed to this material?

...I have this new theory that, the "collective-consciousness" of humanity as a whole is, manifesting itself through our Art, Technology, Inventions, etc... literally, practically, everything...

To the point that it would seem silly for anyone to claim his or her idea is his or her own. I think we are all sub/un-consciously driven to create and express, that which our greater "hive-mind" of humanity compels us to...

It would appear as though we live in some sort of Hybrid Reality, one in which humanity has 'Free-Will' to come and go as it pleases, and yet in the *background* there is a definite, overall "storyline" taking place whether we acknowledge it or not. I can imagine it in video-game terms as a cross, between, a linear-style single-player game, and an open-world cooperative-style game; in which the world of the game is massive, and there are endless quests and fun adventures to keep you busy...but, lurking behind it all, is an incredibly mysterious story that somehow keeps you within the boundaries of the game-world created. You, never, have to *consciously* participate in The Story, but, it's there *unconsciously, always.*

"A man decides after 70 years, That what
he goes there for is to unlock the door, While
those around him criticize and sleep, And
through a fractal on that breaking wall, I see
you my friend and touch your face again,
Miracles will happen as we trip, But we're
never gonna survive, unless we get
a little crazy"
Seal|Crazy

Here Now

6/8/20|Late

    I AM, HERE NOW!

"Everyone must figure out their own way
to climb up the mountain."
Master Shi Heng Yi

Star River|Be Here Now

A Hundred Aeons

6/8/20|Dawn

"Talk as much philosophy as you please, worship as many gods as you like, observe all ceremonies, sing devoted praises to any number of divine beings—liberation never comes, even at the end of a hundred aeons, without the realization of the Oneness of Self."
A. Shankara

"I am the call of awakening from sleep in the Aeon of the night."
Gnostic Text

"We find ourselves, Our hearts alive, Awake from the night, Our souls defined"
JODA|We Find Ourselves

Words Have Power

6/22/20|Late

When in Communion with Others, come from a humble place, consciously listen, and allow for space. Like a witch, my words have power. I have that, *witching power*. That is why they are *limited...*

My words, should be chosen wisely.

"We woke like Gods, all-seeing
A tethered call, and you left
And the void was all that there was
I hear voices coming closer
I hear voices coming close to me
I hear your voices over water"
Talos|Voices

Saving Truth

6/22/20|Dawn

> *"Indeed, the saving truth has never been preached by the Buddha,*
> *seeing that one has to realize it within oneself."*
> Sutralamkara

> *"I'm on the rise I'm on the edge, I'm not*
> *afraid to step into this world, I see the light,*
> *I feel the love, I see the joy, I saw them all*
> *come to life, in my mind"*
> Scorz|Come To Life

I Had To

6/25/20|Late

> *"...she smiled at her fears now and sat down tranquilly by the fire..."*
> J.M. Barrie|Peter Pan

Today, I had to face death. Look at it in the face, in all of the darkness, in the shadows, and know that it is the end for me, for him. The end of this body, with all the carnal pleasures and pains. Today, I faced death, but from a place of knowing, that we don't truly die. Not the essence of who we are. The "I Am" inside of me. Inside of, him. The "I," never dies.

I looked at Death in the face today. And, I saw that our death on this earth is, *the Final Realization of it all*. Then, knowing it all, ...our "I" is truly free. That freedom will come for us all. Knowing that...it makes me want to truly...*Live*. Not wasting a single minute of this self-realization journey, I am on. He is on. No matter the time, months, years, decades...I am Forever His. He is Forever Mine.

> *"We are the wild youth, Chasing visions of*
> *our futures, One day, we'll reveal the truth,*
> *That one will die before he gets there"*
> Daughter|Youth

The Perennial

6/25/20|Dawn

"When poets or metaphysicians talk about the subject matter of the
Perennial Philosophy, it is generally at second hand. But in every
age there have been some men and women who chose to fulfill the
conditions upon which alone, as a matter of brute empirical fact,
such immediate knowledge can be had; and of these a few have left
accounts of the Reality they were thus enabled to apprehend and have
tried to relate, in one comprehensive system of thought, the given
facts of this experience with the given facts of their other experiences.
To such first-hand exponents of the Perennial Philosophy those who
knew them have generally given the name of 'saint' or 'prophet,' 'sage'
or 'enlightened one.' And it is mainly to these, because there is good
reason for supposing that they knew what they were talking about,
and not to the professional philosophers or men of letters, that I have
gone for my selections."
A. Huxley|The Perennial Philosophy

"I see you in the darkness, I see you in the light,
I see your eyes shining, In through the night"
Zoe|Sunshine On a Rainy Day

One Day

6/26/20|Late

Text message from, *The Beast*!

"It's not for you to respond, or, do anything, literally, at all...I just want you to know, that, I look forward to the days when I don't have to be separated from you 5 days or more per week. I look forward to waking-up, together, just being each-others shadow and mirror. I hate, having to spend half my life, apart from you. There's nothing for you to say, or do, so you, really, don't even have to try to respond. Seriously, I just want you to know, that, I am happy and in love with you, and our life is amazing, and I looove that I can provide, in a way that allows you to, not have to work or, be out of the house and, getting exhausted and, everything that goes along with participating in the outside-world. I love that, and regret nothing!!!! But, even with, all that...I can't wait to break-out of this, Cocoon...and become a butterfly, one day, with you. Free and fully formed, with no job or care in the world. Living for Us. xoxo"

One day! It'll come!! Patience, Love, Understanding!! It's all about timing!!!

"Give me patience, I thought I learnt it
already, Give me patience"
Kinnship|Patience

Self-Knowledge

6/26/20|Dawn

"In other living creatures ignorance of self is nature; in man it is vice."
Boethius

"Ignorance of self is something that answers to this description. In its origins it is voluntary; for by introspection and by listening to other people's judgements of our character we can all, if we so desire, come to a very shrewd understanding of our flaws and weaknesses and the real, as opposed to the avowed and advertised, motives of our actions. If most of us remain ignorant of ourselves, it is because self-knowledge is painful and we prefer the pleasures of illusion. ...The importance, the indispensable necessity, of self-knowledge has been stressed by the saints and doctors of every one of the great religious traditions."
A. Huxley|The Perennial Philosophy

"A man has many skins in himself, covering the depths of his heart. Man knows so many things; he does not know himself. Why, thirty or forty skins or hides, just like an ox's or a bear's, so thick and hard, cover the soul. Go into your own ground and learn to know yourself there."
Eckhart

"You can't await your own arrival, You've twenty seconds to comply, So let go, so let go and jump in, Oh, well, whatcha waiting for? It's alright, 'Cause there's beauty in the breakdown, So let go, yeah, let go, just get in, Oh, it's so amazing here, it's alright, 'Cause there's beauty in the breakdown"

Frou Frou|Let Go

A Year of Wonder

7/3/20|Dark

Today I woke up, feeling, *so much.* I couldn't pin-point it... I asked myself, "*what could be bothering me;*" why I felt, sadness... It felt cleansing, releasing, to cry...

Still, I was confused at, *why* I felt that way.

I was actually excited about this birthday. This upcoming year. Turning thirty-eight. But, I still felt sad. Later, telling him about being a bit sad, ...his own sadness and struggle came out. I don't think the sadness was mine. Not sure if what I felt was, his... All I know is that I still can't come up with a logical reason for feeling so sad. For wanting to cry... *for,* crying.

I called-back my mom. I knew that her call was to say '*happy birthday*', and at some point in the convo, I told her that I felt like we would be getting a bigger earthquake. ...*At 4:49 pm, we had a 5.3 magnitude.* I, stayed calm this time.

I think it was more a feeling like, it had finally arrived. What I had intuitively known! The kiddos did great. *The Beast* felt it pretty strongly in the *Tower. It feels like it's all connected.* I told him that, I *feel electric,* as well as feeling certain aches and discomforts in my physical body.

Thirty-Eight, feels like a powerful year! A year of wonder, magic, and change!

Loafy Building|Sleepless Wonder

The Knower

7/3/20|Dawn

> *"Knowledge is a function of being. When there is a change in the*
> *being of the knower, there is a corresponding change in the nature and*
> *amount of knowing. For example, the being of a child is transformed*
> *by growth and education into that of a man; among the results of this*
> *transformation is a revolutionary change in the way of knowing and*
> *the amount and character of the things known."*
> A. Huxley|The Perennial Philosophy

"There's nowhere left to hide"
J. Isma-Ae|Left To Hide

Made Allowance

7/12/20|Dark

Today, during meditation, I made allowance for *automatic* "doodling."

It was the weirdest sensation... I felt my hand wanting to draw these squiqqlies, and perfect smooth circles. My whole arm felt *heavy*, felt like it would be *too* heavy to move.

In my mind's eye I could sense, the circles, small tight circles and squiggly lines, and the pencil, it felt, like it glided on grooves on the paper. Like all I had to do was relax and stay within the smooth grooves, and the rest would flow.

The feeling lasted about 10-15 mins and then it went away. I was so excited to see what I had drawn. I ended my meditation, turned on the light, and when I checked the paper, *it was completely blank*, except for a small smudge.

Incredible! I could have sworn that I had even heard the scratching of the lead on the paper. Wow!

Hevi|Mind At Ease

New Worlds

7/12/20|Dawn

*Nor are changes in the knower's physiological or intellectual being
the only ones to affect his knowledge. What we know depends also
on what, as moral beings, we choose to make ourselves. 'Practice,'
in the words of William James, 'may change our theoretical horizon,
and this in a twofold way: it may lead into new worlds and secure
new powers.'*
A. Huxley|The Perennial Philosophy

*"Stay wide eyed and questioning
Find the color in the chaos
Stay open
Close-in the distance
Warm up your heart"*
Double Touch|Wide Eyed

Back To Love

7/16/20|Dark

No matter what...It ALL comes back to, LOVE!!

Tritonal|Back To My Love

Divine Ground

7/16/20|Dawn

"The divine Ground of all existence is a spiritual Absolute, ineffable in terms of discursive thought, but (in certain circumstances) susceptible of being directly experienced and realized by the human being. ...Out of any given generation of men and women very few will achieve the final end of human existence; but the opportunity for coming to unitive knowledge will, in one way or another, continually be offered until all sentient beings realize Who in fact they are."
A. Huxley|The Perennial Philosophy

"I'm calling your name, I need your light, Every lonely day's on fire, You're not by my side, I'm calling your name, I scream at the night, Tell me can you hear my voice, I'm losing my mind"
S. Isoyan|Where Are You

To Know

7/26/20|Dark

What does it mean to know, "*I Am*?"
What does it mean to be, *No-Thing, No-one*?
Non-duality...No "*Right*," No "*Wrong*"...

Tenno|Gatekeeper of Thoughts

PK Effect

7/26/20|Dawn

> *"And if the PK effect can be demonstrated in the laboratory*
> *and measured by statistical methods, then, obviously, the intrinsic*
> *credibility of the scattered anecdotal evidence for the direct influence*
> *of mind upon matter, not merely within the body, but outside in*
> *the external world, is thereby notably increased. The same is true*
> *for extra-sensory perception. Apparent examples of it are constantly*
> *turning up in ordinary life."*
> A. Huxley|The Perennial Philosophy

> *"There's a power in your soul*
> *There's a power in your soul*
> *There's a power in your soul*
> *There's a power in your soul*
> *And I wanted you to know"*
> gardenstate|Take Me There

We Are Evolving

8/27/20|Dark

> *"We are the first species, ever, to know we are evolving. We are the first species to know that we're living in a shift point in evolution itself, from the devolution of our species, towards the evolution of our species to some unknown future. And we also are the first species to know we're affecting our own evolution by everything that we do, every impulse that we have, every thought that we speak. And we are, therefore, becoming conscious evolutionaries."*
> Barbara Marx Hubbard

Raimu|Future's Beyond

Communication

8/27/20|Dawn

*"...the divine Mind may choose to communicate with finite minds
either by manipulating the world of men and things in ways,
which the particular mind to be reached at that moment will find
meaningful; or else there may be direct communication by something
resembling thought transference."*
A. Huxley|The Perennial Philosophy

*"You used to bring the smell of rain into
my bed, And lie so close to me you could
be inside my head, Maybe it's a once in a
lifetime kind of thing, To feel the kind of
magic that your love brings"*
Above & Beyond|Reverie

The Flow

8/31/20|Dark

What is my deepest desire?

...Highest-Self, what do you have to say today?

> *Just start writing. Stop thinking. Go with the flow. Don't resist. Stop resisting. Go slow. Appreciate nature. The beauty of all that is natural. Relax! Stop, and look at the butterfly. Feel the breeze. Enjoy your life. Turn it off and just go with it. It. All that is. Pause. Breathe. Breathe. Remember the deep breath. Excitement is emotion. It is separateness; ...an illusion. Calm. Notice your breath. Stop gripping! Let go. Let it all go. Notice the clouds.*

Do they notice me, noticing them?

...Is it why they paint pictures in the sky for me?

> *Notice the clouds. Breathe. Acknowledge the wind.*

As it caresses my skin. The way it dances around me.

...Playing. Twirling.

> *Breathe. Let go of the grip. Soften. Communicate clearly. When necessary. Otherwise, quiet. Contemplate silence. Taking it in. Taking it all in. Breathe. Pause. Stop, telling, the story. Just be, in, the story. Fully in it. Feeling, all of it. Exactly as it it. Exactly as it presents itself. Breathe. Soften. Let go of the grip.*

Thank you, Highest-Self!!

Raimu|Meditative Flow

The Way

8/31/20|Dawn

> *"We should see that artists, far from being the neurotics they are often*
> *said to be, are, on the contrary, more healthy psychically than many*
> *modern men. They have understood that a true new beginning can*
> *come only after a real End. And, the first among moderns, the artists*
> *have set themselves to destroying their World in order to re-create an*
> *artistic Universe in which man can at once*
> *live and contemplate and dream."*
> M. Eliade|Myth and Reality

> *"Thus enlightened, the Avatar can reveal the way of enlightenment*
> *to others and help them actually to become what they already*
> *potentially are."*
> A. Huxley|The Perennial Philosophy

> *"That's the way"*
> Sultan+Shepard|The Way

CHAPTER 3

A New Reality

"You don't have to be afraid
You don't even have to be brave
Living in a gilded cage,
The only risk is that you'll go...
Go, Go, Insane"
Flume|Insane

Waking Up

9/2/20|Morning of the Full Moon

As I sit, I hear a bird song near, then another. Then two more. A trio of beach-birds land near the pond.

The sky a pink, orange hue.

A chirp, chirp, here, then there, then everywhere. How beautiful it is to, hear, the world waking up.

The air calm, barely a gentle breeze. Smells new. A bit chilled. The palms barely sway. You have to look, closely. The clouds move slowly, floating and slightly moving.

Then Frank, sings his song. It stops me. Makes me pause. It's beautiful. A smile begins to part my lips.

I'm in love.

I close my eyes. I hear the early morning Rooster call... a beautiful island reminder. Oh, the Sun. You peek-out on the horizon. I see you through the palm leaves.

How beautiful it is to, see, the world waking up.

Ornithology|Birdwatching

The Moment

9/1/20-9/4/20|3:00am

> *"...they drew near the Neverland; for after many moons they did reach
> it, and, what is more, they had been going pretty straight all the
> time, not perhaps so much owing to the guidance of Peter or Tink
> as because the island was out looking for them. It is only thus that
> any one may sight those magic shores."*
> J.M Barrie|Peter Pan

I am, *so happy*...that is, *an understatement.* I am, *overjoyed! ...Why?!* I *know* why; but, cannot accurately *express* this, in any conventional way...

I am, not suicidal...and yet, at this Moment, I am filled with 'anxiety' over, the Beauty, of it *ALL!* It is, so much! My mortal-self, struggles under the weight of, it All. I am in, complete *AWE!*

I've never, *felt* so much, palpable, overwhelming, joy. So much joy & beauty & awe that, I find it difficult to think upon... So much, understanding and happiness...literal, Ecstasy! I am arrested at my own thoughts, of, desiring nothing more than, to become One with it, All...

Suicide, ...as an expression of joy, not sadness, ...*suicide as a vehicle*...to join in the cosmic dance! Suicide, viewed from the vantage point of, if everyone knew, realized, what I do, have...we would ALL hold hands as we walk in-step, into the eternal abyss of Love and Understanding...understanding of, the Magic of, it All.

Pure Magic. Wonder. Beauty. Ecstasy. Awe. Connectedness. No separation. One.

To rejoin, the Universe at-large!

"They recalled with contempt that not so long ago they had thought themselves fine fellows for being able to fly around a room. Not so long ago. But how long ago? They were flying over the sea before this thought began to disturb Wendy seriously. John thought it was their second sea and their third night."
J.M. Barrie|Peter Pan

"Next, we must bear in mind that the fundamental characteristic of shamanism is ecstasy, interpreted as the soul forsaking the body. The shaman is the man who knows and remembers, that is, who understands the mysteries of life and death;... He is not solely an ecstatic, but also a contemplative—a thinker. In later civilizations, the philosopher will be recruited among these beings, to whom the mysteries of existence represent a passionate interest and who are drawn, ...to know the inner life."
M. Eliade|Rites and Symbols

"Stumbling out of the fog, I've been lost for so long, No more silence and lies, Maybe this is what it means to be alive. In the darkness, I bathe in light, I found grace in the falling sky, now I'm awake, I'm awake, I'm awake to feel the wonder"
Genix|I'm Awake

Be Still

9/5/20|Dark

Be Still, Heart of Mine. There is no you; There is no me. There is no landscape away from, us. As I look out, there is no There, there is no Here; I'm engulfed, within it. Engulfed, in, It. There is no separation. I am, It. Everything I see, everything I smell; All I touch and sense; It, is a World of my making. This is the World, I am creating.

I think that makes me, a Creator.

Tenno|Heart of the Mind

All You Need

9/18/20|Dark

What does my Higher-Self want to tell me today?

How big, you really are. You, are all you need.
That's all. That's enough! Stay in the feeling. Feel
it in your body. You, are all you need. Now, breathe!

Nothing can phase you. It's all an illusion of the ego!
And, Breathe!

BluntOne|Under Your Skin

◆◆ ─ ◆◆◆ ─ ◆◆

Listen To Self

9/19/20|Dark

What is best for, the highest good of all?

Remain grounded! Listen to Self. Listen
to Others. Center Myself! Come Back to Self!

Raimu|Tranquil Thicket

◆◆ ─ ◆◆◆ ─ ◆◆

Intuitive Energy

9/20/20|Dark

"The intuitive mind is a sacred gift and the rational mind is a faithful
servant. We have created a society that honors the servant and has
forgotten the gift."
A. Einstein

Creativity, is an intuitive energy... Maybe, this is why I was drawn to Theater as an adolescent... Without even knowing it, I was exercising the muscles of empathy...

"Theater is like a gym for empathy. It's where we can go to build up the muscles of compassion, to practice listening, and understanding and engaging with people that are not like ourselves. We practice sitting down, paying attention & learning from other people's actions. We practice caring."
Bill English

What does my Higher-Self, want to tell me today?

Expansiveness. To grow yourself, far beyond the physical body. Do not be afraid, to feel. Deeply. It's part of the human experience.

A reminder & affirmation on giving power away:

"I call back every piece of myself that I have ever given away, I call back all of my power."
Lee Harris

Lilac|Honey and Lemon

Shamanic Journey

9/21/20|Dark
New Moon; Waxing Phase energy;
Near ovulation of period cycle.

> "Look closely, however, and you may note that there are here seven
> large trees, each with a hole in its hollow trunk as large as a boy.
> These are the seven entrances to the home under the ground, for
> which Hook has been searching in vain these many moons."
>   J.M. Barrie|Peter Pan

Today, I embark upon my first *Shamanic Journey*... Really, it is a journey into *the unknown*... All from the comfort of my meditation room. I call out to my guides...aspects of, my Higher-Self, energies from elsewhere, "I'm ready!" My ego says, "hmmm..."...My humanness goes, "eek!" But my, oh, ...*my sweet Heart*... says, "*Yes, Lets!*"

1st Shamanic Journey Meditation:

I imagined myself traveling, first, through a giant, me-size oval opening, in the middle of the giant tree... I also saw myself, sitting on the beach...Getting up, walking towards the ocean... At first, I remembered my fear of open vast bodies of water, it made me pause, but, I continued forward... And, as I approached the edge, saw the waters part, and I was able to head, down...

I saw a spiral, through which I traveled. I saw a dove, white, it reminded me of the angels. The angelic realm. A human-looking Being walked or appeared before me, he reminded me of Abe Lincoln; long face, long arms, and legs that morphed much larger. I thought that, if I looked up, I would see the rest of him, as it appeared I was so tiny, standing between his two long legs.

I asked if He was my guide, I quickly heard, "*yes*," ...almost before I could even finish my question. I asked again, I quickly heard, "*Yes!*" Finding his answer to be a bit abrupt, and deciding his answer sounded a bit rough, I told him I was going to keep walking through the forest.

I had my first "shamanic trance dance"...more like, intuitive spontaneous, ...*movement*. I felt surges of energy coursing through my body. It felt deeply feminine. It was a, sexual energy. I realized that, I'm tuned-into my sexual energy. I thought of my sacral chakra, it looked like it was on fire. I saw the color orange. I thought of passion. How it awakens when my sacral chakra is activated. And, I hear the words: "*Passion seeds Creativity.*"

And, I got a quick vision, of how that sacral-sexual energy, transforms from passion, into creativity. Creativity, into something that is, Birth, that is, *New*. The basis for inspirations, for any artist. I felt like I wanted to own that, *strong, sexual energy*, that, *sexual-feminine-energy that flows, ...creates, ...births*.

And, the way it flows. It is liquid, it is silky. Refined.

For a moment while I was dancing, I saw my myself as a revered Queen, Oracle, Shaman, Healer, ...naked and shrouded with a see-through flowing robe. Dancing, in the middle of a circle of Warrior-Men getting ready to go to battle. A battle, they would be fighting for, me.

It was a, sacred ritual; powerful, shamanic. Tribal and indigenous. The men were the strongest, most handsome, most fiercest warriors. Carefully selected. I felt revered, honored, worshipped. My role, was to prime them. Get them ready, to face possible death.

The movement of my body was, hypnotic; moving the energy around the circle, affecting each man differently, but powerfully. Each, getting ready. Each, would deposit their seed into, The Queen, me. One by one. Assuring that, a Strong, Fierce, and Handsome Warrior would be carried forward.

It started with, The Chief. It was ceremonial, sensual, powerful, and, pleasurable. This was done, *before every great Battle!*

Raimu|Call of the Wild

❧⋯•◆•⋯☙

Upper World

9/23/20|Dark

I took my 2nd shamanic journey; this time, I set my intention on the *Upper World,* to see if I could meet-up with my, or, one of my, guides.

I tried using the beach as a way to travel and, while it was a great place for a short gratefulness-meditation, I couldn't visualize how I would use the ocean, to go, Up. So, after I meditated on the sand, I got up and headed towards the water. But, before reaching it, I remembered the Tree from my first journey.

I would use It to travel.

I went in through the "me size" opening, and from there tried to fly up the tree. Fairy wings appeared, but, when I tried flying with them, *they went too fast for me.* I saw that there was an Air Balloon, waiting for me. I floated up; up in the sky, and, was met with an almost never-ending layer of clouds. Packed tightly. I thought I would never get through.

When I finally did, past the clouds, stars started to appear, and I saw I was in space...nothingness.

Although I didn't get any strong visuals, I did *realize* some things:

I realized that my life, today, has gotten to a point where, I find myself overeating; ignoring the discomfort in my stomach and, even gaining some weight. But, all of this is easily resolved by simply, recognizing it, and then being hyper *Aware.*

Aware of when and what I eat. But, not just that. To take my time with it, savor it, enjoy it, bless it, and honor all that was involved in growing or making everything that I drink or eat. A gratefulness for the ability to eat, the fuel it provides for our bodies, how it nourishes us & provides health.

That's the secret! Not giving over my power to my cravings, emotions, habits. An awareness, a mindfulness, a conscious-in-the-now type of way to carry on with life.

No diet or pill, or crazy health fad. Things I've known for a long time, that it starts with, me. Inside, of me. The thoughts, rolling around in my head and, the emotions of my heart.

Today, I also practiced just, "sitting" with the feeling. While I did a chakra-tune-up meditation, prior to journeying, I felt lots of strong energies and then felt my whole body go into a "swirl," a sensation that lasted some time after I was done with the tune-up.

I had a vibrational feeling on the back of my head, towards the nape of my neck, on the Left side. I felt a pressure towards my, Right temple; it wasn't painful but, it was pretty intense. This time, I sat with all of it. I just, let be what needed to be.

Raimu|Picnic with Fairies

＊＊＊＊＊＊＊＊＊＊＊＊＊

Soul Lessons

9/26/20|Dark

"Soul Lessons Commonalities Meditation":

I started at "Childhood": for me, I chose 19 years old. I was transported, back to our first apartment. A simpler time. Spent it mostly in the clouds, blissful with my new husband. Everything seemed possible. We were on top of the world.

Forward 5 years: 24 years old. A time of painful learning, church, religion, jealousy, attachment to others, and struggling with motherhood. Relationship rocky, but, came out of all that connected, stronger, and we matured. Forgiveness.

Forward 5 years: 29 year old. Huge change! Independence. Moved to P.R. Psychedelics. Openness. Marriage overhaul; absolute & total focus on each-other. Anarchy.

Forward 5 years: 34 years old. Start of transformational, *paradigm shift*. Maria. Meditation. Sparks, of true Awakening.

Forward to now: 38 years old. Huge shift in Consciousness. See the world with, brand new eyes, or, better said, I see reality for *what it is*. Bliss. Peace. Love. Grace. Awareness. Humbleness. Nature. Optimal Health. Exploration of, the Self, *like never before*.

Jhove|What If It All Turned out Fine

)) · •◆• · ((

Many Paths

9/28/20|Dark

There are as many paths, as there are Souls! This kind of perspective, brings about more compassion, understanding, non-judgement, and acceptance!

Last night, I had a realization while lying in bed with, *The Beast*, on feeling nostalgia over the "good-ole' days." The "me" that I am, *today*, is different from the "me" of the past. The "good-ole' days" would not be the same, today, because of the simple fact that, today, I am a different person from, that person of the, "good-ole' days."

Having this realization, "cured" me, of those past daydreams and desires, *for what once was*. To look at it, all, ...this means I look at, right Now. For time is an illusion. Time, is made of, the Now moments. All happening in, the *NOW*!

"The greatest thing a human soul ever does in this world is to see something
and tell what it saw in a plain way. Hundreds of people can talk for
one who can think, but thousands can think for one who can see."
John Ruskin

Tenno|A New Beginning

Frank's Aura

9/29/20|Dark

I heard your song. It quickly caught my attention. I stared at you. Perched on the top of that virgin palm. You are my sweet reminder of all that's beautiful in this world. How wonderfully big Nature is. And, how small "human" is, compared to all the Beauty that is.

I was grateful for your song. Your Beauty. Your Perfectness. You stared, perched for a long time. In my mind we were having the greatest of conversations. And, then, as if to say "thank you" for my gratefulness, I saw your aura.

At first, a thin, white, bright haze that went around you. And, all around the palm. Your aura and the palm, indistinguishable from each other. Like it all merged together. Then, for just a few moments, I saw further out. A beautiful yellow glow. It reminded me of the divine.

Nvmb.|yourcolors

You Are Mighty

9/30/20|Dark

Higher-Self, what do you want to tell me today?

*That you are a beautiful soul. There is nothing
you can't handle. That is the human, and its
limitations. But you, my dear, you are mighty.
Mightier than you can imagine. Don't let worry
fill your heart. It's futility, at best. You know that
already. Feel yourself in your greatness. Don't dim
it. Don't diminish it for others' comfort. Including,
those closest to you. Speak your truth. Do it gently.
Softly. As to not hurt others. For then, it's in the
highest good for all. Highest good, for all!*

*"All souls are channeling soul & spirit energy
through the body, all the time."*
Lee Harris

BVG|Silk Touch

All Adds, Up

10/2/20|Dark

All, ...*ALL*, adds up to living a fulfilling, passionate, joyful, compassionate, and fun life. And, on the universal level, as a drop in the Vast Blue Ocean of Consciousness, I live my truth, and, by doing so, do my part in the shifting of collective-consciousness. *How?*

By, *BEING*, the change, ...so I can see *that* world that, I want for my children, and all generations forward.

cxlt.|Your Light

Glowing

10/2/20|Dawn

...just, ...Glowing;...

Angus Stone|In The Glow

Around Me

10/17/20|Dark

Meditation:

How am I navigating all the high feelings, coming up on Earth at this time? Both, unconscious and conscious feelings?

I need to have an Awareness of, what I might be "picking-up" around me. Let the emotions, the feelings, go through-me; not letting them get, "stuck", and then later come out in unhealthy ways.

Peak Twilight|Magical Connection

Said The I

10/25/20|Dark

Am I willing, to have an experience, with no expectations as to how it goes? No resistance; *to see*, life play out in my full power. I feel a small, sometimes, teeny-tiny resistance, deep inside my heart chakra. A fear, as to what it would look like to walk, act, think, see, *be*, ...in my full DIVINE power! *"No Fear Beloved!"* - said the I.

hi jude|Companion

‹♪♪·—·♦·—·♪♪›

The Call

10/26/20|Dark

I heard The Call, to Oneness! A recognition of, the Relationship, between "me" and "other." See the connection to the All, God, the Universe; *where we all come from and are a part of;* fully and completely.

I'Outlander|Higher Calling

‹♪♪·—·♦·—·♪♪›

A Place

10/29/20|Dark

...*The Beast* told me he was working on, something...and I heard the following words pop-up in my head: "*Write not from a place of desperation, but a place of, KNOWING!*"

Nuver|The Place Where I Belong

My Heart

10/30/20|Dark

The heart is the core; leader of my soul. Every morning, first thing:

Place hand on my heart and just feel, be in the heart. Be aware, of being distracted, by my feelings, or emotions. Be aware, of all the different feelings coming up; do not run away or push or fight or ignore... See, acknowledge, let them pass through...not identifying with them... I am not my grief, or sadness... I am not my happiness, or joy... Let them, all, come and go...they, do not "belong" to me. Always, come back to my center, My Heart.

When with others:

Own my healing heart. Do not give-away my healing, or, pieces of My Heart to others. Instead, see the power of my heart, and use that, energy. I am, the Master of My Heart. In difficult times, uncomfortable times, hard times, and sad times...just, ...listen and, stay centered!

Kainbeats|Heart of the Ocean

Winter, Is Here

October 31, 2020|Dark
Full Moon-Blue; Halloween

Happy Samhain...A Blue Moon on Halloween, 2020.

Just as farmers see this time as, the end of the agricultural year...a time to celebrate all the hard work, everything harvested. A time to, look back at everything done all year, and to look ahead for all that will be, *after* a time of Winter rest...

I, see this time the same. A celebration, of how far I've come, how I've expanded, how the seeds were planted, and then flourished. A time, to look back at the last year and see the Harvest of my Soul...where I am, at this point in time.

I celebrate my growth, my expansions, and, my new understandings. I'm thankful, so grateful. As we go into the winter time... I too, take this time, this energy, to go inside. To remember my connection, to Source, to the Power inside of me, and, my ability to, truly, live a magical life. To remember the human, and the Self, forever intertwined, but not the same.

As I enter a brand new year, and I get ready to sow the seeds for my next harvest, I take this time to ponder on what those seeds are:

Seeds of love. Seeds of connection. Seeds of responsibility for my life and choices. Seeds of passion and creativity. Seeds of courage. Seeds of grace, forgiveness and understanding.

Otaam|Dreaming of Snow

As Humans

11/1/20|Dark

As Humans, there is so much we don't understand; and, somewhere along the way, probably related to survival, we have been conditioned to fear, almost as a "knee-jerk" reaction to, anything that is different, and everything we don't understand. Quickly making the polarized separation of "this" is "good" and "that" is "bad."

Is that how the "asleep", find their footing in this world?

steezy prime|misty nights

Irradiated

11/1/20|Dawn

...just, ...Glowing;...Irradiated;...

cxlt.|Rays Of Light

Friendship

I am free. I am free! Free.

Free. Free. Free. Free. Free. To be free is to let go of fear. Death is not the end. Free. Free. Free. Free.

To fully accept death, is to fully accept life. To run away, shy away from, to fight, or to fear death, *it to do the same with life*. To forge ahead, having full awareness that what I'm headed towards is, ultimately, death, is to fully embrace all of, life.

Life, the path that leads to, Death.

So, I have a choice... I can push away or accept. To push away is to live a foggy, numb sense of reality, constantly carrying an underlying feeling of what I, deep down, know to be true. That in the end, despite all of my "efforts", I will, someday, die.

Or, I can *accept* that I will someday die, everything I've ever known, will *also*, someday die.

Accept, that the moment I was born, I had begun to die. That each day I live, every birthday I "celebrate", inches me closer to one day dying in this life. By accepting that greater truth of my reality, it teaches me, in a instant, to accept the everyday, small, sometimes mundane "happenings" of my daily life. Accept them with joy, with appreciation, with love. It teaches me to fully, and truly enjoy this life.

To accept death as the reality of the end of my life on this earth, *frees me to fully engage, accept, love and appreciate it.*

The connection between life and death seems strong, almost interchangeable, as if to say, "life is death and death is life." I feel this, even if I can't fully explain it.

On Fear and Anxiety:

Anxiety is the body's physical response to the energy of fear circulating and being 'stuck.' The energy of fear being perpetuated by looping thoughts and emotions tied to supposed memories.

Repetitive anxiety in a person can be diluted by, a repetitive response: *Morning routine, connect with the heart, mindful breathing. Movement, nature walk, dancing. Meditation practice.*

I have found these, and several other examples, of what some may call routine or ritual, to be most effective in helping me come back to my Self.

Coming back to Self, I find peace, power, grace, calm, joy, passion, knowing, magic, bigness and smallness, understanding and knowledge, hope, laughter, strength, compassion, adventure, lightness, the dreamer, and the inner child that sees the world clearly and honestly, as if seeing it for the first time.

To notice the bee flying by a tree and the almost translucent dragonfly that landed at the tip of the virgin palm leaf. I see dragonflies, a lot. I notice them often, hummingbirds, too. They seem magical to me. Small in size but fierce in will. This small dragonfly, sat on top of the palm leaf, I felt it "staring" right at me, as I write in my journal.

I wonder what it would be like to have it land right on my nose. Even if for a moment, just to say hello.

Does it notice me, noticing it? I close my eyes, take a few deep breaths, just being in its energy. The only way I know to "hang out." I hear the heartbeat of my heart. So loud, purposeful, powerful...and then calm.

Eureka! You are calm, little dragonfly!

I open my eyes...it is still there. I am grateful it still is. That I was allowed to draw it into my perception. I thank it.

As I write about this Dragonfly, I have an impulse to write "he," *the energy felt more than an "it."* Did I perceive a masculine energy? Grounding, secure, yet calm? Or, is it my human trying to rationalize...

I guess I perceived him to be conscious of me... A feeling much like when I "feel" a person staring at me from out of view and then, on instinct turning towards his or her direction.

After my communion with him, and opening my eyes, and pondering on what I felt, ...I began to write...a few moments passed and when I looked up...He was gone.

This felt like an incredible act of, Friendship.

Towerz|good friends

◆

Slow Down

11/3/20|Dark

> *Slow Down... All in good timing, Beloved!*
> *Continue on your Path. Check-in with your heart,*
> *constantly. Go deep, anything you need is found*
> *inside. Remember the Self! Remember what is truly*
> *important, and whatever might be shaky, cement it.*
> *Adaptability and Flexibility!*

I began to think, *more like daydream,* of what it would take for a Dragonfly, to land on my nose. The absolute stillness, the total control of any "knee-jerk" reaction to seeing it approach and, eventually land. The absolute hyper awareness it would require. To be *that* aware...all the time.

I ask myself, would I instantly swat it away, or, would I allow time to slow down, enough so I could see every movement, of every moment?

WYS|Backyard Memories

Non-Resistance

11/5/20|Dark

Akashic Meditation:
What is my purpose for the world and my self?

Purpose of Hope!

Felt further guidance of, *"not resisting"*; to stop pushing away.
Stop resisting.

Bcalm|calm descent

Magical Stars

11/7/20|Dark

Learning about the energy of Jupiter; I think about how *The Beast's* vacation is happening, right smack in the middle of the Jupiter-Pluto conjunction; and it just got approved.

A time he'll take to, formulate his thoughts, and organize them in written form. That was intuition. The timing is so perfect. More and more, I see Astrology, as just *awareness of what, already is*. A tool; a map, a "*video game hack.*"

And, the "magic" is, *Us*, ...the *Aware*, ...harnessing that energy; like an Avatar energy-bender. Using that energy to our advantage, in our daily lives. *It's quite simple, really.*

I can also see why the "controllers"; the "freedom takers"; want these simple truths, these universal realities, to be seen as scary, negative, and from ..."The Devil."

It's unbelievable how we, humans, have demonized the *Stars*...the beautiful, sparkly, magical stars.

❧❧·◆◆·❧❧

Energy of, the Jupiter-Pluto conjunction, in the sign of Capricorn:

Deepening of growth; digging-into roots of circumstances, to see what truly matters; *"Birthing Ambition and Passion from the Core."*

These are energies of maturity and responsibility, cultivated through the acceptance of the natural cycles of, change and growth. Jupiter and Pluto's intense ambition for power, is softened by the Capricorn (and it's ruling planet, Saturn) energy of seeing the realities of life, and working with them, even if they seem like limitations or restrictions.

Difficulties or perceived road-blocks, will shed light as to what serves and what doesn't. Let go of what does not!

Jupiter and Pluto in Capricorn, *guide from beneath the surface*, and urge us to tap-in to the roots of where the visions lie, so you can then manifest from the super-conscious.

Jupiter and Pluto energy urges us, to forge ahead; *even with what may seem impossible*. This energy is felt most when creating. This energy urges us to look inside, the knowing of our own self, for validation, ...not the outside world; and there, inside, you'll discover the ultimate truth.

No Spirit|Field of Stars

⸭ ⸭ ⸭

Fingertips

11/8/20|Dark

> *"...these things cannot be long hidden,*
> *the Sun, the Moon, and the Truth."*
> Buddha

Know Thyself!

Be, in the most intimate relationship, with the Self.

I am light, full of love. I live a happy existence. The more I know who I am, the fullness of who I am, the less I will pick-up what others are giving-off.

See, and accept my empathy, my intuition, and my sensitivity. Be a loving and happy space for others who are hurting and need healing.

The healing will not come from my acts, just from my, silent, subtle frequency. A loving frequency. Not taking responsibility or making it my burden what their outcome is. Having compassion, with the knowing that the grand majority of humans really want to just, talk-it-out...to have someone who will, listen.

Most humans have yet to realize, that all they will ever need is inside of them. So, those of us, the *Light Bearers*, just hold space; a loving, "high-frequency," divine space for those that need it, until, they find their own way. Holding zero expectations.

It's about having the objectivity of a psychoanalyst, with the everlasting love and compassion of, the Cosmos. No judgements, no opinions, no emotions, no attachments, no expectations. Just pure love, compassion, empathy, happiness, peace, and gratitude.

The divine spark, which is a part of the Whole "Om," that lives within me, is mightier than the illusions and delusions of this physical world.

To be affected by the outer, is to be affected by the illusion. It is choosing to play that game. That part in the "play." And, to temporarily...forget. To forget that, I am truly Free. Truly Divine-Love-Energy!

❦ — ◆ — ❦

Tarot Pull, 8 of Swords

Personal Meaning:

Choice...it's all about choice...if I ever feel stuck, and in times past when I have felt stuck, it has always been because of the illusion of my self-limiting beliefs. The choice comes, in allowing that to continue holding me back even after fully recognizing it.

The time is now. To see things as they are, taking action when appropriate and then, sitting back and watching it all unfold, exactly as it should. I must be aware, of, not falling in the same vicious cycles of, reacting based on old, limiting beliefs, and still expecting different results.

Everything, is truly at the tips, of my magical finger tips, if, only I will see it.

To have the courage, to take the blindfold off, untie the binding around my body, and walk the path before me.

The old shit... I've chosen to let go. Do not pick it back up!!!

møndberg|As Far As I Can See

❦ — ◆ — ❦

Connected

11/11/20|Dark

We are one; the word "*one*," echoed through the cosmos...*one...one...One*. Makes me want to say, "Om," *all that is...*

A call to *unification*, to see through the veil of separateness, the division between me and other.

We are connected, all is connected, we are the Universe!

Jhove|It All

Witness It

11/14/20|Dark

Meditation:

Is there anything; thoughts, past events, ideas about the future, that, I am obsessing about? Anything I am, holding onto? Even though, my highest knowing, is aware, that it's time to let go?

These are good questions to ponder.

What does true forgiveness, letting go, and not ever looking back, actually look or feel like? To, not even have a recollection of, a past hurt? Where it fades away, not in the land of forgetfulness, or denial, but of transcendence. Where, if remembered, it's almost as if it's a retelling or remembering of, a stranger's storied past. No emotions. No hurt. Just facts. Just a, story.

Why? Because, I can see it all as just steps in, a path. A path that, brought me to my now. Each situation, each moment, each hurt & joy, ...all just pieces to the overall story of, my Life.

To bring up the past, especially hurtful or painful things, is to send a little (or sometimes a big) piece of my Now-Moment to the past. Stuck in a perpetually frozen moment in time. It will not allow me to fully, truly, move forward. Instead, it will be a "re-living" & "re-telling" of the same narrative.

Face it. Face it all. Even if it hurts. Even if facing it, leaves me uncertain or insecure. Trust in the NOW moment, above all else. Not at what once was. *What is!* Not what could have been, but what *did* happen! Not what could possibly happen, but what is *happening right now*. It's about opening my eyes, to see, to really see, feel, and be in every single moment.

Consciously taking it all in.

I have seen how far my spirit can stretch... can grow... can expand....can adapt! Do not fear! Feel...embrace my Cancerian nature. See how I navigate this world, as a gift. To hone in my Inner, built-in radar "super power," into a fine-tuned instrument.

Go inside often.

That is how, I'll tune and attune my instrument. Continue to get to know myself, in the deepest ways. Fine-tuning my sensitivity...used, to bring the highest good to myself & the world around me, my Love & little Loves, and, beyond....

Love, Healing, Peace, Calm, Health, Contentment, Joy, Passion, Creativity, Compassion, Grace, Understanding, Priorities, Forgiveness, Awareness.

To be so aware, that knee-jerk reactions, are a thing of the past. To instinctually take a literal breath, before answering, doing, and acting. To just, be, in that Moment. Truly, Be.

Wisdom ~ Discernment ~ Calm Focus

Let go of all worries. Anxiety and worries are all hypotheticals. Not real. They cloud. They take me away from the magical reality of being fully present to the unfolding of my life. As it is happening. Live!

Nature, you great healer! The freshness and lightness of the wind. Playfulness at a grand scale. The power of the sun to brighten-up, to energize, the Star that brings light to all on Earth and beyond. That heals. That wakes me up!

All that is green. The jungle that surrounds our house. Full of life, sound, a world of its own. Alive, so alive! A mixture of shade and glow from the light of the Sun. Dancing and playing by the wind.

To take off my shoes, feel Mother Gaia's current, connect through my feet and ground my whole body. Security, balance, solidness, ...all, is found within her.

The clouds with their ever-changing shapes; a reminder that life is art & the imagination is great.

Ultimately, a reminder to take notice.

⋘⋙ ⸱⸱ ◆ ⸱⸱ ⋘⋙

December marks 2 years since we moved to this house. Our dream house in The Mountains. Surrounded by nature, in its tropical glory. Peaceful, safe, and quiet ...most of the time. A retreat from "big city" life. A place that truly feels like, home.

This island...we've created paradise inside paradise.

But, that has been a choice. To roll, with it. No matter what is happening around us, we've, I've, chosen to focus, within. To stop looking outside of self, and, the four of us, to create our beautiful reality. But, understanding, all, is found, within. Always within.

Beware of fear. Such a grand illusion. But, believable to the human. So much so, that it can literally make me sick. Disease comes from the body's disharmony, being out of, ease. How easy healing is available to me. I must listen to my body, and that takes being intimately connected and taking each moment to connect with self and the physical body. It is always speaking....if only I'll listen.

Give it rest, when it needs it. Nourish it, when needed. Take vitamins and holistic meds when illness comes. And, be aware of, the Mind, above all. As I think, I will be.

I must see, imagine, and feel myself healed. Healthy and strong. It all comes back to the mind. And, the stories and narrative rolling around...that are creating my reality. I must see myself well. I see what happens when I do. I feel healthy. I'm not laid-up.

Even today, as I meditated, I could feel a pulling on my lower back... But, now I see it all as, energy... So, I focused my attention to my back, mentally moving that energy. At the same time I massaged my lower back. I stretched and sat up straighter. By afternoon, no pain!

Do not forget that greatness. It is also a responsibility. I create my reality. As I think, ...I am.

But, if I live in each moment, fully aware, invested in each happening, I won't have to think...no judgement, no expectations, no daydreams of the past and or future...I can just, be. Fully, completely immersed.

That's life. And, I get to witness it.

Raimu|Camden to Chinatown

Stability

11/15/20|Dark

Tarot: 4 of Pentacles

Personal Meaning:

I see stability. My life does feel, super stable right now. Our family is in a pretty awesome groove. Our finances are stable. Everyone is healthy. We all feel good. All are happy. And, this small taste of, the retired life, has been amazing.

The Beast said the other day that, he could totally get used to this. It's been awesome. Lots of family time. Everyone with their own crazy schedule, and, with me being an Early-Bird and he a Night-Owl, there's a parent always *awake*.

There's been lots of reading, writing, movie watching, yummy food eating, meditating, sun-bathing, tree-decorating, car-fixing, weed trimming, and, lots and lots of coffee drinking.

Retired life is just around the corner, and it will be awesome. In the meantime, we enjoy it all, because it's all awesome. The whole trip of it. The Journey. And, yet...I also see a call to, see it all for what it is, and not the source of my comfort, or happiness, or security. To not cling, to anything.

To just, enjoy what is, when it is. Life is ever changing. Nothing ever, truly, stays the same. To not hold to what we have, so tightly, that I'm blinded to those that have much, much less. To not have fear or worry over anything material. As it comes, it can go. Here today, gone tomorrow.

Ultimately, a call to live for today, exactly as it presents itself. With its highs and lows. Taking each thing, situation, happening, as it appears, marveling at its uniqueness in the now moment. I also see a confirmation that, what we have been doing, or better said, the choices made in how we live our lives, have led to today. To what we have created as our reality. So, I see this as a call to stay the course.

Do not get bored with the routines and rituals, habits and life philosophies that have led to the happy healthy existence we all experience. Coupled with a gentle reminder to always stay flexible, to whatever life throws our way. A, go-with-the-river mentality. Not pushing. Not fighting.

It's astonishing to me that we were able to create such a stable reality for ourselves smack in the middle of a world pandemic. This tells me, confirms to me that, we'll always be able to create stability, calm, peace, joy, love, health, ...no matter the exterior circumstances. If, we want to. ...All is choice! I remember my mantra: *"To create a magical home and life, despite the world lighting itself on fire."*

Creating that sanctuary for ourselves and our beautiful children. The White Dome of Protective Light. No harm may cross, here, or wherever we may go. We truly are magic!

Laffey|Together

Fully Immersed

11/18/20|Dark

> *"And, in your wondering about yourself, you forgot what you came*
> *here for, what you came to be a part of."*
> Guy Burgs

Time and time again, I learn that, it all points to a forgetfulness, *...a personal and collective amnesia of, our True nature...*
I want to learn...to observe....to experience...to expand...
All happening by being fully immersed in, the Moment.

Tibeauthetraveler|Childlike Wonder

Simply Looking

11/19/20|Dark

I can understand, why it's so hard to look at one self. To really look, at the shadows and corners where we shove all that is, disagreeable. All that, makes us uncomfortable. Ultimately, all those things that hurt. We don't like the pain. So, we shove it away, hide it, ignore it, deny it...

Sometimes, just simply looking at the shadow, shining a bit of light (awareness) on it, is enough for us to transform it, transcend it, and move past it. Letting it pass through us, ...yea, even the painful.

Feeling the joy where there is joy, the pain and sadness where there is pain, and then, letting it go. Seeing it for what it is. An aspect of Self. All the little aspects that make up the Whole. Just as "above." Everything...little aspects of, the Whole.

And, I know it's more comfortable in what we perceive to be joy, or "good," ...but all makes up, the Whole.

No fear. Look at the shadows. Shine all the light on it. See it for what it is. And, let it go.

See the anger for what it is...the sadness...the disappointment...false and unmet expectations. Emotions. Feelings. All fleeting...All part of, the Thing, that makes us human. This learned experience!

See it all for what it is. All pieces and players, mirrored reflections, distortions and illusions. And, let it all go...

A smile always comes upon my face...seeing the "game" of it all. The silliness if it all. The stresses and worries. The planning and analyzing. All for what?! That is not what we are here for...

We are here, to experience it, All; and, to do that, you must show up to the moment, free of the jumbled silliness fogging you...

Your mind...thoughts, ideas, analysis. Your heart....emotions, feelings.

Bring your Whole Self to, the Moment.

No Spirit|Mirrors

A Warrior

11/20/20|Dark

Does a Warrior, after a life spent in battle, recognize peace and harmony? Always in conflict, do they realize when, they don't have to fight any longer?

Do I see, I don't have to worry...? Do I realize The Battle is over and that, I'm truly free? Nothing to fight about. Nothing to fear. It is possible. Peace, harmony, joy! Days full of love, and hugs, and kisses. And, smiles, laughter, and good memories being made.

Healthy minds, hearts, and bodies. Connection, growth, and expansion. Wisdom and learning.

Dreamlike kids, dreamlike partner, dreamlike life! Happiness, calm, peace, love, ...so much love. All the time.

Do I see it? All of it....? See how far we've, ...*I've*, ...come?

j'san|outer peace/inner demons

Great Illusion

11/21/20|Dark

The great illusion; ...thinking, obsessing, analyzing, planning, ...and all of it taking place in some past event, conversation, mistake or grievance.

As if it will change it, or, make it disappear. So easy to get lost in it. Holding on so tight. Gripping it for dear life. As if our very breath, life, depended on it.

The truth is, to see behind the veil, is to see that, what is crucial for us to be present in the now, and be able to move forward, toward our future, ...is to let it go.

To let it all go. To leave the past where it belongs. To give it, it's proper place.

Yasumu|Illusions

❧ ·· ✦ ·· ☙

Dreamy Block

11/23/20|Dark

The Sensitive.

A way to validate each others' feelings and emotions, is to lovingly ask, "*I can see this is making you emotional, do you want to talk about it, or, would you like some time alone?*"

Everyone, is entitled to, feel how they feel, and, the space to process.

With our kiddos, it's about giving them that safe space to feel and express and process. And, all the support that they may need. Sensitivity is not a "bad word," it isn't something to have to hide or suppress.

Awareness is key. Recognizing the need to be still, to have peace, calm and quiet, has been key to working with, my own gift of sensitivity.

I see the incredible wisdom that *The Beast* had when picking our home in the mountains and *campo*. Having so much quiet and peace, I see how bothered we all are with noise and chaos. How good this space is for us.

❧ ·· ✦ ·· ☙

Important to be self-moderating with what we read, watch, and what we are exposed to. The influences around us. Bringing the Self back to harmony and balance. The heart. Being centered brings about clarity of mind.

Coming to center for me is to meditate, to be with myself. To connect with the highest part of myself, my Soul.

Recognizing the vital importance of cultivating peace and stillness is a super-power for the rest of our lives here in the midst of the world's story unfolding.

❧⟫ · · ◆ ◆ · · ⟪❧

Yesterday evening, I found myself becoming emotional when doing financial projections and seeing that, ...we still have a bit to go...yet, emotional also because of the, being able to feel it, see it "peeking around the corner." But, seeing, knowing that, it's not quite time yet.

It became hard to hold back the emotions, and tears streamed down my face. Such a feeling of impotence, of not being able to hurry along the path, ...the journey to what we want. *To Retire and to be Free.*

Thank goodness I have such an amazing partner who sees and knows and understands and gives great discerning counsel...my own live-in *"King of Swords."*

Once I saw my emotions for what they were, and reigned them in...almost instantly felt clarity of mind. I was able to see my humanness in all of it, but also see, the much bigger picture. Not from that place of impatience or sadness or frustration, but from a calm, still place that understands the journey.

While we talked last night, I shared an image that I get when thinking of our road towards retirement.

We are like the sculptor...who "sees" the final beautiful sculpture inside the big block of clay or rock. Who knows, what it will look like, feel like, smell like. Who can see the "complete picture" and, slowly chips away at the block, ...shaping, adjusting, analyzing, and chipping some more, bit by bit. Resting...stepping back...coming back and chipping some more. Until, one day, there is no more chipping, no more sweating, just admiring of all the work done. At the masterpiece accomplished. And, remembers that it all started out as a huge block of clay or rock.

To stop half-way or when exhaustion comes, to want to quit although it's around the corner...a few more chips here or there and the sculpture will be defined...is to dishonor the original artist's vision, to dishonor the Dream.

No matter what, we must stay the course!

S. Hunt|Dreamscape

Beautiful Reality

11/24/20|Dark

I wake up, everyday, in such a beautiful reality. Excited to start my day. Nourish my soul and mind. To spend some time connecting with Mother Gaia, through the rustling of the wind and the rays of our brightest star.

It's my passion to take care of our home, our kiddos and, work in partnership with *The Beast*. I cook, I clean, I read, I watch, I meditate, I sit, I smoke, I have interesting conversations with myself, my family, and the Magical. I don't really fret or worry about anything.

Is this what it means to live an awake life? To live content, and in awe, and amazement, to not have expectations and be wonderfully surprised with the mundane? To know the gift of every now moment? To savor it? To notice it?

Is this wonderland? Is this what you find at the bottom of the Rabbit Hole? To make the shift, from one reality to the next... to, this One? To this, Now Moment?

Tibeauthetraveler|Reality

Who And What

11/26/20|Dark
Full Moon, Partial Lunar Eclipse in Gemini

Remember who and what you are; —Highest Self

This is an opportunity, to truly let go...release...but first, for me to take a look at...*analyze*....*shine the light* on all of those shadowy aspects of Self...originating from childhood, society's conditioning, memories and perceptions, ideas and viewpoints...see how it creeps up...how it is sometimes easy to forget...to step back, to see the whole picture...to see the illusions, the habits, the programming...to not grip because it's known, ultimately making it comfortable...but to let go. To not fear the unknown, the new, the potential greatness which is only felt...but to welcome it all...open heart, open arms, to the adventure...to this thing we call *ALL*!

Hevi|Ethereal

Doing So Much

11/28/20|Dark

Tarot: Ten of Wands

Personal Meaning:

A reminder how I can become, sometimes, *obsessive* over something, *to the point of exhaustion*, whether physically, emotionally or mentally.

Know when to ask for help and, when to delegate. Don't feel guilted into doing so much, a lot which is not even asked of me, that I end up not taking care of, mySelf.

When enough is enough, be aware to recognize the "finish line."

Softy|We'll Be Alright

In Love And Truth

11/29/20|Dark

Throat Chakra

I communicate with ease. I clearly state my needs. I have wisdom over what words I use. I am a confident communicator (*lose self-doubt over past communications). I speak in love and truth. I take comfort in the silence and stillness. I set clear boundaries. I am an effective communicator, and there is ease in being understood. I am a compassionate listener, active and balanced. I create speech reflective of my loving nature. I speak from my true, inner voice.

As authority over my world, I am aware of my thoughts, those inner thoughts, ideas, and perspectives. I voice my feelings and emotions with discernment and wisdom of, appropriate place and time. Sweet balance of speaking and listening (outer). Awareness of memories, thoughts, inner voice, feelings, and memories (inner).

> *"Astrology is assured of recognition from psychology, without further restrictions, because astrology represents the summation of all the psychological knowledge of antiquity."*
> Carl Jung

WYS|True Love

❧⸱◆⸱☙

Dreaming

11/30/20|Dark

I woke up from another *vivid* "nightmare." I woke up with a headache...general malaise...

This is the *third* dream in the last few months that, *I remember and it "stays" with me awhile.*

The dream, from what I can still remember (a few hours later) was not pleasant. I remember the mother-in-law being angry with me over something, and me being so frustrated with trying to tell-her-off and, not being able to...until finally, I think I remember saying something angrily toward her, and then I must have woken up.

At first, I tried to just really forget it...ignore it.

Had my water, went outside, had a cigarette and some weed, watched some Astrology stuff and, went back inside...I grabbed a bit of leftover coffee and sat down at the dining table...to meditate a bit...to be with myself.

I did a quick chakra tune-up meditation... And, the dream came up again.

At first all of my thoughts were directed at all of her faults...*like a movie*...things, conversations, situations, ...*started to replay*...wrongs and offenses...losses and disappointments. But, my Third Eye was activated. I started to see more clearly.

I saw that, I still carry anger and resentment towards her, instead of compassion and grace for her ignorance and personal pain. I saw that I regret us not being closer, but that it is irrational to put the whole breakdown on just one person...and I imagined for a second that she never was the problem, and could see that there are many players...*that she is just a small piece of a greater puzzle*...that all of it, has brought us to here.

Would a closer relationship, mean drama and a disruption of our peace and life? In the today; in the now? Two sides of the same coin.

I saw clearly that even having "cool" parents doesn't guarantee a "close" family... That in the end it all becomes peripheral...that outside of my three, who the hell matters anyways?!

When and if the peripheral shows up, let it be like a cherry on the proverbial sundae. Or like sprinkles. Meant to add to the already goodness of our lives. Anything that doesn't add, just keep it away.

All played-out as it had to play out. We are, where we are, precisely because of how everything happened.

Therefore, I am grateful, not angry. I am joyful, not resentful. Angry and resentful, over what?

Would I trade, even a small slice, of my Now? To change anything? *NO!* Resounding! So, let it go....let her (you) go. Forgive her (you) and release her (you).

Cut the tether that bound us...We are both *FREE!*

Sleepermane|Dreamtime

Aflame

12/1/20|Dawn

...just, ...Glowing;...Irradiated;...Aflame;...

"Whoa, Heaven let your light shine down"
Collective Soul|Shine

More Than Words

12/1/20|Dark

I love what the magical tools of astrology, tarot and the likes do,...confirm what I'm already feeling inside...I look to the stars and celestial bodies...the activity for this month, and it matches what I feel inside. A flurry of energy, sometimes intense, sometimes calm, all good!

I feel ...upgraded, this year, like ...I did a bit of "leveling up"...and now get to live my life accordingly. It feels exciting, big at times... It feels as it should, being a human, living life on this earth, at this time. Wow!

With an openness to whatever shows up, no expectations, just openness. So unknown, and for the first time ever, I'm unafraid. I smile, even as I write this. Because I love life, not because I anticipate anything or am headed towards a specific goal, but, ...just to live it. To wake up to the bright intense sun, to be with my family, to just be and live this life. When I focus in, on my life, it can take my breath away...

To the mystery of it...what will today bring? Who and what will I see when I go out into the world? What will catch my attention? What will I see...smell...touch...hear...feel...taste, today? This, as simple as it may seem, has become enough. Even my breath, becoming conscious of it, becomes a miracle... To breathe in, take a big huge breath in, and then let it all out emptying.... emptying... gone.... and, *in again.* Ah...a true miracle of this machine.

Reminder:

Find the balance of when to quiet, when to speak, when to listen, when to put forth what is rolling around the mind. *Not all has to be said.*

A moment, can be worth more than words.

Hevi|let the notes speak

❦ ——•◆•—— ❧

Much Calmer

12/2/20|Dark

I woke up today, much calmer...the energy felt a lot less, intense. I feel more integrated in my new reality, as viewed through the lens of my newfound perspective. It has always been about perspective.

On and off for the past few months, and more so maybe the last few weeks, thoughts about purpose have risen. Do I have a life's purpose, goal, "mission?" Is there something I'm "meant" to do...

Back and forth, between those questions, and yet I get a sense that, —*I'm exactly where, I'm supposed to be.*

I found myself looking to *The East*, and to, *Mr. Alan Watts...*

Purpose, ...what purpose? Other than to *Be, fully* Be, ...present, *aware*, eyes open, heart open, mind open, to each and *every* moment.

Watts likens it to a song. Which we listen to, and enjoy it *for what it is*, not trying to get to the end, as a goal. So, the same with this life. We are here to just...live. Fully. Not worried about the end (death), but just enjoying the unfolding of this, *Thing*...we call, Life.

Akin|Calm Afternoon

❦ ——•◆•—— ❧

The Outsider

12/3/20|Dark

Have the Confidence, to be *The Outsider*... to be *different*... to be *mis*understood... to be labeled *weird*. Not apologizing for being my *True*, authentic Self.

Standing in truth, confidently; *yet, humbly*. Not preaching. But, sharing with love when approached. All done through the lens of wisdom and discernment.

casiio|passing by

❦ ·◆· ❦

Here, Now

12/4/20|Dark

The birds *chirp, chirp*...man *hammers* and, engines *roar*...is it the same thing?

Birds being birds, letting their presence be known. Man being man, finding purpose. With man, it sounds so mechanical. So loud. Disruptive. Would I feel the same if instead I heard an old lady singing? I try to not let it bother me. To not let it disrupt my peace and quiet. Thank goodness for *noise canceling headphones*...

But, it often spawns questions:

Why with the noise so early? Why go so late? Do you not have anything else to do? Why so often? Do you not tire? Does the noise not bother you, too?

I know this is pure judgement...selfishness, for wanting my surrounding world to be *...still, quiet, and peaceful.* Thank goodness for the still, quiet, and peace we've fostered, *inside, our home.* So, we go Inside. Inside, where all the answers lie. Inside the home. Inside the cave. Inside the heart. Inside of, *me.*

Go within and find the Still...the Quiet...the Peace.

Mavine|Bird Watcher

❖❖——◆◆——❖❖

To Be Seen

12/8/20|Dark

"*The Boy...into The Man*":

Last night my son acted in his manhood.

He expressed himself, eloquently, lovingly, full of wisdom, grace, and forgiveness. He stood in his courage! Asked me to better our relationship, *because...he immensely cares.*

Taught me to be better...My Son, The Man.

❖❖——◆◆——❖❖

It makes sense that, shy of his 16th birthday, we had such a profound discussion. He asked to be seen. To be seen, deeply. For what he is. What he is 'morphing' into. For respect, and more love. I had to be humble, accepting, and make amends.

To look inside myself, and see, that I must let go of the little boy...to let in the man that he is turning into. To give him maximum space. My heart beats so fast and deep. I feel pain. Loss. It's the Mother's heart.

I saw in my mind's eye, a cutting of a spiritual umbilical cord, and more of a heart connection. An ethereal line between his heart and mine. But...with all the freedom to grow, expand, explore, and play. It's a transforming of that eternal bond. A transmutation!

Transmute: *"to change or alter in form, appearance, or nature, and especially to higher form."*

All that is ever left is, *LOVE!*

Yasumu|Growing Up

❖〜・◆・〜❖

Philosophoetic

12/9/20|Morning

"Let the Waters be separated,
let the Heavens be formed, let the Earth be!"
Io

I am,
Balanced;
Torch, in hand,
Here; *Hear*; ...I stand,
In the midst of, the Neverland,
Shining bright, with Inspired Might,
Made possible indeed by, this, brilliant Light,
That all the Other may, equally See, with New Sight.
...Philosophoetic...

Firmly On The Now

12/10/20|Dark

Ego, seeks to protect always...gathering information from past events and time. Intuition, gathers information from present moment, launching me into the inspired future.

As a healer it's important to recognize times when I've harmonized/healed others, at the detriment of myself and my wellbeing. Learn when it's wise to retreat, Self-care, and, to be able to say "no" without feeling guilty.

As December comes to a close; as I approach the New Year, I have to ask myself to, hyper-consciously look at all I've overcome, my new ways of thinking, how I now view and live my life. The grand percentage of the time, my thoughts are firmly on the now. Enjoying every bit of it. Taking mental snapshots of my husband and beautiful kids.

Every now and again a random thought will pop-up, a past hurt, a doubt or unanswered question, a weird feeling of jealousy, or resentment. Some of it resolved, some unresolved, left in a limbo of uncertainty. This year I practiced letting it go. As stuff came up, I looked at it. Sometimes quite painful...I let the emotions come up, I felt them, and then practiced releasing it. I can still feel some holding on. Still wrestling with silly 'what if' scenarios.

The big question here, isn't if those few remaining things can be resolved...instead, the question is, and will always be, ...can I let them go? Will I let them go? So that, I don't take them into the new year... Can I practice, now more than ever, present-mindedness? A tuning-in, to the precious now moment....that I'm so joyfully engaged, I don't have the mental, emotional, psychological space to entertain things of the Past. Thoughts, memories, ideas, ...that just don't serve.

The Past is the Past! Stop throwing stones, everyone is fallible. I may never know everything, in fact, I just won't. Accept the unknown. The darkness. All is safe! The ego, fears it all happening again...But, the ego is not in control. To let go, is to be released of it.

Habitual thinking will try to once again focus...it's a comfy place, while horrible, still comfortable... What if my rebuttal is, "*I release you from my present, into the past?*"

Recognize, and give proper place. Let it go! Release it all. It will always give way to future; the New. Which direction is my compass focused on, ...backward, or forward?

Osaki|New Beginnings

❖❖ — ◆ — ❖❖

Sexual Healing

12/11/20|Dark

Healing Sexual (*Creative*) Energy; 2nd Chakra, Sacral

Questions to ask myself: *History of childhood sexual abuse? Shamed for sexuality, or, sexual behavior, by caretakers? Criticized for playing? Was I allowed to play? Criticized or discourage for creative tendencies as a child? Pushed towards non-creative careers?*

Healing 2nd Charka:

-Transmuting Old Karma (personal and collective), this lifetime, past lifetimes. Always start with the Self, then collective. Ceremony and invocation (can be as simple as a quiet, still, deep-contemplation, ask higher self, guides, to help transmute)

-Clear Guilt and Shame. "I can't heal what I can't feel." Be aware, feel the emotions and feelings. Awareness to 2nd chakra. Then, let them pass. Let them go. Shame is believed to be the densest, lowest vibration. Moving pelvic area, dancing with lots of pelvic, round hip movements, helps one become aware of that chakra (reminds me of Kundalini experience, early 2020, compelled to move hips/pelvic area. My shamanic journey, the indigenous queen before the battle, very compelled to move hips and dance.)

-Honor Sexual Energy. Retrieves the sacredness (which is the essence of all creation) of the sexual energy. Using sexual energy in honoring way. Establishing connection before act. Aware that through the act, your are creating an energy bond, regardless of how small. As with all acts, all creations, big or small.

-Honor Body. Tantric belief: Get to God through the Body. Recognizes sacredness of body, uses that sacredness to further connect with God; Creator. Most traditions/religions reject the Body. Shame it, and belittle it. Eat well. Lots of water. Activity, and taking care of physical needs. Getting comfortable with nudity, dancing in front of the mirror, naked. Honor the Body, by brining awareness to it! Connecting with the Body, as it was made. The more free I feel, the more healed is my 2nd chakra.

-Work Closely with Feminine Energy. Sexual energy is always moving and wanting to create, give birth and *express*.

DaniSogen|Healing Touch

◆◆◆——◆◆◆——◆◆◆

Change Is Good

12/13/20|Dark

Stay present to, the Now! Don't overburden my Self with busy-ness. *Rest.*

Take care of the body. Meditate. Create. Stay in Heart chakra. Stay balanced.

Focus on loving partnership with *The Beast.*

Space and Love with James and Elizabeth- Let them *Be*, Let them *Grow!*

Change is good!

Kinissue|Always knew

◆◆◆

Today I Rest

12/14/20|Dark

Welcome, New Moon...

Seeds have been planted...

Now we can watch it grow...

Today I rest. I take a calm, deep, breath.

Today I rest. My mind, the searching.

Calm. *All is calm.*

Rest in that. Rest. Breathe. Rest.

cxlt.|The Clouds Stood Still

◆◆◆

To Cook Breakfast

12/16/20|Dark

I had such a realization this morning...as I sat outside, smoking a cigarette and watching a streaming show. In a moment, I thought about my sleeping family, our family movie-day-watching plans...that Elizabeth wants to be woken up to cook breakfast for us...my calm...my contentment...my wonderful life... —tears streamed down my face.

I'm finally, Free.

Bcalm|free

Third Eye

12/19/20|Dark

"*Third Eye*"

I see now...

I see you Ego, trying to protect me, comfort me...

I see you bring up the past, the memories...habits...it is, what is known. It is comfortable.

I see now... The inner child just wants to be seen...healed...comforted...and, when it doesn't get its way...it hollers...it screams...it cries...acts out...

I see the inner conflict...the mind wants control...it tricks....it is overbearing...needs to be in control... But, the Soul knows, intuits...it is subtle... I know the difference.

That is what I take forward.

tomcbumpz|eyes shut, mind open

⊹⟩⟩ ⋯ ◆ ⋯ ⟨⟨⊹

Aquarius

12/22/20|Dark

Energies of Aquarius:

An energy that goes from individualism, to, collective *source* consciousness. Freedom to be authentic Self. Breaking away from "the Pack" (family, society, etc.), to forge New path. Healthy sense of community that, supports each unique Self. No judgement to choose essence of own path, all is valid.

This energy takes us, away from religion, into True spirituality (*even if in its manifestation, is tied to certain religious practices*). From extended focus (*extended family, friends, work, gurus, saviors, celebrities*) to more of an, interior focus, (*nuclear family, and the Self as the Guru*).

No Spirit|Together

⊹⟩⟩ ⋯ ◆ ⋯ ⟨⟨⊹

Often, Constant

12/29/20|Dark
Last Full Moon of the Year, in Cancer

   What does freedom mean to me? What does it look like to live my life on my terms? Not looking to society, family (*my upbringing, parents, siblings, ancestral baggage*), or anything else "outside," for validation and total guidance. A going within, my Self, to connect with the highest good for mySelf and all involved.

   An authentic Being, exactly as, I am. A raw honesty. A wide-lens view of, Everything. An intimate, deep, connection to the Heart chakra. Often. Constant. To stay grounded, remembering that, I'm an Earthling, communing with Mother (Earth) Gaia. Often. Constant.

Towerz|Constant

❧⟫ · ◆ · ⟪❧

Resorbed

...just, ...Glowing;...Irradiated;...Aflame;...

...Resorbed;...

"Home is behind, the world ahead
And there are many paths to tread
Through shadow to the edge of night
Until the stars are all alight
Mist and shadow, cloud and shade
All shall fade, all shall fade"
The Steward of Gondor

Give Space

1/2/21|Dark

My son turns 16 today. I get a lump in my throat...
A sense of loss; the little boy gone... *Did I do enough; was I enough?*
But, I let go...give space, for him to be free & grow!

potsu|letting go

Hierophant

1/3/21|Dark

Great Conjunctions: historically seen as, turning-points for Humanity.
2020's Great Conjunction, took place in the sign of, Aquarius...carries a revolutionary energy; an energy of great change, but also, very hopeful...a New energy.
2021, A year to integrate experiences, understandings, and changes from 2020. Action in all that was meditated upon in 2020, understandings that were elevated...truly letting go of what was shed, to make room for, New.
Be okay in transitional periods that may feel - void.

❧⟩⟩—•◆•—⟨⟨❧

2021 Tarot Card Pull: the Hierophant - Reverse
   represents something bigger than oneself
   * *family unit, community, like-mindedness*
   unorthodoxy & breaking-free from tradition
   look at convictions & dig deeper
Personal Meaning:
A call to look at things in a new way...break out of stifling traditions...to challenge beliefs (own & external)...stay true to values & convictions...embrace the unorthodoxy, the non-traditional.

Kalaido|Teahouse Spirits

❧⟩⟩—•◆•—⟨⟨❧

Coincidence

1/9/21|Dark

I woke up January 7th, at around 1 a.m., with excruciating pain in my right shoulder blade... pain, that radiated towards my sternum, back and forth...sometimes a 'burning' sensation when I took a deep breath... I barely slept that night...the next day it lessened...phew...not symptoms you want persisting in the time of Corona.

I thought maybe I had slept wrong...or hurt myself while cleaning the shower floor...I never did figure it out. I'm basically back to normal with some sensitivity in my sternum & shoulder blade. But, thank goodness, today I woke up with energy after a great night of sleep. Feeling more like myself.

After watching some astrological videos, I decided to re-read my previous notes...seeing what I had written, re-affirming all the good shit...and saw my notes for the 6th of January:

Venus, would be in Sagittarius, at 27°, conjunct the Galactic Center; Activation of, the Heart Chakra...coincidence???

A[way]|Warm Nights

❧◦◦◦◆◦◆◦◦◦☙

Why Doubt

1/10/21|Dark

What does my Soul want to tell me today?

> *You are not blocked. Always connected to*
> *Source. Why do you doubt it, Dear One? Why*
> *do you block it? It is your emotions. They*
> *take a hold of you. They control you. But, you*
> *are in charge. Always have been. Why do you*
> *doubt this, Dear One? You have the power.*
> *Always have!*

Peak Twilight|Magical Connection

❧◦◦◦◆◦◆◦◦◦☙

First Kiss

1/11/21\Dark

I remembered our first kiss...*it was like Time Traveling via a Feeling*...it was, his lips...

I remembered the *Feeling* of discovering them for the first time...so many years later! He told me for him, it's my scent. It takes him back!

"Haunted by the ghost of you"
Lord Huron|The Night We Met

❧ — ◆ — ☙

To Trust

1/12/21\Dark

Elizabeth was born 10 years ago. Ten. *A decade.* Already...such a wonderful, smart, funny, beautiful young lady.

I have to let go, too. To trust she is ready. Ready for the space and freedom to put into action all we have taught. Now, it's all about support and connection. Love and compassion. And, always a helping hand when needed.

No more lectures. No anger or frustration. No fear of the unknown and hypotheticals.

They, both, need total freedom to just, *Be.* To expand and explore. To make mistakes, to learn.

My babies will always be my babies in my heart. But, they are growing up everyday... *They are meant to grow up. Let them.*

And, take pleasure in all of it. Delight in them and the Fruits of our labor. They are ready, they have been.

Love Love Love Love

Deep seated in the ancestral collective-consciousness, may exist a mythical narrative that *'The Astrologer,'* is somehow connected with the Divine, rather than, a person well versed & studied in a particular tool; skill: A tool of, Self-discovery; Self-empowerment; Self-awareness; and a, blue-print for the Psyche. Astrology, today, needs to be seen as a Tool; —anything, *other than that*, is misunderstanding.

cocabona|Planet Buddies

Accept It All

1/15/21|Dark

Bringing all fragmented parts of myself into a divine union, accepting the wounded inner-child, and by doing so healing *all aspects of her*, she is seen. She is heard. She is loved. She is wanted.

Personal Mantra:

I call in all fragmented parts of me, back in divine union. I accept the wounded inner-child, into my loving arms. I see all the past pains & programming. I accept it all. You are free from all that, sweet child. You are healed from all that. Inner-Child, I see you. I hear you. I love you. I welcome you back, into me. We are One, you and I.

Yes, you can play. Yes, you can create. Yes, you can laugh. Yes, you are loved & wanted. Yes, you can have fun & be excited.

You don't have to cower anymore, hide behind walls, or inside closets. You are not in a prison; you are absolutely Free. There is unspeakable joy, inside. And passion, and creativity. And, energy.

You are safe!

Dream, imagine...let the visions excite you. There is nothing to fear. *There is nothing to fear.* You are safe. You are loved. You are wanted. You are healed. See the divine, inner-child; welcome her in.

Hoogway|Beauty In All Forms

body, mind, soul

1/17/21|Dark
Full Moon in Leo

Leo, rules the Heart Chakra. Goes to the heart...*(calm...slow...peaceful),* with an intense; disruptive; *shake-up* energy. Associated with personal power.

Watch for explosive, erratic emotions. Make time for Self, ...*body, mind, and soul.* Seek balance & grounding; consider slowing down. Stay grounded as potentially explosive, chaotic, things occur. All is for my highest good!

cocabona|You

Journeywork

1/22/21|Dark

Reading; ...I see the quote from Walt Whitman...

> *"...And have distanced what is behind me for good reasons; And call*
> *anything close again when I desire it."*
> Leaves of Grass

We are Magicians, and often fail to realize it...wow! *Man...journeywork of the stars.*

M e a d o w|Leaves

Look Around

1/23/21|Dark

You have more than enough... Look around... You have so much and more. Do not be afraid if it all goes away. Do not be afraid of having "too" much. It is time to let go of the pain of the past... The fear and uncertainty... The stress and worry at such a young age.

I realize my childhood still has so much pain attached to it. Just thinking of how poor we were, breaks my heart. How hard they worked, *I worked,* to have a decent life. The struggle...

The feelings of "less than..." of, "not enough..." ...And just feeling helpless.

Today, I have so much. Too much. In my heart, pains of the past sprinkle onto the acceptance of it all. Feeling like we are at the brink, of even, *greatness*, why does the question, "could I handle more?,"... comes up again & again?

Self-worth. How do I define this concept?

Is it, *the personal sense of whether you are deserving of something?*

What does it mean to "deserve" something?

I looked it up, it means: "*be worthy of, qualified for, be good enough, merit, to earn, warrant, justify*"

I've often asked the question, "*what justifies that I deserve this?*" and, "*what did I 'do' in life, to warrant such a good one?*" ...when, I am so fallible. Imperfect; still learning. Can anyone ever do enough to deserve anything?

Dumb luck? Personal efforts? Does it even matter? Is this more about, a total focus on what I do have, *NOW*? How I feel, *NOW*?

All else...nonsense...

Not the questions of "why" I deserve such-and-such, but *an acceptance of Now*. Isn't it a waste of time and energy, questioning why? Is this questioning, just a way that the little girl inside uses, to not be forgotten? What would happen if she just, felt safe, secure, well cared for?

Does it take, looking at the mirror-of-life and saying, "*that was then...this is now...*" Looking at that little girl inside and telling her, "*hey, you are all grown up... yes, life was hard, yes, you were so poor, yes, it was painful & scary & sad...but, you grew up...moved on...moved up.*"

It feels as if letting go of the past, or, better, *integrating it & acknowledging it* as what made me who I am, *today*,...is, *the way.*

It is welcoming the wounded little girl inside... I think I would be letting myself free!

May the highest outcome be manifested. Trust this, be open to being a vessel, vehicle...for my creator power.

WYS|Rapid Eye Motion

Still Here

1/24/21|Dark

Yesterday, through a guided meditation, *in my mind's eye I traveled back, in time,*...to my childhood home.

The little wooden house; my first and last childhood home.

There, I met "little girl" me. We sat on the cement half-wall of the open driveway, with its zinc covering. Legs dangling, facing grandma's house. I held her hand. Her small hand firmly in mine. We walked over to the door, walked in, saw the small kitchen with it's singular counter along one wall; I saw the round table where we ate our meals. To the right the tiny living room.

We stood at the beginning of the hall...where the bedrooms and bathroom were. We didn't go down the hall. I barely wanted to be in the house. Too painful. Too scary. For both of us.

In the meditation, I was guided to look around and see if I see anyone...? I didn't. I realized where the feeling of 'alone' came from. I just wanted to leave. But, we stayed. I realized as emotions and memories surfaced...that home was always a scary space for me. For her. Not feeling safe, cared for, loved & accepted, ...*or wanted*, was normal for her.

The dark, the most scariest place. That is where the boogeyman was. I realized that even though I didn't acknowledge it back then...I'm happy the house was torn down. And, with it, all the unhappiness and cruelty.

While still inside the house, never letting go of her hand, I looked at her, her sweet little face, and told her, "*But, you survived! You did it!*" We walked back out. I led her back to the driveway half-wall. We sat there together, for a long time, a couple of hours, she sharing stories and memories, me telling her, her future.

It *felt* like, *I had really done that for her.* Telling her, everything would eventually be All Okay! Never letting go of her hand, I told her about who I married. How wonderful he is. How loved, accepted, wanted, cared-for and seen, I feel from him.

I told her about the kids we made together. How dedicated I am to them. How absolutely perfect they are. I told her about our home. How spacious, beautiful, close to nature, and SAFE it is. More than I know what to do with. I told her how brilliant, smart, beautiful, kind, funny, and wonderful she turned out to be.

How there is no fear. We are so completely safe! I told her how badass she is in crisis, and how creative she is. I assured her, her spark would never die. That throughout her whole life, she would have wisdom beyond her understanding, which would guide her in that life.

As I squeezed her hand, I assured her, all would be okay. That she would emerge stronger through it all. I let her know, telepathically, that my "mommy senses" were tingling, and that I had to go back to 'real life.' I didn't want to go. As I released her hand, I told her to, come-into me. ...Warts and all. In my mind's eye, I saw her come-into me; I said to the Cosmos, *that she be returned to me healed and whole.*

I told her I would never leave her. That I would always be here to tell her all is okay. And that above all, she was safe, and so, so, so, so loved and adored.

I stayed in a meditative state. Every once in a while feeling, a nudging from her. Like a child tugging at momma's skirt hem...seeking that reassuring look that says, *"I'm still here...You're safe!"*

Mecklin|The Feeling Is Still There

Wild Abandon

1/31/21|Dark

    To experience joy, with wild abandon. To love passionately, without limits. To be utterly amazed, even with the mundane; possessing an inquisitive wonderment. To trust with an *open* heart, fully and *whole*-heartedly. To dream big; to dream, the impossible.

DaniSogen|Voice of the Wind

Deified

...just, ...Glowing;...Irradiated;...Aflame;...
...Resorbed;...Deified;...

"Be all and all, together something"
Kings of Leon|The Immortals

Always Has Been

2/5/21|Dark

A little after the one-year anniversary, of, the last time *The Beast* was *really* sick, ...he fell ill again.

We actually had to call a physician, who simply confirmed, what *The Beast* had already Self-diagnosed. He's now on a cocktail of chemicals. He is finally starting to get better. First couple of days were difficult. As he was so sick, and I ...adjusted.

Yesterday, I told my mom that I learned a lot, matured a lot, in the sense of, how I give of myself. To be there for my Love who needed me, with all of my love. A love that, would show up limitless. To find inner strength. A great lesson in, underestimating myself.

On one of the drives, to get supplies, I had the thought of how I felt lucky to be well, strong & able to be there for him. Since then, I've had a slow-drip of adrenaline going through my body, pushing me forward, ...even when tired. One goal in mind: —*Him getting better! ASAP!*

❧ · ◆ · ☙

Today, *The Beast* (*I don't know where he got the strength*), Elizabeth, and I, had the proverbial *'little kid fearing parents dying'* talk, ...except, a million-times more elevated. She shared that, she's been thinking a lot that, as the Baby of the Family she would, probably outlive us all, and, that *she feared being alone.* How scary. Poor baby!

The Beast, in his genius and awesome communication ability, was able to explain, what I struggled to previously explain to her. And, many tears (she's emotional like me), hugs, jokes and, more hugs later, she fell asleep.

Exhausted, but I think more at peace. More learning. Maturing. She is turning into the most genius of young ladies. She knows & sees, and ponders so much. Such a tender heart.

Studying the energies of February, I see the similarities. How it is all, connected.

❀────◆────❀

Realize the *Whole* of, *who and what you are.* Accept it. Be empowered by it. No nose turning, to the pieces of you that you disliked...were ashamed of...*it's all you.* Makes up the *Whole,* of who you are. Embrace it, *it's all beautiful. It always has been.*

Yasumu|Midnight Thoughts

❀────◆────❀

Integrated

2/7/21|Dark

Ego: A mental construct, of who I, *think,* I am. The Ego creates a boundary, a separation between, mySelf and the outside world. Gives me, Identity. Ego is not your enemy. Ego helps me survive. Ego *can* "get in the way" - when not feeling safe, it wants to control.

Self-sooth. Assure Self "all is ok," "all is well," "all will work out, eventually."

❀────◆────❀

Inner child wounding = wounded Ego
Heal inner child = heal Ego
Balanced. Trusting. At peace. Quiet.
Knows it's place. Connected to source.
Allows for Higher Self to lead!
Integrated; All aspects of Self.

less.people|Capturing the Light

❧ ——— ◆ ——— ❧

Sigh...

2/18/21|Dark

Sigh...

Unconditional acceptance, is unconditional love. Nothing is happening, *to me*, everything is happening, *for me*.

idylla|beauty in everything

❧ ——— ◆ ——— ❧

So, Just Chill

2/21/21|Dark

When we sit in silence, we allow our *vibration* to rise, and we can sit back, without resistance, to watch 'the movie.' So, just chill. You have already created what you want; all you have to do is find the "path of least resistance." Therefore, there isn't a need to, regurgitate, "how things are..."; wow! *Which*, prevents me from going where, I want to go. So, fucking chill!

Requires Trust & Love.

❧ · ◆ · ❧

Human Experience:

The human labels, names, and tries to understand. *Contrast helps the human see itself.*

To not name the Experience...just to be...always being, even when analyzing or labeling experience. Focusing on what you've already created...that's the "path of least resistance," and it allows, that, to continue.

Bcalm|pathway

❧ · ◆ · ❧

Foremost

2/23/21|Dark

Recognize, first and foremost, I am a Creator, whom sometimes co-creates with, other Creators.

I am a creator; *The Beast* is a creator; James is a creator; Elizabeth is a creator.

What I give thought toward, is what I invite into my, Experience.

A magnet, attracting unto me, *that* which I am thinking and feeling...that which I say...and do...awakening to the realization, that, I am more than this Body; that, I am guided from, the Inside; the part of me that, is non-physical. And, the need for blending the two.

No matter how sick a body is, it can achieve perfect health.

> *"Man is constantly looking outside of himself, for what is standard,*
> *what is right, what is truth, a set of rules, through which he can*
> *compare or pattern his own life experience, then spends the rest of his*
> *life trying to live within those rules, and wonders why he can't find*
> *happiness within those rules. But, the world is too diverse, 'too many*
> *rules to choose from,' when what man is seeking is within himself, an*
> *internal guiding system. Rather than seeking relic of old, go within*
> *to connect with the same thing he seeks, that he sees in another,*
> *as an image revered."*
> Esther Hicks

Nogymx|Painted Skies

An Extension

2/24/21|Dark

Leave everyone, out of it. Takes not giving a fuck what, *anyone*, thinks. It's irrelevant, because it's all about, me.

As long as I reach outside of me for comfort, approval, guidance, I will feel un-ease, because, the higher guidance & all the answers lie within me. That which, is an extension of all that is. *Source.*

Laffey|Mirrors of Our Sky

Liberated

3/1/21|Morning

   ...just, ...Glowing;...Irradiated;...Aflame;...
   ...Resorbed;...Deified;...Liberated;...

> *"First thing to starting over,*
> *I made sure I was dead"*
> E. Sharpe|If I Were Free

Cause & Cure

3/6/21|Dark

> *"...The older notion apparently is that the essential fact of life is
> Man himself: and that the external forces, so-called, are in some
> way subsidiary to this fact - that they may aid his expression or
> manifestation, or that they may hinder it, but that they can neither
> create nor annihilate the Man."*
> E. Carpenter|Civilisation: Its Cause & Cure

...found this note from, *The Beast*:

"Good Morning, my Love; Thank you, so much, for nursing us, all, back to Wholeness; my Love, you truly are, One, of a Kind; I am so happy we are, resuming our life, all together again and, healthy. I adore you! I Love you! So happy! xoxo"

Hoogway|Healing

Risen

4/4/21|Morning
    ...just, ...Glowing;...Irradiated;...Aflame;...
    Resorbed;...Deified;...Liberated;...Risen;...

A Forest Mighty Black|Rebirth

What Comes Next

4/8/21|Dark

I think, part of the healing process is, a loss of identity. Healing "that" part of yourself, leaves a type of void.

..."*What am I, without 'that' pain?*"..."*Who am I, without 'that' story?*"...

It takes a type of courage to be, in the Void. To wait. In stillness. Patiently. For, *what comes next...*

Jhove|beyond the stars

The Language

4/9/21|Dark

> "*Astrology is the language of the cosmos, it connects us to the divine...
> It is the level of consciousness that determines how magnificently
> that birth chart is gonna be played out.*"
> P. Gregory

Kalaido|Stars and Chimneys

⧉

❧ ⸺ ◆ ⸺ ❧

In A Way

4/14/21|Dark

In a way, it feels as if it has taken me almost all of our 20 years, to personally, "get here," ...to this, "now" moment. I think the trick, for me, is to not get distracted...to not lose sight. 2020 was, pivotal in my walk. I saw so much. So much awakened. Sparks and magic. Deep, deep wounds, resurfaced; healed thru transmutation. My view grew wider, ...bigger, brighter. Glimpses of the big puzzle, as the pieces fell into place. The realization that when I was a child, I saw...spoke...acted...thought, *as a child.* And, saw, that the simple key is...*growing-up.* To see; Be, fully aware. Accepting of what is, and floating towards the light, allowing the river of cosmic-consciousness to take me Home.

Beware, of anything & anyone that, will distract my eyes away from my truth. I release anything that isn't for my highest good, I surround it with love & light, ...and send it back to its source. Timing is everything! Even the greatest thing, in a premature time, will just be, disastrous.

...found this note from, *The Beast: "My Love; I am proud of, you; For, who you are...your essence; You, are special! xoxo"*

Kainbeats|Midnight Journey

⧉

❧ ⸺ ◆ ⸺ ❧

Cultivate

4/16/21|Dark

Calling all Empaths, Sensitives & those with a High-Sense of responsibility for, Others...*cultivate a culture of, Self-Care!*

Remember the Breath connects the Body to the Spirit!

Towerz|familiar feeling

Bring Me Joy

4/20/21|Dark

Joy, is a... question. *"Does this bring me joy?"* If the answer is yes, keep that. If, the answer is, "I don't know." or "no," then you move forward. How often should a person ask that? All day, everyday. Humanity has been taught for centuries & centuries to do what they, *"should."*

Recognize your own divinity, and once you do, you'll recognize divinity in *all* things, then, you'll know you are not severed from god, you can never be severed from god, and you'll see that neither is your brother or sister here on earth...they also can never be severed from god...and then you'll never be able to mistreat, yourself, or another.

Best way to slow down aging process? Living best life. Remember: to grow old, is to grow! To evolve! Humans aren't meant to stay in youth forever; great wisdom in aging. I am ready.

My purpose is, to communicate healing!

Raimu|Sprouting

❧⟫ — ✦ — ⟪❧

Fret Nothing

4/25/21|Dark

I have on my left hand, index finger, what appears to be four "bites," or, blisters. Right where the finger meets the next one. It itches like a mofo. I'm trusting my body to heal. Made some lemon-balm tea, and putting lemon-balm on my finger, and, I'm keeping it covered.

In a weird way, it feels connected spiritually. When I discovered the Bumps...yesterday...I just thought, "*I gotta take care of my body.*" Be mindful of all that goes in it. An awareness of every morsel I eat. Keep it properly hydrated. Properly exercised. Do not undermine it.

Stay focused on what is. Fret for nothing, keeping the mind clear, the heart pure & loving. Be totally in the moment. Do what brings me absolute joy...see the joy & fun in anything & anyone. Remember that, I am always connected to Source, for I am part of Source, and can never be separated. That makes me, divine...that makes me, powerful.

To create, live, experience, exactly the life I want. And, to realize, I am already living it.

"*Ong Namo Guru Dev Namo Guru Dev Namo Guru Deva*"
I bow to the Creator (source), I bow to the Divine Teacher (within)
During meditation, while I listened to this chant, a memory of my family calling my singing ugly, resurfaced. Forever marking me as a bad singer. Inhibiting me from singing to my children...out-loud in front of others...disliking, my own voice.

So, I started to hum...then to sing...and I liked it. Today, I learned to love singing, for mySelf again.

Elior|Soaring

❦

Losing His Soul

4/30/21|Dark

Yesterday, we reached a "breaking point" - a, "fork-in-the-road."

The Beast, broke down an hour before having to leave for, *The Job*. There was so much, ...sadness. He talked of depression, of, becoming grumpy, of, *...losing his soul.*

I mentioned selling the House; downgrading our lives to fit a much smaller budget; and him retiring, now.

After many hours, ...*the hours just melted away*, ...we decided, we are selling the House, taking a One year sabbatical, using that time to recharge, and, think, where we want to go next.

He stops, *The Job*, June 11th. Hallelujah!

Direct|One Step Forward

❦

Undeterred

5/1/21|Morning

    ...just, ...Glowing;...Irradiated;...Aflame;...

    ...Resorbed;...Deified;...Liberated;...Risen;...

    ...Undeterred;...

I Will Not Be Sad In This World

Come True

5/1/21|Dark
40days!

Reiki Session:

We don't have to feel guilty for what we have accomplished. Retirement at 39, is a dream that many will never achieve, yet we prove, ...dreams, come true.

Trust, that it will all work out. We don't have to worry about our needs being met. Trust. Everything we have worked for, sacrificed, given, given-up, dreamt about...has led us to this. Achieving our dreams. Take time to rest. Recharge. Take care of Self.

Dream about adventures, family togetherness, relationship strengthening, shenanigans, relaxation, growing, and learning. Having fun! So much fun! Rediscover parts of Self that feel lost in childhood (they were never lost!). Learn to play.

Be joyful! I am free. He is free. We are free. Be, in freedom. Be, in love, Enjoy having nowhere to be, no time to watch, no bosses, no co-workers, or costumes. No to-go lunches and rushed embraces. Sleep when we want. Wake when we want.

Eat, Play, Rest! What could be better *than just living life* on our terms, *TOGETHER?!*

> *"James Allen retired in 1903 and he devoted the remainder of his life*
> *to writing. He wrote a total of 19 books, most of which were written*
> *after he retired from working."*
> J. Allen|As A Man Thinketh

*"All I need is the simple life, Make believe
the world has vanished around us, We could
sneak away and not come back, Slow it
down for awhile, We'll be alright,
You and I"*
Washed Out|Great Escape

❧ — ✦ — ❧

Wu Wei

5/3/21|Dark
38 Days!

"Wu Wei" - *Don't force, anything!*

Tears stream down. I'm so happy. Sometimes my mind feels like mush. Like it doesn't even know what to focus on. I don't know if, awe, is the word to describe it, all.

Ready for adventures. For rest. For freedom. Our own lives, seem to prove time & time again...that amazing and miraculous things still happen.

We will, no longer be held up by time, or places or people. What does it mean to be free? To be accountable for Self only? What does it feel like to have, total, freedom? To feel, the world, wide-open? —*So many possibilities.*

BluntOne|Blank Canvas

❧ — ✦ — ❧

A New Beginning

5/6/21|Dark
36 Days!

> *"Listen, pay attention to, and follow the signs. Then you enter co-operative & co-creative relationship with our guides, the gods, and divinity itself."*
> A. Elenbaas

A purification of anxiety has to happen. Anxiety happens because we are trying to control Everything. Must surrender to it, *the Everything*, in order to experience freedom

Sun in Taurus square Saturn in Aquarius = *stick to it, persevere, no matter what. Mind the transition - you'll get through it!*

June 10th - Solar Eclipse = *powerful New Beginning in our lives.*

Carufo|A New Beginning

❦ — ◆ — ❦

This Adventure

5/7/21|Dark
35 Days!

All I can think about, is going on this adventure with, my best friend, him. A few more weeks, to endure what we've endured for ...so long. Of course, we can endure a bit more.

It's the last leg, before we embark on ...whatever comes next. My Soul craves this. With him. The four of Us, together. Me and him, forever. A landing pad for, our kids.

A grand adventure. Discovery. Curiosity. Contrast. Perspectives.

Freedom:

To choose. To go. To stay. To rest. To create. To love. To enjoy. To capture. To release. To take things slow. To be inspired. To be explorers. To be content. To appreciate. To take it, all, ...in. Together!

Tarot Pull:

4 of Swords-Reverse,

10 of Cups-Upright,

the Lovers-Upright

...a need to spend time recovering, healing, resting...consciously decide to slow down and process...before, sprinting-ahead...harmony in relationships and family...heart opening & expansion, wholeness...dualities...relationship & friendship...soulmates...on the cusp of, profound connections...Self-love, is the Key to, Balancing the duality of, any, relationship...

Jupiter in Pisces

(May 13, 2021- July 28, 2021)

*an energy that will, come back,

at end of 2021, through 2022.

Highly creative time. Jupiter symbolizes good fortune, luck, expansion & opportunity. Pisces symbolizes spirituality, mysticism, creativity, charity, compassion for, Others.

Jupiter in Pisces, deep understanding of Others' feelings & experiences, and, an inspiration to give to Others, out of own abundance.

A great energy for the Arts, especially film, photography, painting, and artwork in general. For visualization and meditation, and, manifestation.

Jupiter in Pisces themes:

Pay attention to what comes up individually and collectively, positive manifestations, to get a glimpse of those themes that, will be more greatly experienced in 2022.

Tarot Pull:

3 of Swords

...separation can come in many forms. From a loss of a relationship, or identity, to the disintegration of beliefs, purpose, or goals...know that, this too shall pass...the severing, although painful, is a necessary part of the process...the brightly lit future comes, because of the experience of loss or separation...nurture tender heart...give Self time to heal...know that I will love, thrive and find joy again and again...

Mondo Loops|Ancient Map

Changes Coming

5/15/21|Dar
26 Days!
  Reiki:
  Abundance, as *not* material; (money).
  Money, as *energy*! "My energy is abundant." Trust in my future! "*I'm deserving, worthy of, the big changes coming.*"

Do not ignore feelings as they come up. Face them. Replace them with new awareness. Pay attention as it shows up in the Body. Pay attention to thoughts in the Mind. Trust that, like always... We'll come out ahead! Stronger! We can deal with anything!

Laffey|Forever Changing

❧ ⋯ • ◆ • ⋯ ❦

I Will Project

5/22/21|Dark

19 Days!

Reiki: When old baggage comes up; Understand it is the "old" me feeling a sense of loss. Ask Self: *what really was lost vs. gained?* Understand that my ego will want to control...I will project that outward, if not aware. I will want to control outside of me (people, situations...)

When others come to me for help; Practice not fixing right away. Ask questions that encourage someone to do their own analysis. Via inquiry, each can come to their own solutions. Practice not being in that "role" of, The Nurturer, or, The Fixer.

Chau Sara|Space 420

❧ ⋯ • ◆ • ⋯ ❦

Connection

5/23/21|Dark
18 Days!

  *Compassion * Joy * Love * Truth*

Tonion|Connection

❧⸱⸱❖⸱❧

En Rincon

5/27/21|Dark
14 Days!

Phew! Day after the Lunar Eclipse, in Sagittarius. Super Blood Moon.

We went on our little *staycation* in Rincon. I was so exhausted, I think we all were. It was a chilled time. A day at the beach, and then *we were all ready to come home*. Left a night early. True homebodies.

On the 25th, I did a gram of shrooms, *Chilean*. What a trip, indeed.

I went through *The-Mouth-of-The-Skull*, into My Kingdom. A kingdom ...ruled by iron fist. I knew, I had to let it go. Come from the heart. To soften everything. No more '*cutting off the heads.*' Time to relax. To play. *No more, ruling.* 'The Shrooms,' have lots to teach & heal.

❧⸱⸱❖⸱❧

Tarot Pull: *5 of Wands-Reverse, Queen of Cups-Upright, 3 of Swords- Reverse*

Back-down; the conflict, isn't worth the hurt it can inflict. Come from the place of wisdom, intuition and above all *love*...the heart. Let it go...let the pain from the past go...don't let it hold me captive...let go...let heal...keep heart open and tender...there is power there.

Eclipse Season:

Lunar Eclipse - Mega Full Moon

Solar Eclipse - Mega New Moon

next one: June 20th, *Massive New Beginnings*.

hi jude|close to home

Found

6/1/21|Morning

...just, ...Glowing;...Irradiated;...Aflame;...
...Resorbed;...Deified;...Liberated;...Risen;...
...Undeterred;...Found;...

"Merchants and liars,
they have hearts of coal,
Selling rich-man's dreams,
to a beggars soul"
Thievery Corp.|Philosopher's Stone

The Unknown

6/1/21|Dark

...*The Beast* retired, ...*yesterday!* Like, fully retired! We are finally free...fully free.

There is a bit of shock after the plunge. Maybe not fully integrated. A fear of, *the Unknown.* Memories of the Past. A wanting to, control the outcome. All of this requires a trusting. A letting go.

I want to feel the adventurous spirit. Of discovering what is not yet known or experienced. A remembering that, *we live like many won't, so we can live like many wish they could.*

To identify more with family, love, and togetherness, than the material...*the old ways*...the false senses of security in, the illusion; the game.

To break free of all of that. To say enough. To be free.

Don't fear it. There is nothing to fear.

Laffey|Floating, Drifting

❧——◆——☙

Able To Create

6/5/21|Dark

I am able to create a new story...

By not, fixing and being *everyone else's* Hero, I'm setting my Self free.

<hr />

How to keep "*honeymoon-phase*" forever? *Stay in the present moment!!*
Freedom...

j'san|a new world

<hr />

Hermes

6/8/21|Dark

Double-Bodied Signs of the Zodiac: represents dualistic nature - "of two natures." Gemini - the twins. Sagittarius - the centaur, half man, half horse. Pisces - the fishes.

Gemini; represents that time of the year when, *the light is at its peak*, seasonally, then moves to the time of year when, the light is starting to diminish in the 24 hour, day, cycle. This sign is known; for being changeable, due to being associated with *the turning-point between Light & Dark*, for letting go of something as soon as has tried, or becoming disillusioned as soon as it reaches pinnacle. Ruled by, Mercury; represents the one that guides you to Hades, after 'death'... —the "guide of souls."

A reminder that, *all*, is impermanent.

Hermes had love affairs with *many (nymphs, semi-goddesses, etc)* in places like; *a clearing in the woods, waterfalls, streams, beaches, etc.* Didn't live forever, but lived a very-long time.

A reminder that, it's okay to fall in love, (have *love* affairs), even with "shiny things"...as long as you can let go.

Kinissue|Amorous

⟨⟩ ⋯ ✦ ⋯ ⟨⟩

Inner Sage

6/15/21|Dark

Overall theme of, Saturn in Aquarius: *evaluate what does not serve highest Self; get rid of it, so nothing hinders my future. Authenticity in, Self.*

Tarot Pull: the Hermit-Reverse, the Emperor-Reverse, 10 of Swords-Upright, 7 of Pentacles-Reverse.

Go within, seek inner guru; sage...stay connected with heart...release need for control, rigidity & pragmatism...be confident about the world we are creating...be secure...painful endings, but also opportunity to find hope and resiliency...can signify an abrupt end, but illuminates greatest strengths and innate ability to heal any situation...losing faith, giving up too quickly, impatience.

As I give thanks for what I am about to harvest, I know that, my life is headed in the right direction.

Sleepermane|Shimmer

⟨⟩ ⋯ ✦ ⋯ ⟨⟩

Trans-Medium

7/1/21|Morning

   ...just, ...Glowing;...Irradiated;...Aflame;...
   ...Resorbed;...Deified;...Liberated;...Risen;...
   ...Undeterred;...Found;...Trans-Medium;...

                    cxlt.|Into The Void

Solar Return

7/2/21|Dark

One day before my ...Birthday. *My Solar Return.*

I think about who I, think, I am. I think about freedom. All that has happened in the last year. All the "aha" moments. I think about the rabbit-holes...the shadowy corners. Moments of meditation and, deep, contemplation. Moments of magic. Of manifestation. Divine timing. Intuition and visions of the future.

Paths laid before us. The unknown, the adventure. The will. Times of stepping forward...speaking...stepping back...listening.

What will this solar return usher in? I don't quite know...*it's new*...it's exciting...it's only a feeling...and that's ok!

Nuver|Sunrise

In Front Of Me

7/9/21|Dark

Reiki: Where does my loyalty lie? I can have, involvement, with family (i.e. mom, etc.), but not, entanglement. Be thankful to parents (ancestry) for life. Gratefulness for life, and living well, honors the past.

Visualization:

Mother to the left of me, Father to the right of me, and all ancestors behind them. In front of me, my life, *The Beast* and the kiddos. What I've created for Self. Keep focus on that.

The past can be…in the Past, so that, it doesn't hold me back.

i'Outlander|Past Things

More Than Well
=

7/20/21|Dark

Yesterday, we found out, his father died. We'll tell the kiddos in a day or two. It's a weird feeling…his father dying…

There wasn't a relationship there, nor with his mother. So, it's a bit awkward. But… I do honor him for creating, my *Beast…such an excellent human being.* Grandchildren, who carry his ancestry.

I took some shrooms, 1/2 gram. I just had an image of the family, together, *…illusionary "happier times…"* And, his father just, disappearing. That's how it goes. All that is left are ghosts of memories past.

This morning, as I drank my morning coffee…I put my hand over my heart. I honored his father, for who he was on this earth… 'Good'… 'Bad'… 'Pretty'… 'Ugly.' For, the role he played, in bringing life to, *The Beast.*

And, I set his energy free, untethered from our lives. His energy now free, back to source…all is well!

The Beast turned out, and continues to be, excellent. Grandchildren, straight out of a, dream-come-true. All is well…more, than well.

mell-o|Sleep Well

❦ ⸺ ✦ ⸺ ❧

Tiny Roach

7/27/21|Dark

This morning as I finished my coffee, and inhaled a few puffs of a tiny roach, ...*I realized something.*

We've always wanted, to be able to, do our life, live our life, experience our life, without the worry of, money; —Even, *to create & give it away!*

Not worry about finances, ...the business of it all... the stuff that, *stifles creativity.* Well...I just realized we, *have,* created that for ourselves. That, is our life, now!

Raimu|To Be Continued..

❦ ⸺ ✦ ⸺ ❧

Unfathomable

8/1/21|Morning

...just, ...Glowing;...Irradiated;...Aflame;...

...Resorbed;...Deified;...Liberated;...Risen;...

...Undeterred;...Found;...Trans-Medium;...

...Unfathomable;...

Jacob Haage|Above below

Already Perfect

8/2/21|Dark

Uninspired...Unmotivated...Direction-less...Uncreative... So, I sat outside. Listened to some music, and connected to Self again. I sat with nature. With the birds & the clouds in the sky. And, the space in my mind. To let it come clear, uncluttered...untethered to all that exists outside of me, and come back to Self.

Come back to, me. Let my soul breathe. Be calm. Be still. And, feel the sparks of inspiration, once again!

...found this note from, *The Beast*: *"I adore you. Never forget, you are, already, perfect. xoxo"*

kudo|Off

Hybridized

8/8/21|Dark
New Moon in Leo

Had an idea the other day, that I shared with, *The Beast*, while we sat outside. Instead of rejecting, this or that type of Astrology, I thought about, combining different types of Astrology, for a more Whole-*istic* view of the story that, *Astrology is trying to tell.*

This is my Idea: Traditional Astrology - *sets the stage. Lays down the foundation. Tells the story of the tangible. What happens on the 'outside'; the Body.* Modern Astrology - *speaks about the Psyche, a more psychological view; Story. Why we do what we do. Habits, conditioning, etc.; the Mind.* Sidereal Astrology - *takes into account the "wobble" of the Earth. Ascendant sign based on actual position of the Stars. The "now." Maybe, speaks about the person's greatest potential....?; the Soul.*

All Three, hybridized into, One. Just an, Idea.

Bcalm|Together

* * *

Meteditate

Meditate

8/28/21|Dark

Meditate on how I can be of support to my family unit. Invest in my family! Meditate on whether I need to go deeper...to put action when it's needed...or whether I am being too passive...know when I need help...know when to ask.

Kanisan|A Meditation

* * *

Disclosed

9/1/21|Morning

  ...just, ...Glowing;...Irradiated;...Aflame;...

  ...Resorbed;...Deified;...Liberated;...Risen;...

  ...Undeterred;...Found;...Trans-Medium;...

  ...Unfathomable;...Disclosed;...

"When I'm with you, I got nothing to hide"
Cosmic Gate|Nothing To Hide

Everyone Competing

9/10/21|Dark

It took me a few weeks but, I've arrived at the place where I will not be moved, no matter what. Be it here, or there. Surrounded by this or that. It just doesn't matter, not anymore. The world is moving too fast, everything & everyone competing for your energy & attention. Trying to persuade you about, this, that, or the other.

Pulling to the Left...pulling to the Right. *"Everyone is wrong, only I am right,"* ...*bullshit.*

But, enough is enough. I'm choosing to just be me; to raise my family as my convictions and intuition tell me; to be in the moment, as much as possible; to enjoy the Kids, my *Beast*, and myself, always! Because, if not, I'll be swept away. Taken away by the strongest current.

Steady...Courage...Non-attachment...Love...Grace....Understanding... Compassion!

sleepermane|Levitation

Your Road

9/11/21|Dark

> *"It's your road, and yours alone, others may walk it with you, but no one can walk it for you."*
>
> Rumi

...found this note from, *The Beast*:

"Good Morning, my Love; Thank you for, Your, love; Your attention; Your care; Your affection; Your spirit; Your, entirety; All of You!"

Nick Cave|The Road

◆»·—·◆·—·«◆

To Recognize

9/26/21|Dark

To do *everything*, as if I were doing *it* for good, is to recognize everything & everyone as part of divinity. All, a piece, of the whole, of, Consciousness.

...found this note from, *The Beast*:

"My Love, I hope you rested well; I am so happy, and, thankful for, You...You, amaze me, and, I am just so proud, of who you are, and who you continue to, Become; Life Is Easy. xoxo"

amies|Fragments

Reporting, Alive

10/1/21|Morning

...just, ...Glowing;...Irradiated;...Aflame;...

...Resorbed;...Deified;...Liberated;...Risen;...

...Undeterred;...Found;...Trans-Medium;...

...Unfathomable;...Disclosed;...Reporting, Alive;...

"There will come a time (There will come a time)
When love will blow your mind (Your mind)
And everything you'll look for you'll find
(Take a look inside, yeah!)
That will be the time (That'll be the time)
That everything will shine (Forever)
So bright it makes you colorblind
(You will be color blind)
If I gave you diamonds and pearls
Would you be a happy boy or a girl?"
Prince|Diamonds and Pearls

I Hugged, Me

10/1/21|Dark

This experience taught me... —*there's layers to, ...this.*

A couple of weeks ago, had a visual meditation. In my mind's eye I traveled back to my 15-year-old bedroom, to visit with my 15-year-old Self. She was there. I could see the whole room. My twin bed on one wall...ceiling-to-floor glass closet on the opposite wall...my double-cassette grey Boom Box.

I hugged her. We fit like a perfect yin-yang. I told her she was loved, and, that she would be alright. We started to dance, slow at first, then faster...funner.

I told her I would lend her my eyes, so she could see the Future that I was inviting her to. I opened my eyes so, she, could see. She saw her life. Our life.

I told her about, *The Beast*, and, the Kids. *All would be her reality.* She looked out to the Mountains...Paradise.

I closed my eyes again. I hugged her, asked if she wanted to come... And, we merged. I turned towards, the mirrored closet doors, and saw, me. Just me.

⊰⊱ · ◆ · ⊰⊱

In our conversation, I told my 15-year-old Self, that, we would be getting our 6-year-old Self, who, *was still back in our childhood, tiny, wooden house.*

That meditation exercise was tough! A classmate, a Psychology Counselor, later explained that it may, possibly, get tougher the further back you have to go... It was hard to go back there. Even writing it, I get distracted easily.

We, eventually went. We separated again, hand-in-hand we walked up the inclined driveway, towards the covered car-port, and, there she was. Sitting on the side ledge, legs dangling. I, sat to her Left; 15-year-old me, sat to the Right of her. We held her small hands.

Not much had to be said. But, we told her, how loved she was, and, how all would be okay. I lent her my eyes, so *she* could, see. I opened my eyes; and, she saw with such purity, newness. And, that is when, I knew, *I was seeing "The Balcony" of my visions.*

Everything she saw, was through the Eyes of Infancy. It was beautiful. I closed my eyes again and, asked if she wanted to come. The answer was, ...*we all merged into her.* And, there I was, as I am today, legs dangling, on the ledge, eyes towards my grandparents' house.

I felt, Whole. Complete. No part of me missing. No chunk felt missing. I was Whole.

I am, Whole.

⋅⟪⟫⋅ ⋅◆⋅ ⋅⟪⟫⋅

The Dream

A couple of days ago, I had a dream. At first, forgot, but a trip to the bathroom later, and I could remember enough. I sat outside with *The Beast*, and told it to him.

In the Dream, I was a weary traveler. Tired and worn out. Dirty. I was in the City. I went into what, at first, seemed like a hospital... Later, morphed, into a hostel-type of place.

It was chaotic, a bit dirty. In need of some bathroom time and, desperate for a shower, I meet up with someone with plenty of "know-how" of the place. Knew all of the ins-and-outs.

Reminded me a bit of Melx; a bit naughty, really street smart, and really, ...*not giving a fuck.* She clued me in, on how to, lock myself in the communal bathroom, so I could have some privacy. The downside... It would make, the Others, very mad, and, could cause a riot.

I had to choose between, my needs and desperation for a peaceful, alone, shower....or, a riot.

So, I took my chance...locked mySelf in, and, had my shower. Sure enough, the People got pissed... banging on the Door.

The "Melx" person gave me all the tips & tricks of the place, so, I was able to escape. As I was leaving the place, I could see, it wasn't a hospital, but a type of, hostel.

So, there I was, in the City. Alone. Dark.

I knew the general direction of my destination and it would take me through a, ...*very dark tunnel*. The only other choice, was to head further into the City, more people, more lights, but I knew, it would take me, ...much longer.

I decided the Tunnel was too dark, too scary and dangerous to go, *alone*...a woman...in the big city. So, I headed towards the City lights. And, then, I faced another choice.

There was a man, *tall, tan, not fat*, but big enough to overpower me. He didn't seem threatening at all. Still, he was a stranger.

So, my choice, again, was, scary and dark...tunnel...or, strange man? I decided the Man, was the better choice.

As I headed towards the City, towards the strange man, I saw he was, *headed towards me*, too. As we met up, he warned me, not to go towards the dark tunnel, and although he seemed hesitant himself, *he offered to walk it with me*, if that's where I needed to go.

It felt like, two, would be better than, one, so, I agreed. It just felt...Right.

We turned away from the City lights and started, *our*, walk towards the Dark tunnel. When, suddenly, we see a car approaching us. It's an older man, not super well educated, but, I could tell he knew the Neighborhood and the City, very well. He seemed almost a little "tweaky" but, very friendly.

And, again, non-threatening. He warned us that, it wasn't safe, to go walking through the Tunnel. That, rather, He, *could drive us*. After discussing it with my new companion, we decided that it would be safer if he drove us. So, we hopped in the Car, ...*I believe we sat in the back*. I felt like I could finally rest. I felt, at ease.

The Old Man, did a u-turn, away from the City lights, and towards the Tunnel. And, then... —*I woke up!*

"You're safe, The curtain's drawn, And
we're all alone, Inside, In our special place,

Where we can get away, Escape it all
tonight, Inside, We're all alone tonight, You
and I, We're far away from it all, Inside,
We're all alone tonight, You and I, Tonight"
Washed Out|Paracosm

<hr />

The Whole House

10/14/21|Dark

Time, is weird as fuck right now. Probably the excitement. *We are moving, to Colorado.*

We decided that, ...it's *Time*...that, it's *Time* to, spread our wings and, Fly.

On the 8th, we got our Cali.-Canna, and, *by the 9th, we had decided*; ...our *Time* here, ...is up. Next stop: CO.

The Whole House, buzzes with excitement. No one can contain it. But, we all are trying. Even, *The Beast is excited and shows it*; A rare sight to see.

We are ready! We'll take, all the good we experienced here, ...and Shine.

Softy|Snow in October

<hr />

See, The Ocean

10/20/21|Dark
Aries Full Moon

We went on a drive with Elizabeth, stopped at a gas station to get smokes and, see the ocean. *The Beast* and I, decided that we would start the big move to the Mainland, and, *moved the move*, up, to 2-3 weeks. Kiddos are so excited, everyone is ready! Let's Go!

❖⟫ · ⋅◆⋅ · ⟪❖

Aries Full Moon trine Natal Moon in Sagittarius: Big personal transformation. Be secure in who I am, 'warts' and all. Show up Authentically - Always!

"Something's changing"
Myon|Moon

❖⟫ · ⋅◆⋅ · ⟪❖

Birthed, Us

10/27/21|Dark

Wow! I am beyond words. So happy.

We met with our former broker yesterday, *and within an hour*, our house came under contract, and we sold both cars! Wow!

...we can leave, the Island, *with zero obligations*.

We can totally and completely close this chapter, and properly say goodbye to, this beautiful island that, birthed, ...Us!

❖⟫ · ⋅◆⋅ · ⟪❖

These last few months, it was small lesson after small lesson, of learning to *let go...trust...submit*, and, *get out of the way*...letting things....unfold....taking charge of, my, emotions and feelings. All, ...to see, bit by bit, ...all unfold before me; like, *a beautiful Storybook, come-to-Life.*

Living it, in every moment; present. Enjoying all, as it was. As it is!

Tibeauthetraveler|Liberate

Observant

11/1/21|Morning

...just, ...Glowing;...Irradiated;...Aflame;...
...Resorbed;...Deified;...Liberated;...Risen;...
...Undeterred;...Found;...Trans-Medium;...
...Unfathomable;...Disclosed;...Reporting, Alive;...
...Observant;...

"The sky looks like it's burning
The world feels like it's ending"
BetweenUs|All I See

So, Bright

11/1/21|Dark

My heart beats, fast with excitement. For all that is up ahead. To watch it, all, unfold before me...as I live it. Moment to moment!

Today is November 1st. We have exactly 31 days left on this beautiful island. We'll leave, having said a proper goodbye.

So thankful, for all she gave...taught. She raised my kids. She mothered, me. She matured my relationships. Even distant ones. She purged me, cleansed me, healed me. She protected us, united us, solidified us. Individually. In partnership. As a family.

We take all the good. It was, all, good. That's what we'll take with us.

I took pictures of the Sunrise today.

Watched, ...as it 'came up'... watched it, hide the Moon. ...inspire the rooster to sing, and, the last Coqui Song at dawn...before once again waiting for the night to fall. The greenery came alive. The birds woke up and started to take flight. The bright light, covering every surface. The Isla del Encanto; *light, blue sky, so bright.*

Purrple Cat|Breathtaking

Step By Step

11/2/21|Dark

Step by step, all falls into place. As long as I get out of the way.

It feels so good, to get out of the way. *Peaceful...calm...quiet...just nice.* The more I get out of the way, the more space for, the New to be created.

Words fail me! And, that's okay!

Dimension 32|Trust Fall

◈◈ — ◆ — ◈◈

Because, Every Day

11/3/21|Dark
29 Days!

Seems, not so long ago, that it was a foreign concept to me, that I could live a contented existence.

That, all of my life, could be lovely, exciting, and, an adventure. That, my lips would part, to show a smile, while I cook a simple meal, or watch the Sun come up.

That, mothering could be enough. That, I wouldn't go looking for more. Because every day, gave me all I needed. All I ever wanted, and more. The sky will be the same...but different.

The Beast and I have grown so much!

Things are as they should be. Hot; Strong; United; In Love.

◈◈ — ◆ — ◈◈

Laffey|Simplicity

❧ — ◆ — ☙

Make Noise

11/4/21|Dark
Happy New Moon in Scorpio

Mornings and Nights, are starting to get and feel, colder. Yesterday, *The Beast* commented, that it was starting to feel like, Winter.

I love this time! Now, we'll have much more of it, as we make our way West, seeking, our new home.

But, for today...I enjoy each and every sunrise I have left here in paradise. To enjoy the Art pieces the sky creates every morning. The Sun *rays*, the Clouds *cloudily color*, the canvas sky. Animals *come alive*. Wake-Up, make noise, take flight.

fourwalls|Out West

❧ — ◆ — ☙

All Unfolding

11/8/21|Dark
24 Days!

Another beautiful day in paradise. It is all unfolding, as it is. As it's going to. Reminder:

Steady. Know Thyself. Solid Ground. Unmoved! Breathe... Breathe... Breathe...

Sleepermane|Unfolding

I Need Not

11/10/21|Dark
22 Days!

I am, who I am. My convictions are my own. I need not, from anyone or anything. I stand on my own two feet, I am unmoved.

Today, I woke up with a disquieted heart or spirit. I'm still getting used to being comfortable expressing, my authentic Self. I used to take-on everyone's drama & trauma. But, now, that feels like sandpaper.

People, in their Un-awareness & Selfishness, confuse my empathy and nurturing spirit, for a dumping-ground, for all of their problems. But, for what seems to be a great while, part of my Self-Awareness, was to come to understand that for my own spirit & mind, sanity, *I have to be super Aware of where my "giving a fuck" goes*...I have to budget it.

I have mySelf...that is, enough.

But, I also have the love of my life, and, the two amazing wonders we created.

To an extent, I have my parents, and already the account is running low...to a larger extent I have my longest standing friend, and siblings. And, I still have to have a few fucks for while I drive, or interact with the grocery checker...

So, no...*I'm no-one's dumping-ground*. No one gets to decide that for me. Not sorry!

People's lives are, a product of their own path, karma, choices, thoughts, etc., etc. There is nothing I can do or say, to change their circumstance. And, I don't have to listen to it, or invite that energy, into my reality.

A reality that, for me, is full of joy, growth, fun, so much love, peace, and easy going flow...

No-one or nothing will fuck that up. And, fuck anyone that doesn't like it. Because, I need not, from anyone or anything. Whatever goes, goes, away...it's excess! Let it come & go!

W.G.A.F.?

That mentality, all this that I wrote, has to be my mantra. My life mantra in this season I am in...

I am who I am. I am comfortable in who I am. I Know!

Take it or leave it, I care not. I stand on my own two feet. It is solid ground. I will not be moved. I need not, from anyone or anything. All I'll ever need is, ...*inside me*. Always has been!!!

midnight alpha.|Winter Gardens

Feels Electric

11/13/21|Dark

I've awoken the last few days, ...full of energy.

Be still, heart of mine. Probably a combo of a lot of things...the Day is getting closer...the upcoming Eclipse. It feels electric...I can feel it, all over my body. It takes me a bit, every morning, to calm my mind.

Morning routine is crucial. How you start the Count, dictates all!

Raimu|Morning's Chant

❦·◆·❧

Being Alive

11/14/21|Dark
18 Days!

2022 and Beyond...

I feel like this next season we are stepping in, has a lot to do with up-leveling. And for me, it feels like it's a lot of, listening and giving space. *I've done a lot of talking.*

20 years of incessant talking. To the point where *my stories repeat themselves.* Let *OTHERS* do the talking, telling the stories, sharing opinions and ideas, ...dominating the conversation and room.

I feel a call to be left alone. I don't want much stimuli. It just feels unnecessary. And this feels more like myself than ever before. Like the Cancerian crab, it decides when it comes out of the shell and into the world. Otherwise, it wants to be left alone.

I feel the utmost contentment with my little family.

Raising my kids, and more than raising, just being there for my kids. To listen, and to advise when asked, and to give room for the ton of growth they have left to experience while still being dependent on us. And they will be ready, when they decide to fly. In the meantime, space, love, so much love, and, support above all else.

I need of anyone, absolutely nothing, and my cup is overfilled with my partnership. He is all the friend I need; companionship to the max; adoration and love and care. The absolute best mirror and, amazing to look at. Mesmerized by his Mercurial nature and, entertained by his Magician side. He is me. It's why I married him.

Just like my children, he also needs space to grow, space to explore those realms he is curious about, space to mature as we age together, and space to never be judged.

I must trust, as I Trust myself. To have Grace as I give it to myself. And to show Compassion as I show it to myself. As I know myself, I know him. As I am sure in myself, I am sure in him.

As I love myself, I love him.

<hr/>

Don't hold on to anything too tightly. Don't hold on to *anything at all.* Let it all come, and go, as waves in an ocean.

Know myself above all else. In truth and in clarity. Firm, steady. Unmoved. More than moving forward, staying ever present. Aware. Absolutely aware of, myself, and everything else around me.

Breathe-in every moment. Soak it all in. Nothing is mundane and everything is. It doesn't matter. Be in it. And I'll never miss it.

Remember the breath. Be the breath. Slow it down, observe everything. And surely, a smile parts the lips...

Hear it all, the soundtrack of your life. Smell it all, creating memories in the mind. Touch it all, it's all experience; The gifts of this earth. See it all, pay attention, *be quiet, stand back*; the big picture. Slow down.

Speak it all, but only when necessary; better, not to fill the Silence. No *dödprat,* "dead talk." Always in truth, brief and concise.

Sense it all, this, all of this, is My Experience. There isn't anything else. But, discern what I focus on... where will I put, my point of focus? That, will become my reality.

Be so immersed in, it, that instead of calling it work, I call it play. Alan Watts says it better... but remember that all of it, is just the game I play in this world. With my roles and titles and perceptions and ideas, all, the Video-Game of what I call my life.

I'm the Avatar, and everything else is, the Game. How will I play it? Meditate on that. Learn from this time, what relaxing did. What slowing down did. What quieting the mind does for creativity and thus creation. How easy it all became when, I started to go with the flow, instead of trying to paddle against it.

How everything unfolds like the thousand-petal-lotus. Above and beyond anything I could have imagined or ever dreamt of. How enjoyable the piece of pie is, when, you take and savor each and every bite as it comes instead of trying to gobble the whole damn piece down.

Remember always what matters. Myself, and, what I helped, create.

And, then carefully and tastefully budget the rest of my energy to those 'extra' things that truly matter and bring me joy. Otherwise, what is the actual point of any of it? Like we say in our family, —'*if it isn't fun, stop doing it.*'

Fear not! I just heard in a song, a spoken word; "*what if I fall? What if I don't, and I fly...*"

Trust! Everything has always worked out for the best of me. Always what brought me to, today. To who I am today. If I am to feel anything, just feel gratitude for all that has made up, the Story, of me, my existence, which, is all founded upon, how I perceive my reality.

Stay light. Remember the bliss of peace. Of being ever present. In staying in non-judgement and in full-acceptance. Surrendering, to what is. Because, that is, all there, is. There is no past and there is no future. Just the ever present experience of, being alive.

kyu|Beyond

Individuated

12/1/21|Morning

...just, ...Glowing;...Irradiated;...Aflame;...

...Resorbed;...Deified;...Liberated;...Risen;...

...Undeterred;...Found;...Trans-Medium;...

...Unfathomable;...Disclosed;...Reporting, Alive;...

...Observant;...Individuated;...

> *"Mama was queen of the mambo, Papa was*
> *king of the Congo, Deep down in a jungle,*
> *I started banging my first bongo, Every*
> *monkey like to be, In my place instead of*
> *me, 'Cause I'm the king of Bongo, baby, I'm*
> *the king of Bongo Bong"*
> Manu Chao|Bongo Bong

Truth About, Truth

12/1/21|Dark
1 More Day!

Today I came to understand, a basic truth about, Truth. That, it's better to show and live our lives, standing in our Truth, than to merely speak of such, Truth; thus, allowing for others to stand in theirs.

No need for convincing. For arguing. Trying to make, The Case. Respect others' thinking; space. Understand that everyone, all, ...me, us, ...are only capable of playing the game we've created for ourselves. Any other supposed reality, won't ever work for me, nor vice versa.

Only I, am capable of changing, my, reality.

To remember that, means I am filled with compassion & grace. Recognizing everyone's individual journey, as I recognize my own. Love, grace, compassion, understanding. Stay in my highest vibration. Meditate, daily. Ground, often. Stay ever present. Let go...let go... —*let, Be.*

DaniSogen|Strong Minded

Adventuring

12/2/21|Dark

Today is the day, I caught my last sunrise. 32 days straight of catching them. A picture perfect beautiful dramatic sunrise.

The roosters singing their song. Waking up the whole world. Letting us know it's time to get up and get going. The clouds wispy & dancing with the sun's rays. Shades of peach and pink, against the light blue sky. The world coming alive!

It's our last day here. I'm not sad. But, there is a pulling in my heart. *So,* much happened here. So much growing! So much good.

And, at the same time a gentle pushing out. Like our time here is done. And, a jittery, electrical, feeling of anticipation of, what comes next. A fondness for all we created here. All the many, varied experiences. An excitement for all we have left to create.

And, at the end of the day, my mind goes to Us. Him and them. Together. *Let's go...let the adventuring begin.*

DLJ|Adventure

CHAPTER 4

Solunarukh

"Chasing stars in our galaxy
Making our own make-believe
I want you when the sun goes low
Your body warmth wants me close
You say you're always by my side
'Till my blood runs dry"
Glades|Drive

Illumined

1/1/22|Morning

...just, ...Glowing;...Irradiated;...Aflame;...

...Resorbed;...Deified;...Liberated;...Risen;...

...Undeterred;...Found;...Trans-Medium;...

...Unfathomable;...Disclosed;...Reporting, Alive;...

...Observant;...Individuated;...Illumined;...

Marsh|The Whiteroom

Arrival

1/13/22|Dark

Two days ago we got email that the house, *officially sold!* Yesterday, the paperwork was fully signed.

After traveling across the country, we arrived in Colorado. We are at a great & cozy Airbnb, where, we'll stay the rest of the month.

Plant Guy|Towards The Mountains

❦❦ · ◆ · ❦❦

Dream This Day

1/20/22|Dark
Cancer Full Moon

I had a dream this day.

In the dream, *The Beast*, was checking Us into a Hotel...It was, evening. The "Hotel" was, Dark, tended by an overweight, older "lady" - I couldn't really tell. She was just a, ...dark figure.

I watched from across the room. Focusing on *The Beast's* hand, cupped, resting on the counter.

As I came closer, *I wondered, what he had in his hand...* As I came closer, I saw, the head of a baby, bobbing Up & Down in a dark, gel-like liquid. Whether out-loud or telepathically, I asked *why he had a baby. Why?*

He "answered," that he would tell me, later.

Interpretation:

Beast - masculine aspect

Beauty - feminine aspect

Baby - new product of, the masculine and the feminine; united.

This sparked great discussion between, me, *The Beast*, and James. Also, this has inspired me to have a dream journal. I'll get one soon.

Krynoze|Hold My Hand

I, AM

1/25/22|Dark

KNOW, THYSELF! AS WITHIN, SO WITHOUT!

I AM, EVOLUTION! I, AM!

Cosmic Koala|The Player

Self-Governed

2/1/22|Morning

...just, ...Glowing;...Irradiated;...Aflame;...

...Resorbed;...Deified;...Liberated;...Risen;...

...Undeterred;...Found;...Trans-Medium;...

...Unfathomable;...Disclosed;...Reporting, Alive;...

...Observant;...Individuated;...Illumined;...

...Self-Governed;...

"Now when I feel, That weight on my shoulder, I know that I'm stronger, A cloud not a boulder, The power I feel, Just fills me with wonder, I found the way out now, It's over, not under"
Above & Beyond|Chains

Very Honest

2/2/22|Dark

I've decided to write my mother a letter. A very honest letter. It's stressful to confront. So uncomfortable. But, so necessary. To free myself. To free my mind. To free my heart.

The letters, all drafts, have gone from angry, to sarcastic, to insensitive, to cold... The answer, is somewhere in the middle. I don't want to hurt or anger; but I have to just, be clear. If not, it's insanity, to end up in the same position, over & over again.

❖━━━◆◆◆━━━❖

The Letter:

You can accept it, or not, that is completely up to you. You will at least know, exactly where I stand, and you will know, that I am being 100% honest.

Know, that this has nothing to do with my love for you as my mother. If that is ever doubted or questioned, then there are bigger issues than those contained in this letter.

This has everything to do with, ...*my awareness of, me*, ...taking care of, me, so I can take care of, *my own* children, and be a spouse to, *my* husband. It is about the Awareness, ...of how I feel when I become aware of your ailments or loneliness. The burden it puts on me. The responsibility I feel on my shoulders. *How distracted it makes me from, myself, my family, and life.*

For many reasons and, for many many years, you have leaned on me. I have allowed it. At times felt obligated to it, tied to it, this 'leaning' ...responsible for it; burdened by it.

But, I have come to realize, that, for my overall wellness, I can only lean on myself; I have to save myself, nurture myself, soothe myself, mature myself, heal myself, ...no-one can do it for me, not even my husband.

I came to realize that, I can't do it for him. He has to do it for himself.

Only then, can we actually manage to, truly, 'do this life,' *together*;

...his whole Self; my whole Self...

...Him, healed; Me, healed...

I came to realize that, just the task of taking care of myself, ...*which is a daily practice*,... is enough to keep me busy for the rest of my life. Sometimes, when things get "tough," it's a, hour-by-hour, type of awareness.

No room for distractions. No one can do it for me. Which means I can't do it for anyone else. Not for you. Not for my husband. Not even for my children. I came to realize that, in many ways, I do it for you.

In many ways, you expect it of me, and I give it, this care for, your, Self.

But, that became contradictory, to the life I am trying to live and be of good example to, for my children. A life that, says we are responsible for, our own Self. That, we must know ourselves, so deeply and intimately, that we are all we ever need. That we never feel lonely. And in that Wholeness, we bring the best of ourself, to all the places we go, and, it is *that Self* that we bring when we commune and 'do life' with others.

I can't be the best of myself; I can't be focused on making sure I am healthy, 'sane,' happy, etc, ...when I am distracted with trying to help someone else become, all of that. Which, is a futile task, because I am fully aware that it is impossible. No one can do it, for anyone else.

Whatever habits we have established in the past, are in the past. This letter is letting you know that, from now on, many things will change. They are changing, because, —*I have changed.*

It all comes down to letting me go; letting your dependence on me, go. And allowing our relationship to flourish into something that is healthier, and, indicative of a mother-daughter relationship.

You have all the tools (*intuition and discernment and, the internet*) that you need, to take your own life, your own mental health, your own emotions and feelings, and your own physical health, into your own hands. And on top of that, you have a life-partner that is doing this life with you.

I am removing my own Self from being your caretaker, which, this past year-plus has felt, most especially strong, with your health, or lack-thereof, being the bulk of almost all of our conversations. That is not the relationship that I wish to have with my mother. To be quite honest, I don't wish to have that, ever.

I only wish to mother two people in this world, and those are my own children. I wish to mother them until the day I die, and I can only do that if, I am happy, healthy and Whole. And I can only be in a place of total awareness and focus if, I am not distracted by anything outside of me. Yes, even my husband. He is old enough to take care of himSelf, so, I don't have to; so, then he can also show up for our children, Whole, bringing the best of himSelf as a father, until the day he dies.

Understand that, I have learned I need nothing of anyone. I am complete and Whole in mySelf.

When I analyze our relationship, I find that, I am often wearing the hat of a psychologist, doctor, cheerleader, etc. ...when, it should be completely the other-way around. I should, typically, be coming to you for comfort and advice and help... thankfully, I don't need that.

I am fully aware this has been a habit of a lifetime. But, there isn't a better time to change things for the better than, the present moment, ...when something is realized.

I am your daughter. I am not your doctor. I am not your psychologist. This is what I offer from now on; to be your *daughter*.

I am my own person. A mother and wife. Trying to figure out this life just like everyone else. Learning and growing. Dealing with my own physical health. Being aware of my own mental health, feelings and emotions. Making a life and a family with my partner and our kids.

This means that, I don't want to constantly hear about *your* ailments, ...this stresses me out.

What can I do, that you can't do for yourself?

This means that, I don't want to hear about your loneliness or sadness, ...it feels like a burden *that I can't do anything about.*

This means that, I don't want to solve your daily issues, like, *"why is the air purifier light orange?"* You made me responsible for it, just because I bought it for you. This is the reliance that I don't wish to participate in anymore.

"Technology is hard," can't be the excuse any longer; I've seen how often you are on your phone or tablet. If you can figure out *Instagram*, you can figure out the basics of the internet, like researching your daily 'issues.'

It means that, I, can't be the voice in your head, reminding you to take your extra aspirin, to meditate, to take the time to research, to check the weather, to seek and find, to brainstorm with your partner... this, *all*, has to come from *you*.

I must be my own voice, in my own head.

I don't blame you. I have as much to play in all of this as anyone else. Because of my nature, I am compelled towards certain things. Most of the time to my own detriment. And if it is to my own detriment while simultaneously being good for another,...then it is not good for all; then, it is not good, at all.

I am releasing myself from the burden of fixing someone else's problems and issues; being someone's caretaker. That is not my role. All of this simply means that, if you want a relationship, a true relationship of mother and daughter, not of best friends or doctor and patient, I would love that. I am here. Otherwise, I rather that we communicate much less or, *not at all*.

It goes without saying, but, I'll say it, taking into consideration the nature of this letter, ...know that, I love you, Mom. That, won't change. If you accept what I am saying, then, what will change is our relationship, ...for the better.

DaniSogen|Peaceful Warrior

Have To Change

2/6/22|Dark

Decided it much wiser, not, to send the letter. *She'll* never understand.

I, ...have to change! It starts with me!

I, ...have to free, my Self!

Kyle Dixon|Choices

Time To Grow, Up

2/8/22|Dark

> *"An individual is infantile because he has freed himself
> insufficiently, or not at all, from his childish environment and his
> adaptation to his parents, with the result that he has a false reaction
> to the world on the one hand, he reacts as a child towards his parents
> always demanding love and immediate emotional rewards, while on
> the other hand, he is so identified with his parents through his close
> ties with them that he behaves like his father or his mother. He is
> incapable of living his own life and finding the character that belongs
> to him... But, no matter how much parents and grandparents may
> have sinned against the child, the man who is really adult will accept
> these sins as his own condition which has to be reckoned with."*
> C. G. Jung

"Simply put, the greatest gift any parent can bestow upon their children is to be a happy, fulfilled whole person in their own right, since it is this singular achievement recreated moment-by-moment, every day, that sets our children free from having to be caregivers and healers for us and simultaneously be free to be themselves."
W.J. Friedman

Kyle Dixon|Eulogy

Curse Broken

2/11/22|Dark

I don't owe her anything. I don't have an obligation to fix her, heal her, soothe her, be there for her. I am not, her mother. I *am*, a mother. The responsibility and guilt is not mine.

She wants me to feel that, or maybe not...doesn't matter...at the end of the day, I am not responsible for her, nor will I feel guilt for that. I will not play that game; any game.

For far too long, since as early as I can remember, I've mothered others. Who has mothered me? Well, I've learned to be, ...*my own mother.* To soothe myself. Heal myself. Fix myself. Be my own savior.

In that daily pursuit of wholeness & wellness, is how I can show up, in my full potential, for, my own children. So, I can be of example to my children and teach them that, they also, can be Whole, well, autonomous human beings. It's how the "curse" is broken. For the Cycle not to be repeated. So my "sins" don't become theirs.

Every time I feel pulled, I must know it is all in my mind. All starts, in my mind; all ends there, too.

Free my mind, Free my soul.

> *"Now that it's all behind me, I'm just going*
> *to enjoy my day, So good vibes come and*
> *find me, And bad vibes never come my way"*
> Hippie Sabotage|OM

❧ · · ◆ · · ❧

Institute House

2/19/22|Dark

We have about a week and a half left in the *Airbnb*, "Institute House."

...also, our roommate is a mouse.

...we feed it & water it.

...kinda grosses me out...

...and at the same time, weirdly, *like it.*

Very weird.

Clinton Shorter|Prawnkus

❧ · · ◆ · · ❧

Amorous

3/1/22|Morning

...just, ...Glowing;...Irradiated;...Aflame;...

...Resorbed;...Deified;...Liberated;...Risen;...

...Undeterred;...Found;...Trans-Medium;...

...Unfathomable;...Disclosed;...Reporting, Alive;...

...Observant;...Individuated;...Illumined;...

...Self-Governed;...Amorous;...

H. Fernando|Universal Love

We Wake, Up

3/6/22|Dark

20 years ago, today, we legally said "I do!" 20 years ago, today, we moved into our, first apartment.

Today, we wake up to Day 3, in our, *new* apartment; this time with two kiddos. How it all repeats itself. Different, but the same; same, but different. Feels like a re-set; a 20-year cycle reset.

Let's do it, again...this time with our two mini-me!!

Fyfe|Two One, Four

❦❦ ◆ ❦❦

Spend Time

3/28/22|Dark

Tarot Pull: Page of Wands, 6 of Swords, Temperance

Personal meaning:

I found it synchronistic that, the *Page of Wands* spoke on dreams; creativity. I've been having lots of dreams lately. (Jupiter & Neptune in Pisces). A time of high creativity and, letting myself dream the dreams. To, spend time in creative meditation, using the imagination to dream up the possibilities.

The only way forward, is letting go of the "anchoring" to the past. Let go of all that keeps me anchored. Tied. Be free flowing. Ready for whatever comes next; for growth, maturity, evolvement, the transitions from "this" to "that."

All, under patience. The middle way. Not reactionary. No extremes. Always, the middle way.

"Look up to the stars
In the darkness glowing
And when you're out there soaring high
Without your body flowing
Don't hesitate you're dreaming
After all"
Asgeir|Dreaming

Whole

4/1/22|Morning

   ...just, ...Glowing;...Irradiated;...Aflame;...

   ...Resorbed;...Deified;...Liberated;...Risen;...

   ...Undeterred;...Found;...Trans-Medium;...

   ...Unfathomable;...Disclosed;...Reporting, Alive;...

   ...Observant;...Individuated;...Illumined;...

   ...Self-Governed;...Amorous;...Whole;...

"Holy water, Is like real, Ours for the taking,
Holy water, Is like real, Just imagine, Ours
for the taking"
J. Wisternoff|The Bridge

Two of One

4/6/22|Dark

Could the image or the words, I use to describe my mother and father, be a "stand in" for the way I think about, view, describe, or feel, the relationship I have with, my own inner Divine Feminine and Divine Masculine? My earthly mother & father, reflect the divine feminine and masculine inside of me; my consciousness of the divine feminine; masculine? what I lack? want? seek? am?

Am I aware of those reflections, so I can see, the Two faces of the One? So, I can get to know, the One, more intimately?

Early childhood experience; parents, *as surrogates of the Duality of the One?*

"Do you feel something new?"
Fatum|Something New

❧··◆··❧

Heavy Stone

4/21/22|Dark

I closed, my eyes...my body, turned to stone... Every inch of me, ...heavy, unmovable; save the breath... With each inhale & exhale, the heavy stone, moved. The power of, the breath.

In this meditation, I felt 'my body' become bigger, and bigger; as though I could encompass the whole apartment, ...the neighborhood, ...the city, ...the world. Then, my body turned to stone; or, what felt like, stone. Heavy and rigid. So heavy.

But, my breath, my simple, humble breath, ...moved it all. No matter how heavy!

Sling Dilly|Weightless

Momentum

4/29/22|Dark

Tarot Pull: Queen of Cups-Reverse, the Magician-Upright, 3 of Wands-Upright

How well have my emotions been serving me lately? Ability to feel the feels, but go deeper. From emotionality to Emotional Intelligence.

Feel & accept emotional intuition, and, "*listen closely, as the way to understand what, is truly, going on.*" Making sure others feel heard when I communicate with them. Devoting time to their emotional cues. All is precious and divine. Informs and teaches. Wisdom.

Reminder:

I am magic. We have all we will ever need, inside of us, like a "cosmic cauldron." Access *It*, and *Become*, ...limitless.

Recognize the progress made so far, in all areas. Everything from the past has created the momentum for today. Remember, this life is a marathon, not a sprint...so, there will always be "work" to be done, something new to learn, a new "aha" moment, a higher way of perceiving life; "*there are levels to this...*" a wise man has said.

The unknown is...unknown, but, *I am ready to learn, to grow, to expand.*

amies|Destination Unknown

Astro, Logical

5/1/22|Morning

...just, ...Glowing;...Irradiated;...Aflame;...

...Resorbed;...Deified;...Liberated;...Risen;...

...Undeterred;...Found;...Trans-Medium;...

...Unfathomable;...Disclosed;...Reporting, Alive;...

...Observant;...Individuated;...Illumined;...

...Self-Governed;...Amorous;...Whole;...

...Astro, Logical;...

"Kept fooling myself, Lost my sight, But now
I can see you, Sun's shining with you, Dark
days are gone, One by one"
Deeprise|One By One

Self Forty-fication

5/7/22|Dark
Day 1 of 40
Hello

> *Hello*

Nice to meet you...

> *I've always known you.*

How come sometimes, I can't hear you?

> *Because, you aren't listening.*
> *Sometimes you are distracted.*

What distracts me?

> *Others...fixations on, the past.*
> *Fears and thoughts about, the future.*

It's my narrative.

> *The narrative you, ...believe, and tell yourself.*

Conditioning?

Yes. Training. Propaganda. Expectations.

What can be done?

*Become, Aware ...of the "programs" inside, your Astrology.
See, the false narrative you tell yourself and others tell you. Know yourself. Every
inch of your Self. Do not, turn away your sight, from that which you deem Dark, scary,
shameful, ugly and shadowy. The "Devil" can be your greatest ally. It balances, all
which you deem good, light, and, are proud of. Be steady. Within yourself. Within your
energy.*

Sometimes I feel steady, ...sometimes, I don't.

*You are too focused on the Outside,
...circumstances...others... Turn your Sight, within.*

How do I do that?

*Today, today we will start by telling yourself, a new story. A new narrative. Starting
with..."You are not your 'past'; there is no past; a word, that, humans invented, to talk
about memories, perceptions, experience. Not bound to a 'future'; a word, invented to
describe, the unknown, anticipations, visions, dreams." Breathe in the Moment and,
try to describe it, in the most general, non-polarized way...*

...I tried to think of words...
...a list of all the "good," started to form...
...I stopped...took another breath...
...really feeling the moment...
...the only answer that came up, was...
...simply... —*I am Alive!*

And that is enough for today.

"Though you are not around me
Feel this light clear
The universe surrounds me
Sailing out here
I'm the moonchild"
Elysian|Moonchild

Wildflowers

5/8/22|Dark
Day 2 of 40

How to find peace and quiet amongst the noise?

You are in a field of wildflowers. Red and pink, shades of Ruby and Blush, spread out as far as the eye can see. You spot a yellow one, amongst all the rest. It's the only one, inside a Crimson & Rosy sea. But, you see it, start walking towards it, you don't take your eyes off it. You take note of all the other flowers, you see the Fiery and Flushed landscape. But, you are undeterred. Your eyes are set on the Sunny, singular bloom in the Middle of the field. The flowers that you brush past don't bother you. You don't hate them or despise them. They don't annoy or disgust you. You let them be. Let them brush against the side of your legs, as if saying a quick "hello." And, you keep moving on. Because, you remember, the Golden and Honey bud that awaits you. Focused, eyes set on, the Bright and Lemony floret.

Am I the yellow flower?

Yes, but, not what you see on the outside. The Amber Blossom that caught your attention is found within. Always within. Set your eyes on that. Focused. Undeterred. Letting all the other flowers, swaying in the field of Life, gently, softly, hardly noticeable...brush against your legs as you continue to head towards the Bright, Luminous, Shining Golden Flower that sits among all the rest.

no one's perfect|Flower Fields

Birds Fly

5/9/22|Dark
Day 3 of 40

How do I stay in a meditative state, even when life is happening around me?

You stay focused, on the present moment.
Like, this morning...so worried about today's meditation, that you rushed your morning cuddles with the kiddos. Remember, as those photos reminded you, 'time', is precious and goes by too fast. Remember the feeling you got, when you checked on her...finding her asleep and feeling like...you missed your chance. Don't be distracted by the sadness. Instead, look for those chances. With James (his time with you now is shorter) With Elizabeth (you can facilitate so much wholeness here) Simply by...your awareness. Of your past habits...your M.O. Be open to rejection at first. Don't get offended. Don't take it personal. Keep trying! Back off from smothering, from worrying. Let the birds fly... Give them freedom. Stop living in regret. That is a hell of your own making.
Experience, is how you grow. Learn. Expand. Everything, is always, a teaching moment. Brings, awareness. Use that awareness to create, experience, Be. Don't allow the un-awareness to dominate you. Distract you. Be, so ever present, with them. Not with Shame, Regret, or Fear...hanging around your shoulders. Shrug those fuckers off.

And, enjoy the Moment. Breathe it in. Feel it. See it. Enjoy it. Hear it. Sense it. With all of who you are, be in each and every moment. Not judging it, or allowing anticipations. Just, letting it all unfold.

You already know this. You must practice it. Everyday, all the time. Steady. Unmoved. Observing, The Moment. The Moment. The Moment.

Mindeliq|Birds In The Sky

About Love

5/10/22|Dark
Day 4 of 40

    I don't know what to ask or say.

Let it come to you.

How can I be the most helpful to *The Beast*, and, the Kids?

It's not about being helpful, but, about Love. See them through the eyes of love. Not pity. Not regret. Not shame. See that they are perfect! Pure Love. Blameless! See them with the same objectivity that you are trying to view everything else. To accept them just as they are. Love. Just pure Love.

Love does not judge, it doesn't separate. Love doesn't push, it is patient. Love comforts, it does not hurt. Love, it doesn't tally, it does not keep score. Love holds space. Shares. Understands. Love allows, joins, connects. Love calls on Beauty & Grace. It calls on Forgiveness & Acceptance.

Hold this to be Self-evident; First! It surely becomes easy, then, for this to be evident with others.

Tibeauthetraveler|good morning, love

Don't Miss It

5/11/22|Dark
Day 5 of 40

What advice do you have for ~~me~~...*us*, today?

Go with, the Flow. Not everything will go the way you expect, you must learn to stay
in that meditative state, even, especially, when life is happening around you.
This is it. Enjoy today! With whatever it brings. Go with it. Do not trade this morning's
cuddles & love, for rigidity and routine. Do not trade kisses and adoration, for habits
and toil. This is life in action, don't miss it.

Ocha|It's Going to Be a Good Day

Sabbath

5/12/22|Dark
Day 6 of 40

I don't really feel like doing this today.

Not everything has to be a production. Accomplishment.
Don't get caught up in that. The point of it all, is to just Be and live. Rest. Enjoy.
That's it.

Ivylake|Restful

Ever Changing

5/13/22|Dark
Day 7 of 40

What do you have to say about death?

You have to face it. It, shows the impermanence of, this, existence. It's, ever-changing
nature. Nothing stays the same. This life. Your life, it isn't static. Ever moving. Ever
changing. The body does not last. Merely, a vehicle for this world. Enjoy it. Fully.
Completely!

Why can't I stop crying over his eventual loss?

Because, you are holding on too tightly. Let go. And, be free. Enjoy him, while he is
here! Adventure this world with him. Grow and mature with him. Laugh and love
deeply. No fear. And, no holding back. That way, you won't be filled with regret.
Do not be afraid of feeling pain. Be afraid of missing it all. Do not put up barriers
and walls around your heart, thinking you are putting up defenses. Love with wild
abandon. And, you will regret nothing. Be clear as crystal, vulnerable, naked. Soak, in
every moment. Do not mourn. Do not fear. Do not look too far into the Future and
do not waste your 'time' on the Past.

Be enthralled, within the moment!

Krynoze|Deep In Motion

The Great Observer

5/14/22|Dark

Day 8 of 40

Important conversations and clarity gained over seeing the greatness that is our children, *not* being children, anymore.

Two paths...

One, to continue blind to the reality. Stuck in old way and habits.

And the other; a chance to elevate, how I view them. Speak to them. But, most importantly, how I, *listen*, to them. More than teaching the "ways they *should* go," *hear* them, *see* them - give space for them to *show* who they are, Becoming. What they know. How they think. To allow for teachable moments, *from them to me.*

Become the Great Observer of, the unfolding of their lives.

Ky akasha|Seeing Beauty in Everything

Togetherness

5/15/22|Dark
Day 9 of 40

Restful, family, togetherness! Enjoying each other's presence.

Blurred Figures|Angelic Particles

❧ ⸺ ◆ ⸺ ☙

Stay Mindful

5/16/22|Dark
Day 10 of 40

Stay mindful. Where is my focus? Stay, in Love & Peace.

C Y G N|Mindfulness

❧ ⸺ ◆ ⸺ ☙

Rooted Within

5/17/22|Dark
Day 11 of 40

Tarot Pull: the Hermit-Rev, 3 of Cups-Rev, the Hierophant-Up
Personal Meaning:

Sometimes, being so introspective, can facilitate losing or lessening the connection with others, or worse, I dive so deeply into my "story" ...of struggles, that I run the risk of, finding identity, in it.

Inner Sage, Mentor, Guide! Sacred connections, deep & kindred, the family I chose. Him. A companion, in the best & worst of times; sacred mirrored reflections, allowing me to, see, who I truly am. Mirrors, to show me if I am stuck in an old, structured way of acting or being...that no longer serve me. Let it all fall away. I make space for, the New.

Notice, the reflections and mirrors, patterns.... But, remember: *I am my own guru; the guidance I need, is rooted within me!*

Loafy Building|From Within

Always, Within

5/18/22|Dark
Day 12 of 40

Make Death (shadow, illness, sadness, regret) a non-issue; (*i.e. not the focus of my attention*) and make Life (the here & now, what is actually happening/unfolding) the Issue.

Always, in every moment, find peace, exactly, where I am. Accepting what is, in, the moment, ...means not wanting to change it. Or judge it. Or regret it.

Relax, in the Moment! It isn't about withdrawing from the conditions of the World; it's about, not being moved by, the conditions. Takes a daily practice of "un-movability!" Of, knowing who I am. Of, being in total alignment with my Self.

Unconditional Love. Unconditional Alignment. Means, it is not dependent on the conditions; (others, situations, the world at large).

In relationship:

Be together; not dependent on the others ability to make the other happy. Be together; due to the ability to be happy autonomously, and, simply, because you can be.

❧ ⸳⸳ ⸳◆⸳ ⸳⸳ ☙

Tarot Pull: the Devil-Reverse, the Empress-Upright, the Hierophant-Upright

Personal meaning:

Anything, that I allow to entrap me or overtake me, can be and *is* harmful. Even *that*, which I *perceive* to be good (i.e *how other's make me feel...*). Be aware, of the shadows and, anything that drains me. Be un-tethered!

Divine feminine; receiving, allowing, intuitive, nurturing, creative, unifying, listening, empathic, aware, abundant.

Be grounded in the Here & Now. Continuing to move calmly and gracefully towards the subtle voice which comes from within.

Ready? Yes, ready to give birth, *to my abundantly rich future*. New paradigms, definitions, patterns, philosophical framework, perspective, set of ideas. Be open, to new ways of doing things; thinking. Others and the World, mirror, teach. Opportunity to look at myself, my habits, my framework... Strive to understand my internal compass.

All is found within, Always, within!

Hoogway|World Within

❧ ⸳⸳ ⸳◆⸳ ⸳⸳ ☙

A Heralding

5/19/22|Dark
Day 13 of 40

Tarot: Knight of Cups-Upright, the Magician-Reverse, 10 of Pentacles-Upright

Personal Meaning:

A heralding of romance and connection. Enjoy the flirtation & be present to connect.

Intuitive and in touch with my emotions. I know what I want and I'm not afraid to wear my heart on my sleeve. Be aware, of unrealistic expectations, though. Allow deep honesty & vulnerability to flow freely between us.

Is there unfocused or blocked creative energy?

"*Every breath in (and exhale) is an opportunity to carve new meanings and new perspectives into reality.*"

See, feel, know the abundance; of love, family, resources, but above all, connectedness and harmony. See it all around! Give and receive, freely, openly. No holding back. No fear!

no one's perfect|Serendipity

Start With Self

5/20/22|Dark
Day 14 of 40

Speak to me about this? Help me transmute, the pain, the sadness; the sting.

See your role in shutting it down. See your role, period. Don't play the victim game. Trust that time heals all. Be patient, overall. Do not fear it will be too late. All in perfect timing. Practice openness. Humbleness. Non-judgment. Practice, not separating everything into either "bad or good." In time he'll come. He already has. Realize that. Stay open. Become, ...more open, to Listen and Receive. Not interject. Not obsess. Not interfere. Not project. Just listen. Really listen. Be still. Be patient. Start with Self!

Arbour|Patience

Unconditional

5/21/22\Dark
Day 15 of 40
Unconditional Love. Loving, or better said, Offerings of Love; not dependent on the actions or perspective of the other. Love; without conditions. Love; out of abundance of the Love within you. Really meditate, on what 'unconditional' really means, within the context of Love.

TABAL|Days Will Pass

Loved, Always

5/22/22\Dark
Day 16 of 40

I am so incredibly sad today. Tears stream down, and I don't know how to stop them. I feel a little, unloved. A little, rejected. Not good enough; perfect enough; intelligent enough; enlightened enough.

One day... One day... Slowly dying, waiting.

For a day that may never come. For love that may never come. For affection and attention that may never come. For approval that doesn't feel condescending; "*Good, good girl...*"

I feel alone, lonely, but, I am not allowed to feel that way. I feel so much. *When? Will I stop paying for my sins. Or, are they never forgiven?*

I, feel ...I've arrived at, a place of convenience. Good for enough things to not get rid of. Like the dusty old toaster, that would be thrown out, except for that one setting that makes perfect toast.

All around me, evolution... But, mine falls short. Not in my eyes... or, maybe my eyes? I don't know. All I know is that, I am trying. To just live my life. To just worry about, my evolution. To just, Be. And, *then I have days like today*, sad and broken.

Where do I go, from here?

You, have You.
You will always have, you.
You, is home.
Come back to Me.
I'm calling you, unto Me.
I love you. So much.
I'll never leave you. Or reject you.
I see you, even when no one does.
I'm guiding you.
I am your voice of wisdom.
Converse, with me.

Forget about the other.
I am, the Other, you Seek.
You don't need, anyone or anything,
to guide you, teach you, praise you.
I, am praising You.
Look! Look! Look!
How far you have come.
Trust Me. Not him. Not anyone.
Trust Me. I'll never lead you astray.
I'll always care for you.
And, watch out for your every need & desire.
Trust Me!!!
You, are more than capable.
Keep learning. Keep reading.
Live. Love. Laugh.
And then, just keep, Being, You.
Don't be distracted by another's metrics.
What do they really know about you?
I know every hair on your head.
Every pore. Every cell.
Breathe! Breathe! Breathe!
I love you. I love you.
I'll never leave you. Never! I love you.

"Always, Sure as the rising sun, Always,
Hmm, morning's begun, Always, The way
that all good things come, Always"
Above & Beyond|Always

Seems Like

5/23/22|Dark
Day 17 of 40

Seems like, there's a connection between, personal conscious evolution and letting go or letting die, aspects of oneself. A sort of, grieving process, *...right before, growth.* Makes sense; *though, I can't understand it fully.*

Before bed ramblings: In all the Seeking, and Seeking, trying to quench 'the unquenchable thirst', is there any living, enjoying, true loving? Or, does one miss it all, or some of it?

Playing games of convenience, others' pawn in a game, with only one player? Avatars, and, pages & pages. Lore and Legend. Stories and Novels. History and Fantasy. Reaching. Seeking... the biggest, the unanswerable.

On that quest, will others get left aside....Cast aside? Slowly. Consistently. Until, there is nothing left?

Squeeda|Lost World

Watch Those, Too

5/24/22|Dark
Day 18 of 40

What is this ...chaos? In the Flow, out of the Flow... Forward... Backward... Feeling it... Not feeling it...

It is all about attachment. It's not about disassociating from your life or yourself. It's all about the value systems you employ. Good, bad, positive, negative. Identification. Labels, divisions. Let it, all, go.

How does someone do that, when the feeling is strong? How does one separate themselves, from the feelings, emotions? How?

Learn to Observe it. Watch. See; really ...See. Your whole experience. Feelings will come. Emotions will be felt. Watch those, too. Practice. Practice this every chance you get.

When people report "*out of body experiences,*" is that, an extreme version of this *Observing* you speak about?

Yes.

I still feel unsettled.

Observe, That, too. Don't wish it away. Don't judge it, "bad" or "good." Observe, how you feel. And, let it pass. Get on with your day. Confident in your essence. And, watch. Really! Try it for today.

❧ — ◆ — ☙

Note:
  It's been 18 days of the 40 days of "*conversations with myself.*" I had no idea how intense it would feel at times. Reminds me of the legends of masters who would wrestle with both the "devil and god," back & forth. Teeth gnashing. Hair pulling. On the knees. Sobbing & pleading. Absolute bliss. Utter clarity and wisdom. Vitality and eros. Unconditional being-ness.
  Back and forth. A pulling and a pushing. Letting go and letting in. Expansion and constriction. A taste, and a glimmer. Then shaky ground. But, *I press on.* I intuit my growth so far.

SwuM|Show Me How

❧ · ✦ · ☙

To Be Me

5/25/22|Dark
Day 19 of 40

Why would the "universe", of which I'm part of, ...become human? *With all its confusion, pain and horror?* I just want to be happy. And, love and be loved. To be free, to Be me. No walking on egg-shells. No watching over my shoulder. Do I measure up? Do I? Do I? It's tiring.

Lenny Loops|Lost in Thought

❧ · ✦ · ☙

Showing Me

5/26/22|Dark
Day 20 of 40

Today feels ...different; *Lighter.* The last couple of days, confusing; unclear. Despair. Sadness. But, mostly unsettled. Basically, ...confused. At a loss. Emotional. Feeling it all. What was real? What was imagined? *So unsteady.*

I'm up, then I'm down. I just want to be, Steady. Steady. Steady. I feel steady, now. And, it's all that matters. How I feel in this moment. This moment.

I "feel" dark things, sad things. Endings. Deceiving. 1/2 truths. Is that what rocks me? Fills me with fear. With dread? Loneliness? Insecurity? I also "feel" that, it all could simply be self-sabotage. Obsession, leads to manifesting what is not wanted. Creating my own hell. I want, so bad, to love mySelf so much that, others don't affect me. That, even if left utterly alone on an island, I would still thrive. Love. Live. Laugh. I'm afraid of losing it all.

Does this mean I still fear intimacy with mySelf?

Yes.

Can I admit, in these moments of vulnerability and honesty, that I still am uncomfortable with the silence? That I still seek "outside" feedback. *Confirmation. Approval.* That I still depend on the Exterior, to bring me happiness. That the thought of ending up alone, is a bit terrifying.

I, still, find myself reverting back to a more, *childish* nature of, craving desire, attention, love, and acceptance. I struggle with, my perception of, my intelligence; my perception, of others' perceptions of, my intelligence.

Did I say it right? Did I sound like an idiot? But, mostly, did I sound 'smart?' Am I being understood? I have, so much more, in my mind, that I'm capable of expressing. Of articulating. Every ...snub; slight; disregard'; ...is felt, deeply & intensely.

I know, I must overcome that.

That, the Approval I seek, *I must first and only, give and receive from, myself.*

Do I think I'm intelligent? If someone doesn't desire what I offer, why insist on offering it? There is no obligation here. Let go of all expectations. Why is that so hard? I find myself fixating on things.

...thoughts; memories, fog my mind...not allowing me to, see, and act clearly.

I get discouraged so easily; feel unsupported and a bit looked down upon. *Is this all me, reflecting back at me?* What is it all showing me? *What am I, showing me?*

Squeeda|Vulnerable

Boomerang

5/27/22|Dark
Day 21 of 40

It, always, comes back to, me!

Team Astro|Back to the Source

Create My Reality

5/28/22|Dark
Day 22 of 40

What is the object of my attention? Where is my focus directed? What are my thoughts? Ruminations? Fixations?

Thoughts, ...create my reality. What reality do I want?

Ponder, on this, my dear!

Yasumu|Questions

A Choice

5/29/22|Dark
Day 23 of 40

It is a fallacy, to wait until circumstances change, to gain a "better" perspective. It is a choice, ...to seek, ...gain, switch-to, see, notice ...a "better" perspective, and, almost instantly, the circumstances become better.

It comes down to, choosing, what energy, thoughts, and feelings to allocate, to what and for how long, and why. It is a practice that leads to a habit, of not pushing; not fighting. Of living life, as it unfolds. Of trusting the Self and the Moment. Of seeing, recognizing, appreciating the renewal of each morning Sun. To be refreshed and renewed by it.

Guard, mind & heart, from the moment the eyes begin to part, until they begin to close. Is the dream state where it is all integrated? I don't know... But, it should be fed purely.

Don't forget the breath!

BVG|The Path You Choose

Keeping It Fun

5/30/22|Dark
Day 24 of 40

Today: Transiting Neptune square Natal Neptune (exact)

Yesterday:

The Beast woke up with the number 4, and the sense of "Square," on his mind. He asked me to read astro-logically for him. Led to a whole day of conversation, looking at the (our) next Profection Year and what's coming up; and, giving words and voice to something I've been seeking for awhile.

I'll spend all of June contemplating what it will all entail... A focus on keeping it fun!

Be aware of possible self-imposed road blocks; Take it day by day.

⟨⟩ · ◆ · ⟨⟩

3 Notebooks

Start each day with, minor-self aspect notes. Before "outside" influences.

Then, research (astrologically), correlations, data & patterns.

Finally, major-Self aspect, higher, broader analysis. Overall picture. Putting all pieces together.

⟨⟩ · ◆ · ⟨⟩

Have fun. Let yourself off the hook. Be open. Stay humble. Stay the course. Employ discipline.

C4C|Enjoy

⟨⟩ · ◆ · ⟨⟩

Self-Discovery

5/31/22|Dark
Day 25 of 40

Today I became aware, via interview, of French Astrologer *Andre Barbault* (*Born: Oct. 1, 1921 - Died: Oct. 7, 2019*). Fantastic interview, first time seeing such humbleness. Said, after 70 years of study, he still considered himself a student. Said, that the discovery of Traditional Astrology, as with anything, has danger of becoming simple rhetoric.

Unless lived.

To easy to read a book, claim mastery and then spew, regurgitate it all unto the world. Without testing it, questioning it, —living it. Really gives a bit of confirmation that, others have also done it... even if few and far between.

This year-long project is heavy on my mind...but, in the greatest of ways.

A year of Self-discovery, of discovering for myself what is Astrology, and what it's good for; a year of discovering, living, truly, living out my life in this mad, mad world!

A year! The year. *A year.*

mondberg|Living Free

Unbound

...just, ...Glowing;...Irradiated;...Aflame;...

...Resorbed;...Deified;...Liberated;...Risen;...

...Undeterred;...Found;...Trans-Medium;...

...Unfathomable;...Disclosed;...Reporting, Alive;...

...Observant;...Individuated;...Illumined;...

...Self-Governed;...Amorous;...Whole;...

...Astro, Logical;...Unbound;...

*"But you, You take my hand, You pull
me through, You see the new, Now I, Can
breathe new air, You help me see,
What love can do"*
Tinlicker|You Take My Hand

Analyze, The Feelings

6/1/22|Dark
Day 26 of 40

Woke up at 4am. Had a dream. Us, Kiddos, Death...Grandpa.

Analyze, the feelings: Fear or aversion to the thought of death. Ability to look, step-back, see the symbolism.

Elijah Lee|Flying Away

❧ ─ ◆ ◆ ◆ ─ ☙

Time After Time

6/2/22|Dark
Day 27 of 40

Woke up at 4:54am...had a text from, *The Beast:*

"*My old-school musical dedication to you this morning; ...good morning, my Love...*"

And the link for: "Time after Time"

I listened to it many, ...times... Read the lyrics... Many layers of meaning, *unfolded in my heart.* A love dedication, from, him...

A love dedication, from, *my soul*... Went down a Cyndi Lauper rabbit hole...
Listened to; "Girls Just Want to Have Fun"
A great anthem for my upcoming *profection* year.
Listened to; "True Colors," released 1986, I was, ...4...*a 5th House Profection Year. (wow!)*

- Time after Time

- Girls Just Want to Have Fun

- True Colors

I made myself a, '5th House Profection Year Playlist'... Contemplating, what it means to pursue, that which feels fun. Not responsibility... not obligation...

Many avatars and masters have said, become like, a Child... think like, a child...

A child, does what it wants, *simply* because, it wants it. A child does not worry. There isn't a concept of '*what happened already.*' No outlook towards a future it cannot fathom, simply because it's reality, is *happening in the moment.* Not caring so much; not caring *at all*; yet, *there isn't maliciousness there*; just a naive spirit, unaware of, *the cares and weight of the World*; shoulders free, of that burden.

Discovering it all, as if for the first time. Enthralled, *mesmerized by it all.* Flows, going with the Flow of the very moment. The Child is Creativity and, *pure Self-Expression*, ...of desire, joy and pleasure. All 5th House things.

I'm going to meditate more on this.

> *"You have to be here now, take a piece of*
> *everything around you, and use it."*
> Cyndi Lauper

Astrological 5th House:

Creativity & Self-Expression. Sex & Romance. Fun. Pleasure. Art. Joy. Passion. Spontaneity. Inner Child; Children. Games. Play. Music. Entertainment for entertainment's sake.

"If you're lost, you can look, and you will
find me, Time after time, If you fall, I will
catch you, I'll be waiting, Time after time"
Cyndi Lauper|Time After Time

❧⟩⟩ ··•◆•·· ⟨⟨❧

Untapped Potential

6/3/22|Dark

Day of 28 of 40

Thinking of the *minor-self* aspect. Those journal entries, ...the vulnerability, honesty. The *clarity*, will come from the *major-Self* aspect, ...that Sees, all, clearly. Always has, and, ...always will.

But, it will start with *honest, crude if-need-be, raw at times, ...surrender...* to, observing what, is.

Major-Self aspect says:

Look upon Me. Let Me soothe your soul. I will never leave you, nor forsake you. Call on Me. I have the answers. Settle into me, there is unconditional love there. Gentle and soft. Compassionate and caring. It's all here! Can you feel that? No judgements. No expectations. I see you, always. I understand you, the deeper essence of your, Being. There are no misunderstandings there. No words are needed here. Come into Me. Feel what I have for you. Untapped potential. Do not fear. Let it go. Let it all go. What if you woke up, with, absolute blankness of slate? Over what, you ask? Over everything. Every - thing, Every - one! No thing, already exists. Everything, a fresh creation. Viewed, experienced, felt, for the very first time. What if you said instead, "oh, that's interesting..." As in, something that has, simply caught your attention. Not to put it on a scale or hierarchy. Watch it. Observe it. All the ones before, have said; Do not become it. Do not identify. Simply watch, see, observe, view, notice, look, ...appreciate, all, that surrounds you. The feelings, watch those, too. Simply. Humbly. Open-minded. Accepting. Let the feelings go. Feel, notice, Let go!

> *"Tired as we are, When I wake, steal the dawn, Lead my mind, hear me call, I see no other, said I belong to you, Said I belong to you, Said I belong to you"*
> Blanco White|I Belong to You

Ready, Set, Go

6/4/22|Dark
Day 29 of 40

Yesterday, *one month before my solar return.*

Spent the day in *deep* and serious conversation with, *The Beast.* Lots of tears and aha-moments. *Mind-blowing sex; Ready, Set...Go!*

We talked about the upcoming *5th* year. About, *what it means to enjoy this life.* No responsibilities; full of curiosity; moment to moment. Open to trying anything that attracts, pulls, calls to me.

Today, I woke up and, stayed in bed a little while. Stayed, with my eyes closed and, just thought about how I felt; how I wanted to start and spend my day. At first, I was at a loss. What did it mean, to wake up and start my day, through the lens of wonderment, curiosity, and, *possibility.*

Deliberate. Aware. Each moment. Moment to Moment.

Today, I kept it simple. Coffee. Cleaned up emails. Ordered *delicious* Thai food. Now, writing in my journal. Relaxed. Day by day. Moment to Moment. This is nice.

"Wild winters, Warm coffee"
Sylvan Esso|Coffee

Blooming

6/5/22|Dark
Day 30 of 40

I am my own person. I like what I like. I am what I am. No excuses. No explanations. Remember to watch it, *all*; observe. Be in it. With all that I am; —breath it all in.

Steady. Steady.

Worry not. Fret not. Think too much, not. Let it all just, *be*. Let it all land, where it may. Experience, Lived. Open my eyes; open them wide. Take it all in. See. See. See it all.

Oblivion - state of total forgetfulness. nothingness. From latin root word: oblivisci *"to forget, put out of mind."*

Let Go. Walk On.

"...letting life live you for a while instead of trying to make yourself live life. ...the wise man moves with it (the present moment, the eternal), clinging neither to the past nor to the future, making his mind like the mirror that reflects everything instantly as it comes before it, yet making no effort to retain the reflection when the object is moved."
A. Watts|Become What You Are

From a bud, *many which still surrounds it...*it is time.
Bloom. Bloom. Bloom. Beautifully, delicately...opening, Up. Open petals...let the Light, In. Show your beauty. Your scent. Your love. It's time. Bloom. Bloom. Bloom.
Full of Life!

"Breathe in the light"
M83|Oblivion

Let Go

6/6/22|Dark
Day 31 of 40
Let go of the grip that has me, *white-knuckling* it. The grip is also on, myself. Freedom, true freedom, is for *all* involved. Not selective. Not conditional. Stop holding my breath; *Let it go. Be free!*

"Now I'm breathing"
Kinnship|Breathing

Outward Expression

6/7/22|Dark
Day 32 of 40

I realize, I don't want to be babied. Nor do I want mothering. I don't want placation. I don't want atta-girls. Nor pushing, nor pulling. I want peace & quiet. I don't want ever-wondering eyes following me. Watching, analyzing...No trying to figure anything out. No more babysitting.

No. Enough. Stop it.

I like, standing on my own two feet. I like, finding and, maintaining, my equilibrium. Steady. Small spaces. Not a lot of places to go. *Mind, my sanctuary.* That space. I Will it, to my pleasing. It's quiet; it's solitary. It's mine. I rest here. Steadies my heart. Quiets my thoughts. I come back to me.

"May today, this day,
be the day to lead us to peace,
to happiness, and to joy."
Tea Wisdom

The cars pass. The branches sway. A squirrel scurries up a tree. The sun reflecting, *starburst, twinkles of light.* Feeder swinging, evidence of wind gusting. Sitting, here, observing. *Thinking about the Self, thinking about the self.* That is God in Action!

Whatever I was looking for, I already have it. I don't have to go looking for it. It was never lost. There are no gurus; there are no masters; there are no saviors; there are no teachers. Just, ...*people*; ordinary humans, who, wholly realized, understood, knew, what was, ...always, ...*inside of them.*

Through *that* discovery, excitement, and maybe a bit of over-zealousness, these Self-realized avatars put out philosophies, art, books, music, inspired creation.

An outwardly expression, of what was, bursting inside.

And Those who've not, yet, *experienced, this* truth, ...see Them, *the Avatars,* as 'gods.'

Nuit Pluie|Equilibre

Opened Window

6/8/22|Dark
Day 33 of 40

Indeed, today, is the day to lead us to peace, happiness, joy.

Coffee... Good Mornings... Couple's Tinkering... Long Nap... St. Teresa... Coffee & Conversations... Jazz cafe... Showers... Opened Window... Hummingbirds... *Life in Action!*

"That's what we live for"
Flora Cash|pretty things, spotlight and sleep

Brand New

. 6/9/22|Dark
Day 34 of 40
Jupiter conjunct Ascendant

Everything, as if brand new. For the first time. Experienced with awe & wonder. Take it all in. Feel the presence of, the *now!*

‹›‹›——◆——‹›‹›

Quiet, Silence, Peace

6/10/22|Dawn
Day 35 of 40

Zest of life, *come back to me.* Spirit, *come alive.* Wake from your slumber.

I'm 15 chapters in... *St. Teresa, what are you trying to say?*

How do I translate so much religious jargon into words that don't frustrate my soul? *What am I suppose to learn?* What am I suppose to see? *Where is the "aha" moment?* Where is the inspiration?

Tears of frustration form in my eyes...

What "magic level" am I suppose to reach? What is this, *nothingness*, I feel? What is this feeling of being completely lost? Without direction... Times like this, I feel like it's all falling apart. No direction...No where to go...

Been a couple days of "embracing life...", but, ...*I don't know what I want...*

Nothing inspires...Everything seems forced. I thought I was into *Astrology*, but, ...*now I question, everything.* Do I really like it? I don't know...

Without chores, taking care of others, being a mom, being a wife, ...*I feel so lost.* I don't know what to do... If anything at all, would just inspire me... But, nothing does.

I find myself, sleeping. But, I don't want to sleep my life away. I want to embrace it. To grab it. So far...I've acted out fun, in a sexual way. Is that, just habits? *I don't know.* Was I even turned on? *I don't know anything.* I don't feel much right now.

Emptiness. My soul feels empty. Nothing there. Hollow. Empty. In the morning when I wake, I face into blankness. And, I haven't the slightest clue how, or what, to start painting on that blank, blank canvas.

I draw, but I'm not inspired or excited. Just filling the time. I think about learning to sing, ...*but would it just be a sad song?*

I got new shoes. But, so what? *Do I even want to walk?* I know, or understand, or see it...far, far, away...that It, is the point. That there isn't anything more to it than that. The point would be to draw, for the point of drawing. Singing for the point of singing. To walk, simply because I can do it. (*I should be grateful when so many others can't.*)

To live, simply to live. Because, I was granted life. Because, I *am* alive. But, I wander our apartment like a zombie...uncomfortable in my body.

Wondering in my mind, '*how does someone, simply, live their life?*' Not *achieving* anything. No goals. No big plans.

Organic unfolding's.

How easy I can write about it. Or read it... I would so fast burn it all up, ...for what it's been for. I don't want to write about it. *Who cares about damn poetry?*

I don't want to read about it. How many more books do I have to read? Supposedly, *they all say the same thing. All* point, *to the same thing*...yet, I can't see it. I just, can't...

How long do I have to continue feeling, ...so blind?

Am I not, surrendering *correctly*? Not *enough*? *Hard* enough? What else, needs to take place, for my soul to Wake Up?

I've commanded it; *Fucking wake up!*

I've begged it; *Please, wake up!*

I've chased it; *Where are you, soul of mine?*

I've felt it; ...Or, *have I? I question it all.*

Do I dare write the words: my Soul, feels dead inside.

Where do I go from here? I almost can't bare to read of others' divine inspiration. *Their*, aha moments. Moments I thought I had. Brilliant moments of "awakening..." ...*What was that, even?*... *Why didn't it, stay? Why did it go away?*...

Distractions! Arrogance!

Arrogance that I've *overcome myself*. That, through an 'aha moment' or a 'flash of inspiration,' I've managed to change my nature. My true nature. A sort of, cockiness; of thinking ...'*I've made it*.' Of becoming so excitable, enthralled, amazed by the new growth and expansion, that, *I stay there, don't go further*; distracted by the brilliance, in awe of the way it sparkles.

I've stayed there, playing with the flickers. With the sparkles. Stuck, entertained and busied with the new toy. Instead of, seeing, that it all leads...and keeps leading, to greater brilliance. Greater light. Greater understanding.

That is like the analogy of the Teenager. No one denies its amazing growth and expansion, but, it would be foolish to believe it done learning, growing.

So, let's rewind. Let's take this, ...step-by-step. A couple of days ago, I decided to embrace Life. The next day read, "*Becoming What You Are*," which basically says, '*Stop Trying; Now, Simply Live*.'

I realize that, that simple phrase, can be so hard to live out.

Simply live. No, 'buts, ifs, judgements, labeling.' Just simple, *Being*. Human, *Being*. To, *Be*. The Self. Raw. Honest.

And now, ...I read St. Teresa. My mind troubled at her words. Trouble translating. I want to give up. I want to toss it. It's not simple enough. What's with the poetry? What with twisted words. Words, falling over each other.

Simple. *To who?*

If it can't be talked about, why so many try? Why You? And, You?

I'll keep trying. I think...in a bit of horror... *"a year of this?"* I don't want to be deterred, by my wandering of the desert...of blankness, of my calling...Wake...Wake...Wake...Soul of Mine.

⊰❦ ⸱ ⸱✦⸱ ⸱❦⊱

Mother, Father...dying. Going within the Spirit, Soul, to find that ...*Mothering*. No depending on the outside. All within. The Great Mother within. St. Teresa speaks about the Virgin Mother. Mary, Mare - Latin, meaning '*sea, mar, water*'. Water, consciousness. Knowledge.

Coming back to body.

Spirit + Body = *Wholeness*.

What does that mean? If I 'kill' the idea of an exteriorized Mother, dead; then, the only Mother which remains, *is the one inside.*

When St. Teresa says, that whenever she turned to the "supreme Virgin" - Mother, she was conscious, ...aware, ...she knew her aid, and always brought her to herself.

If I 'kill' the Mother on the outside, the knowledge I can find on the outside may subsequently be turned, inside; thus, it is always aiding...and my turning inward will bring awareness of that aid, and ultimately bring me back to, myself.

In a way, you can see the role of the earthly mother, in bringing the soul into physical form. Bringing me into being. A step, a beginning step into, ultimately coming-into my own. Does it all come down to not getting stuck there?

Can I admit that in small ways, big ways, sneaky ways, I still hold onto that *image of being mothered*? Held? Comforted? Led?

I may say that, I've distanced from my own mother. Each day that passes, not so moved by supposed ties that "bind."

But, can I ask myself, honestly, do I seek that mothering from, *The Beast*? If not, *The Beast*, someone else? When will the day come, when I can fully and completely rely on the Great Mother within? Simply put, when do I take responsibility for my life? When do I see, all that is within me?

St. Teresa speaks of graces; *the same as gifts?* Of all the greatness that was inside of her... If I am honest I've always known or been told of my gifts...Of those innate, built-in gifts, unique to me. Many, I am sure, I take for granted.

She speaks of, *solitude*, to offer her many prayers. I tend to fight solitude. Resist the space of my prayers...my meditations. She spoke of her many prayers. Can I just change the word "prayer" into "thoughts?"

She sought solitude, because her thoughts were many. I think of my own childhood... preferred to be alone. The noise, the talking, bothered me. As a young teen & young woman, preferred quiet and solitude in my room. My thoughts, *for they were many.*

My nose in the books, escaping, to far away lands. Was that a form of hermitting? Pen or pencil, journals, doodles. But, mostly my words. Many words. Many prayers. To God. To myself!

Back then, words flowed, solitude - most coveted. I remember, day-dreaming of *The Day*, through much hard work, I would be on my own, alone, by choice, living in my high-rise penthouse apartment. I never saw kids. Never saw a husband.

But, ...I saw myself!

Somewhere, from then to now...I have extinguished that *sense of independence*. Of standing above the city. Above it all. Of being alone and seeing Freedom, not Dread.

See, see yourself, your are, on top of the high-rise, well above the rest; independent, unafraid. Give in to the Height. Do not be afraid to fall.

Repetition. Constant. To be in a meditative state, all the time. My life. Live it. In its simplicity. See its beauty. Simple.

Awake, my soul. Enliven, my soul. Breathe, my soul. Breathe life into me. Open-broadening. Rivers of thought, be all nourishing.

❧ ·◆· ·◆· ·◆· ·❧

Already past midnight of the next day, ...June 11, 2022.

I hope that his worry for me, didn't ruin his birthday. That, he knows, that I am okay.

Even now, I reproach myself, I can't think of him. Not like this. I can't worry for him. I have to worry about, myself. I have to see about my own peace and happiness. I wonder in my head, *'will it always be like this?'*

Unsteady...Unstable...Hot. Cold. Secure. Insecure. On. Off. Up. Down.

I wonder if I just write, and write, and keep reading and learning, will it stick? Will I finally, once and for all, ...*wake up?*

I feel crazy. I don't even know what to write anymore. All I know is that I am done feeling despair, when, I have it all. To feel no inspiration, when, the world is a jewel wanting to be discovered. I wait, and wait. For my soul to wake up. To feel free.

Yes, yes, I know. It already is. Free, free, free. *Why don't I feel it? I don't feel free. I don't feel inspired.*

But, *I do feel,* like I *don't* want to be sad, when my life is pure joy. No more tears.

St. Teresa, in the first chapter, says that if she was ever apart from God, it was solely *her* fault. So, if my soul feels dead, *how do I awaken it?* I recognize it. *Now what?*

Can I tell it to wake up? Is it asleep? Is it an illusion? *Awaken my soul.* Constant repetition. I'll do or not do what it takes. Surrender? *Fine, I give up.* I don't know what to do. Feels...nothing.

Surrender. Surrender. Not to give up... Just give in! Is it a matter of tiring myself out? Of emptying it all out? The thoughts run wild...

To see how wild they truly are. To see the extremes I go. From one side, straight to the other. No anchor. Nothing holding me down. Solitude. *Where is the balance?*

Voices. From all over. Thought I could find answers. Now, a nuisance. *The more voices, the more confusion.*

I desire, *One* voice.

Voice of Reason. Voice of Peace. Voice of Love. Right now, after hours of distress; Not by anyone's fault, or crime; No one; Not one; —I feel peace, I feel quiet. No voices running around my head.

But, in the day time, I get feelings hurt. I get bored. I become self-conscious. I become impatient. *I lose sight.*

I realize in this instant, that, *simultaneously,* I must see the Big Picture and, see my Self, clearly, minutely, microscopically.

See my folly. See my foolishness. See my seeking & searchings. See my illusions and stories. See my trickery. Everyday. See my impatience.

It'll take time to settle all the voices. To sift through the muckery of exterior influences. To give proper spaces to my interior aspects. I have to figure out my voice/s. I have to learn *to hear, my own wisdom*; my own council.

Do not be fooled, thinking a hobby or an activity will fill that void. It will be more of the same. Don't know what to do? *Do nothing.* Don't know what to say? *Say nothing.* Don't know how to be? *Be nothing.* Don't know what to feel? *Feel nothing.* Don't know what to like? *Like nothing.*

I feel like an infant... That I have to *step-by-step,* my next day. Just so I don't screw it up. Wake!

Don't open eyes. Just lay. Breathe. Let the next moment come. Maybe you wish to sleep longer. Maybe, you want to pee. A shower, maybe? Step-by-step. Not getting ahead of myself. Not thinking of the Day before me. *Just, the moment.* Not the Year ahead of me. Just, the moment.

Can I do that?

Please, do that! Do this. *Just be.* Don't screw this up, for yourself. By yourself. Remember, *if it's not fun; don't do it.*

Stop holding my breath. Pages and pages. My hand isn't even tired. Like I am trying to, *write my soul into awakening.*

I long. Like a lover's longing. A wanting. But, *deeper. Stronger. Desperate.* To just feel, Whole. Not needy. Not lonely. Not self-conscious. To be independent. Not *dependent.*

Bowling rails. Babying the ball to hit something. Anything. The side of the pool, holding on to dear life, scooting all around the pool, never exploring the space in-between, *even though I have always been able to swim.* Bicycle training-wheels past their purpose. Someone holding my hand, as I cross the street, *when I can do it myself.*

I can look both ways. I can intuit danger and safe passage.

Stop looking for, the Mother - *out there.* See the Mother, *inside.* Stop, leaning on the Husband *out there, and Husband yourself.* Stop, looking for the Child to instruct *out there,* and tend to the Child *within.*

Realize. I am almost 40. 40 years old. 40 days and 40 nights. 4 - legs on a table. 4 - walls for a dwelling. *Stable. Secure. Perfect.*

How much longer? Retire, already. *Stop working. Stop achieving. Stop trying to get somewhere.* Just, *Be.* Be. Rest.

I'll write it until my pen runs dry. I'll repeat it. And, repeat it. And, repeat it.

It's time. To rest. To enjoy. I'll do this everyday. I'll write until I have no words, or they feel complete. I'll meditate, until I find peace. I've shut it all out before. I can do it again. But, this time, no turning back. No interest. Just moving forward. Pressing on. Life keeps going. It doesn't stop, not even for the lovely parts.

This isn't malicious. No one should take it personal. Life keeps moving. Everything changes. Nothing stays the same. Life doesn't hold on. *Neither should I.* It moves. I move.

Life is not keeping score, not in that way; not in the way I think I understand, to demand anything out of anyone. *I* keep score. *I* compartmentalize. *I* put the good things in the good boxes, which I keep hidden in my closet, and, the bad things in a backpack that I carry around with me, always.

The boxes collect dust. And, the backpack only gets heavier.

What if I took one last look at the boxes, smiled a nostalgic smile, and gave them away? To life. Let life claim those sweet memories. And, took off the backpack, opened it, took a glance and tossed its contents into the sea? Let the ocean swallow them.

The boxes...taking up space. The backpack gives me backache.

Clear out my closet. Make room for, *the New, for, Life.* Take off the backpack, Free Myself.

You'll lay down soon. Eyelids heavy. Soul at rest. You'll sleep, soundly. Restfully, regardless of the quantity of hours.

Dreams will be wisdom, nothing but wisdom. Windows, doors into the unknown. You'll wake.

Slow. Slow down. No hurry here. Nothing to do. Nowhere to go. Breath in, and out. Be okay, having no direction. Be okay, being okay with, being alive. That your body woke up. That you have another day. That the Sun shines.

Be okay, with no goals. Do nothing. Be okay, with nothing. Silence. Be still. And know. Breathe. As many times...as possible. Delay, even the bathroom. Stay, remember.

Tonight, you'll lay down. Mind basically exhausted. Apprehension, *that I'll lose it all overnight.* But, I must trust myself. Trust the Self inside. The Self that animates this animal body. The Self that, is.

What is the first thing fed in the morning? What about a couple hours later? Do not fool yourself. What about a few hours after that? How about towards the end of the day? Do you forget? No tricks! No more!

Matters not, that it's not malicious. That it does not come from a "bad" place. Excuses. Justifications. No more forgetting. No more tricks. Conscious or unconscious. All, *enough*.

No more outside distractions. Or interior ones. Wild thoughts. No one to corral them. Reject all from the world's offerings. Its riches. Fame. Accolades. People, situations, things.

Shut it *all*, off. The news. Opinions. Ideas.

A year of *just me*, life, books, *my mind & thoughts*. No family drama; no outside speeches, lectures, ideas; no twitter, no news; *"if the world is going to burn, let it burn."* No *to-do, have* to, or *should*. Just me, my family of choice, our life; simple-ness, simplicity. Quiet, silence, peace. *Be still Heart of Mine.*

Soul, you are awake. At Peace. Never Apart from Me.

Note to Self:

Everything I read, learn about, pursue in knowledge; let it be casual, as if by accident. No forcing. No trying. Let it be. Unfold. Grow. Open mind. Open heart.

It's okay, not to know!

"The path is clear"
Grum|Disconnected

Melatonin

6/11/22|Dawn
Day 36 of 40
  3:34 a.m.

My soul is well this morning. All is well. Be at peace. See the joy, love, presence of everything. Be, The Moment.

Sun's out. Birds singing. Day's anew. Be refreshed. Love surrounds you. I am, Love. No split here. *Wholeness.*

Be, still. Be, quiet. —*Listen.* Rest. Relax. Enjoy. Rest. Rest. Rest. *Relax.*

11 am.

Guard; guard. my mind, my heart, my ears, my intellect. Guard, as others won't. Unknowingly, it will imprison me. Others' thoughts, opinions, ideas on reality, will overtake my own; I won't know what's mine, what's theirs.

> *"The truth is revealed by removing things that stand in its light, an art not unlike sculpturing, in which the artist creates, not by building, but by hacking away."*
> A. Watts

What stands in front of my light of Truth? What are my distractions? Obsessions?

Boredom. My Thoughts (*illusions, ideas, stories*). Media (*outside news, info*). Others (*those that don't matter, and, those that do*). Comparisons (*compare to no one, ever*). Past (*'hurts', memories, real & imagined*). Future (*what is to come, real & imagined*).

Hack away those things that dim the Light of Truth!

I feel calm right now. My soul is at peace. After so much turmoil, It rests. I wish to stay in this place. Of *peace and quiet*. Of not saying a word, as if not to break its enchantment.

Remember this. Be peace. Be still. Be silent. And, Know! I commune with my Soul. I feel Whole & complete. Keep this union. Don't split from me, soul of mine. I call you near. I call you unto me. Do not depart from me. *Union. Holy union!*

St. Teresa, Chap. 2

"...shall always and in every way see only what is good..."
"...amusement did not have bad effect on her that it came on me."

What is seemingly "good" for others, may not be for me. What doesn't lead others astray, may blind me. Distract me.

Know myself. My weaknesses. Importance of keeping good company. What kind of conversations am I engaging in? What subjects do I talk about?

"These ropes are just illusions"
Field Division|Modest Mountains

Get To The Root

6/12/22|Dawn
Day 37 of 40

I woke up today. Let me focus on that for a bit. The fact that I woke up. I should be grateful. Happy. Elated. And, I could fake it, but here, is supposed to be a safe place. Here, I can be nothing but honest. Because, it is all for me. From me.

I awake, but honestly...rather not. I don't want to die. But, honestly, how I feel...that is dead. I am not happy. *I have all I could ever want and need.* —But, *I don't have, ...me.*

Take the Mom, away; The Wife away; Home caretaker, cook, ...take it, all, away. I've stripped it bare; And, I just feel empty. It's a miserable feeling. I go to sleep with this feeling. I wake up to this feeling. To not know who I am. What I want. I'm very uncomfortable in it.

I think..."*I'll play video games.*" But, I ask myself, "*is that escaping?*" I think, "*I'll bake something.*" But, is that just a habit? I think, "*I'll take my new shoes out.*" But, I just think of the loneliness. I do feel lonely. I want conversation. Then I feel bad for wanting that. Remembering, that, what I currently have to offer, no one wants.

I, ...looked *forward*, to ...so much. The things we would, *do,* conversations, we would have. I have to get that out of my head. The thought, that I'll reach him, one day... That, what I say, has some value past that of a mini-crisis; when all, or almost all, is accepted. That magical day, when I've reached that "magical level." When I'm seen as, an equal. All around, no one cares, or wants to hear, what I have to say. No one is moved, to even feign interest.

Out of rebellion. Out of saving some dignity for myself, I wish I could do the same. Walk away, mid-sentence. Or whistle or hum to drown out my voice. My company. I like it. I enjoy it...and, only sometimes; —even *I* don't enjoy my own company. Truth is. I don't really have anything of value *to* say. I am empty.

I don't know who or what, I am.

Today, if I can analyze, I just feel very alone. A house full of people. Ignored most days. Bypassed. Hugs out of obligation. Conversation, ...mostly annoying. I don't view myself this way, do I? If all is a reflection...

I'm gong to go for a walk to clear my head. I want to scream. I am so sad.

❧ · ◆ · ☙

I let the day be the the day. And, it was a very good day, indeed.

What am I willing to forsake to connect with my soul? What negative company am I willing to not take part in, to be One with the Self? How long am I willing to guard my consciousness, allowing the ways of the world to dissipate?

I see a pattern of St. Teresa fighting her self. Being so susceptible to others' influence; *and, a pattern of finding resolution, within herself.*

What am I resolute about? "*...resolutely persist in a purpose from the beginning.*" Resolutely. Persist. From the Beginning. This requires a meditation. A thinking on things. On *listening*, more than talking. On not being hasty. Of a quieting down of all the senses. Trusting in the Self. Then, nothing is impossible. No fear.

Prayer (otherwise known to me, as meditation) of: Quiet; quieting, silencing the voices of the world, and, *Union; of coming into union with my own Higher Self.* Feeling of, marriage, between Self & self.

⇜⇝ — ◆ — ⇜⇝

Importance of solitude.

If the soul doesn't receive respite from the craziness of the world, might it "force" through other means, *that rest it so desperately needs,* if I am not listening to that need for quiet, solitude, and of union?

Subconsciously acting out. To ultimately get what it requires. What I require.

St. Teresa; "*...cursed be all loyalty that goes so far as to impinge on one's loyalty to (Self)*"

Many ways to deceive the self? "*However good the deed, one must never do the least wrong in performing it.*"

Intentions. Get to the root of it all. *Why do I do what I do? Why do I act the way I act?*

Question it all. Is the root...*fear, self-interest, arrogance, resistance, avoidance?*

"*I look to you to see the truth*"
Mazzy Star|Fade Into You

⇜⇝ — ◆ — ⇜⇝

Understanding

6/13/22|Dawn
Day 38 of 40

I don't understand. I wake up so sad. *Why?* Then, it takes all day to get to an okay place. I don't want to wake up like this anymore. It's like, I wake up grieving. But, ...*what?* My mind tries to conjure up reasons, explanations as to why I wake up so sad. I'm breaking my own heart it seems.

What am I grieving? I've been guarding against media and news. So, this comes from within. Why do the tears fall? *I really don't understand.* I want to wake up with joy in my heart and mind. With a passion for life. This morning, most mornings...I don't feel anything. *What is this numbness?* Who wants to live like this?

I don't know if this is grasping at straws, but, I do think of the year when it all, felt, broken, ...to me. When I saw my partner give up on me. Or, what it, felt like. When, the struggle became real and I saw myself utterly alone. All these years later, and I still feel remnants of it all. Kids treat me with contempt. Husband sees me as a child, needing coddling.

And it fills me with dread, that one day I won't have anything at all. Not even remnants.

I guess I feel that he'll tire of me. That my physical body will only call on him so much. That I'll never be good enough. Not what he desires. When he angers, I get the feeling I am a disappointment to him. Never quite reaching some level that is high enough to feel equal.

I fear, my children never, ever seeing me. How much I love them. How much I've overcome to try to be the best I could for them. And, it still not being enough. I see how I'm overlooked, ignored. My voice, just the mere sound, and I annoy, bother. It's all too painful.

I want to say a big *Fuck You* to *Everyone* that won't accept what I am offering. *Who I am. What I am.* But, I am too weak.

I, still, want and make myself believe I need, their approval. All I hear is, forget everyone else. Forget it all. But, that's so difficult.

I chose him. I love him. How do I just forget him. Indifferent to his praise, his wanting, his approval. We made kids together. Am I to just forget it all? Am I afraid, I'll just be forgotten? Like I never mattered?

Today, I'm tired of this *Red Book* bullshit. My soul is tired. Exhausted of thinking. Analyzing. Watching. Paying attention. I'm so tired.

I think of the illnesses, Teresa endured on her way to enlightenment. *Is this mine? Pain and illness of, 'the heart.'* I'm tired of the tears. I'm tired of the sadness. I want to wake up, just neutral. Yes, joyful would be wonderful, but, even neutral would bring peace to my soul.

What am I willing to endure, to come back to me? What and for how long am I willing to endure it for, just to feel in complete union with my soul? Soul, nurture me. Comfort me. Soul, enliven me. In these moments, it hurts all too much. Death would be relief. In my pathetic-ness, I believe no one would truly suffer. At first maybe, then...a relief for them, too. I can feel it. And, this makes me sad. To feel as if my absence would bring peace to all of them.

I think, to myself. If I don't cook or clean or pay the bills. Then what am I good for? Conversation? Nope. No one wants to hear what I have to say. Wisdom? Nope, I feel their condescending energy. I really despise this. I write until I am out of tears. Until, I am worn out. I'm terrified, ...to be completely forgotten. Un-needed.

What am I good for? Right now I don't feel like I bring anything to the table of Life. What do I have to offer? I don't bring joy into a room. I don't make people laugh. No one comes to me for council. I offer nothing. *I am nothing.* And, this doesn't feel good.

❧ · ✦ · ❧

"As long as I can be talked out of myself, I deserve to be."
Alan Watts

Wow! I'm starting to see a pattern here... The last few days, I've had to come to a place of, utter & total ...*Nothingness*. And, *then*, new insight comes. New perspective comes. Is this what all the Avatars mean, by having to *lose yourself*? Of Becoming *nothing*, to become *everything*?

A change, I can feel it.

Instead of dreading nothingness, —*I start to welcome it?*

It is quite uncomfortable, to be apart from myself. The more I draw within, the more that feeling of discomfort will come when I allow the distractions of this world to grab my attention, allowing it to cloud my thoughts, mind & heart. Steady resolution! Quiet & Silence. Retreat & Solitude.

<hr />

St. Teresa, says troubles lie in... "*...let(ting) my soul become so distracted by many vanities...*" and then I "*begin to lose my joy and pleasure in virtuous things.*"

I, departed from you. The soul's light begins to extinguish. Leaving only darkness. And, noise. What a nightmare. Quiet it all. Remove all distractions. And, see the flicker of light, grow bigger and bigger. *My soul never departs me, it is I, that departs from it.*

I may be "*deceiving those about me by presenting an outward appearance of goodness.*" But, I can not deceive my Self. At the end of the day, I know..."*what I am like within...*"

I can not escape this. "*...that one can see things, with other eyes than those of the body.*" = Intuition.

Teresa mentions the temptation, of trying to help others, while not knowing how to save herself.

Strike arrogance down, humble thyself.

She says, "*I had plenty of friends to help me fall. But, when it came to picking myself up I found myself completely alone.*"

<hr />

Tao Lounge|The Wait

❧ — ◆ — ❧

In And Out

6/14/22|Dawn
Day 39 of 40

> *"...only in the state of complete Abandon-ness and Loneliness that*
> *we experience the helpful powers of our true natures..."*
> Carl Jung

śramana - Sanskrit earliest recorded uses, Brihadaranyaka Upanishad, 6th century BCE.

It was thought that the Buddha went away from his father's house on śramana when became enlightened, then recommended the middle way.

Root word for, *Shaman.* Common theme: *Solitude.* First step in śramana, vow of silence (quiet). Take off all labels, that would identify me as someone, anyone.

❧ — ◆ — ❧

The past almost 40 days, I've gone through a process of finding out what, I am *not.* Who, I am *not.* How, I am *not.*

I've confused my feelings of "nothingness" and "loneliness," as "bad things." Not seeing, the great potential that lies in, getting rid of labels, titles, responsibilities, ideas, theories; and freeing the Soul of all that weight.

I begged my soul, to awake from its slumber. I so desperately wanted to feel "alive" again. I didn't realize that, it had never left me. It was, however, weighed down, under heavy blankets of, —so many illusions and concepts of "reality."

Now, I seek, ...more "nothingness." What else, can I shine the Light on?

I laugh, because there is no "doing." I haven't done anything other than, be in the quiet and solitude. The Blessing, of, having a family, *that affords me the space, to be in solitude and quiet.* The nothingness, just came. The loneliness, just came.

With no distractions, minimal busy work, sporadic, necessary conversations. The quiet sets in; The loneliness sets in. I realized I've *always,* been alone. Without *others, telling me what and who I am,* I realized, I don't know who or what I am... And, I realized, I am nothing.

Without filling roles of "mom" and "wife," of filling my hours with duty and chores, ...*what was my purpose?* I realized, *I don't have a purpose. It's all made up. Make-believe.*

Without goals, and plans and achievements, I begun to ask, ...*why? For what?* And, I realized, *it's all for nothing.* No, thing. No, body. *More,* than a body; *Everything.*

I realized, it's all illusions, games, play-pretend. Made up, by, all of us! *That,* opens up all the possibilities. It overwhelms me. So for now; More *Śramana,* ...*Solitude & Quiet.*

Nothing to figure out. Just be!

Can learn to be spontaneous while still being self-aware. Must become like a child. Freud says, children have innate "oceanic" sensation; feeling of, *being one with the Universe.* Can be at one with the Universe, in other words, become once again as a child, gain back the "oceanic" feeling, without forgetting "the game" of the world.

Playing it when needed, ...in and out, But, not forgetting it's a game.

See my Self, as I am, without judgement. Not by *trying,* I've seen where that gets me; —nowhere.

But, by simply being "*awake & relaxed.*"

St. Teresa, Chap. 8; "*I spent nearly twenty years on this stormy sea, falling and evermore rising again, but to little purpose as afterwards I would fall once more.*" Me too!

One of the most well-known mystics...falling and falling again. I have nothing to be ashamed of.

Meditation, contemplation, solitude, communion with Self, "there is no fear."

I've written often that I want to feel "alive." Called my soul to awaken. Communion with It. Eliminate the outside influences. And the Soul comes alive, it's being recognized! A purposeful Seeking, in a way. Seeking of what fills the Soul. Of turning away from all that wills me away from my Self. The distractions. The outside.

Meditation; A quieting of the outside; A looking within. A coming back to Self. Union. Becoming One! Realize... "*I was not living, but wrestling with the shadow of Death.*" Yes! Again, quiet & solitude! Frequent communing with, the Self!

"*I remember now*"
Field Division|Hollow Body Weather

Something Higher

6/15/22|Dawn
Day 40 of 40

I woke up neutral today! Not sad, not happy, not this or that! *Hallelujah!*

I guess, part of my confusion, laid in thinking that, I *had* to wake - *anything.*

I woke up with the nothing feeling. But, today, it was *not despair*. My mind quickly tried to fill it with memories and thoughts that would explain it all away. But, this time, I let them come and I let them go. I saw the blank canvas. And, moment to moment I get to fill it.

So, I'm going for a walk. I don't know for how long. And, I don't know what I'll do when I get back. But, *for right this mother-fucking-minute*, I'm going for a walk! Clear mind, steady breath. Clear Mind Steady Breath!

St. Teresa, Chap. 9; "*My soul had now become weary...imploring...give me strength once and for all...*"

Moved by an image of a "*terribly wounded,*" battered *Christ*, Teresa threw *herself* on the ground...Resolute, "*once and for all...*" "*...lost trust in herself and put all (her) confidence*" ...on something higher. "*How a soul suffers...by losing its liberty*", "*...began to give myself more constantly to prayer and to be less taken up with those things that did me harm.*"

"*Vibrating in unity*"
Minuk|Aurora

Unto My Self

6/16/22|Dawn
40|40

    Yesterday, was *40 days* since I started to write. To, *honestly*, write. 40 days of desert walking... of, fasting *The World.* Quiet Solitude; *self* in union with the *Self.*

    I don't, know. I don't, want. Nothing. Blank. Unlimited Possibilities. I'm determined to keep going. It's my only choice. To keep, writing. Discovering my Self. *A Red Book Year.* Limited outside voices. A worldly fast. *I am, my own Guru.* Open and willing to say, *"yes"* and *"why not?"*

    Up / Down. *In Union.*

    St. Teresa, ...many saints,... *all* saints, *"fall short of the glory of God."* [10]

    Accepted. Surrendered. Wholly, unto my Self.

    St. Teresa, Chap. 10; *"...walk in simplicity...endeavoring to please Him alone, and not men."* Meditation, contemplation, *"founded on humility"* *"...totally engulfed...soul is then so suspended...seems entirely outside itself. ...mind does not reason...but stands amazed at the many things it understands."* *"...continual tenderness in devotion..."*

    Considering my own loveliness (*animal*), by, thinking what my Spirit has done for me, *...how it sacrifices itself for me, ...its works in me, and its love for me.* Seeing how far it's brought me. Acknowledging the growth within me. *"God will take him into His house and has chosen him for His kingdom, if he does not turn back."* *"If we do not know what we receive, we shall never wake into love."*

    On the gifts of the Self:

    "...will give those jewels to one who will display them, and profit himself and others by their use." *"...impossible for anyone to have the courage for great exploits if he does not know that he is favored..."* *"unless a man realizes that he holds some earnest (in seriousness)..."*, the joys of the Spirit, *"...he will hardly succeed in abhorring and thoroughly detaching himself from the things of this world."*

    In a sense, must choose Self or World.

On Living Faith:

"*Our nature is so dead that we go after what we see in front of us...*" Trust the Self, the unseen. "*...how on a foul and stinking dunghill he has planted a garden of such sweet flowers...*"

St. Teresa, Chap. 11; "*...servants of love...what we become when we decide...the way...*" Comes down to me, always! "*...so slow to give ourselves entirely...*" ...to the Self. This wholly union with, my Self, comes quick by ...not clinging to anything here, turning all of my thoughts and conversations, *within!* No tricks, no putting a veil over the truth; that, while I may "think" that I am giving myself, wholly unto my Self, truth was, I was only "*offering the revenue*" of myself, while, "*still keeping the stock & ownership*" in my own hands.

Resolving "to be poor" but, often resuming my "precautions" and taking "care" not to be "short."

Giving up "all thought" of my "own importance." "Yet, the moments my self-importance is wounded" I "forget" that I have given my self unto, my Self.

Not managing to "*wholly...give ourselves up*", thus we, "*...never receive the whole of the Treasure...*" The Self, "*will not deny to one who perseveres...*" "*...little by little...strengthen that soul...that it may emerge with the victory...*"

The minor-self "*...put forward so many distractions, tricks of rationality...*" to prevent myself from "*setting out on that road...*"

Early stages of this renunciation to, the Self:

"*...it is in those early stages that the labor is the hardest (like drawing up water from a well) for the garden I'm to keep watered, so that the flowers may bloom, filling the air with their sweet scent.*"

Even if I "don't understand," or, feel unmotivated in my Self-awareness, uncomfortable in *the growth of consciousness*, trust that, *I will always be guided by, the Self*, who, all it asks is that, I give myself unto it; "*take up the cross*," as the Self has taken up the cross for my minor-self, in all of my unawareness; unconsciousness. - *All my life!*

Worry not for the garden of others. What grows, or how it is watered. Each path unique. Each Self, speaks to the minor-self in its own way. *Unique Language of, Love.*

Always trusting that my Self will, *always,* guide me; understanding...I am not my own, I am Yours! Submitting, willingly, lovingly. Though I may stumble, "*...draw empty from the well*" of understanding, I need not be afraid of "falling back" if it's begun on "firm foundation."

"*The Love...does not consist in tears or in these consolations and tenderness which we so much desire...in which we find comfort*" ...but in...serving...in... "*justice,*" truth; "*fortitude,*" strength of mind; "*humility,*" freedom from pride or arrogance.

"*...many who make a beginning...never succeeded in reaching the end...due...not having embraced the Cross, from the First...*" I must put my self on the *Cross,* and bring my "Self", down. —*resurrected.* "*...thy will be done...*"

Not mine. ...Not anymore. I look to you, Awakened Soul. I trust You will guide my steps, *as you always have.* You'll open the doorways, windows, portals and paths. And, I'll take courage in *You,* to go through them. *Fearless. Open Hearted. Full of Wonder. And, Love & Peace.*

On my part, at times, when it arises, I'll "*...serve the body...so that on many other occasions the body may serve the soul...*"

Remember to enjoy life. To play. *Let the Body enjoy this life to its fullest.* "*...no one should be distressed or afflicted because of aridities or disturbances or distractions in his thoughts...*" "*...if he wishes to gain freedom of spirit and not always to be troubled, let him begin by not being afraid of the Cross...*"

Seeing how the Self, helps me carry it, I'll carry on joyfully and, gain profit from, *Everything.*

"Safe to surrender now
I release what is not meant for me
I believe what's meant for me will be for me"
Doe Paoro|Divine Surrendering

Take Its Place

6/17/22|Dawn

Another wonderful day. A blank slate, canvas. Ah...my soul is at peace. *I still don't know what I want. Who I am.* And, *for the first time*, I mean it when I say, "*Hooray!*" This, is all, *...just getting started for me.*

Today, completely and utterly open. To ...everything. *Anything.* I feel a spring in my step, a, lightness, more like it; for no good reason.

I saw my love, sleepily make his way to the bathroom, I smiled, for no good reason. We played a random couple rounds of the "*hand slap*" game, just because, for no good reason. I sit here, I write. For no good reason. Because, ...I can. Because, *...I want to.*

I've re-read '*the 40 days*'...

The journey...thus far... through *honesty*. Through, different types of, *surrender*. Through *letting it unfold*, as if I had a choice. Realizing I never did, not in this. Through watching, observing. Feeling, noticing, and... letting it all go. The mirror, the reflections. *In every moment.*

To realize...the only choice I ever had was...*to surrender to, It.* That I, *am*, *It.* ...That, it is, *all*, *It.*

To be comfortable in solitude. In quiet. To, *Be*. In *giving*-it-all-up, ...I *gain* it all. In becoming, realizing, ...nothingness, ...*I experience my all*. To "resurrect" my soul, I only need to take its place; put my *self* on it, take up the cross. As, the *Self*, has done for me.

Instantly, my Self comes alive within me; Finally, Fully, Resurrected.

❖⋙ · ·◆· · ⋘❖

St. Teresa, Chap. 12; "*...a soul can perform many acts to confirm it in its resolution...and to awake to (love) in itself...*" "*...founded on humility...*"

On 'the spiritual path', and, how I won't rise unless, the Self rises with me:

"*...a sort of pride in us...that makes us wish to rise higher when God (Spirit, Self) is already doing more...by drawing us in our condition (just as we are) near to Him...*",

"...*grant(ing) them experience...however slight...they will immediately understand...*", "*For many years, I read a great deal, and understood nothing.*"

Worry not, though, because the *Self*, "...*teaches us everything in a moment, in the most amazing way.*" And, the *Self*, "...*will never allow...to be harmed who endeavors to approach... —with humility...*"

"That wherever I go, I'll find my way home"
Asgeir|Breathe

So Much, Aliveness

6/19/22|Dawn

Yesterday, I didn't journal. But, life was "*a happening.*"

The Beast and I laid in bed *all day*, having sex and just enjoying each other. Watching television. Started my day with a long walk on the trail by our neighborhood. Met a German Lady. But, mostly, ...I was with my Self! And, with *my* thoughts. And, with nature. And, some music. And, it was peaceful.

Came back from my walk, took a bath. Enjoyed my cup of coffee. I had a wonderful day with, my other.

But, I wonder how much of that is connected with, the day I was already having with myself. These days I'm looking after *my* needs. *My* wants. *My* desires. Being mindful not to, judge, separate, compartmentalize. Any of it. Let it flow. Observe. See. Experience. Indulge. Let it go.

This morning I woke up. Many hours still until the sun was due to come up. No other way to put it other than, I woke up *still so horny.* Even after all the *amazing sex* we've been having...I could feel so much, ...*aliveness...* between my legs.

This time instead of ...*fighting* my thoughts, my *desires. I gave in.* Didn't judge it. Nor suppress it. So, got out of bed. And, I sat in my chair, and, felt like watching porn, so, ...*I did.* I wanted to cum, and so, ...*I did.* Then sat and watched something. Had a coffee.

Satisfied; at peace.

Masturbation. A being, *physically*, with *oneself. Makes sense to me.* The aliveness I feel on the *outside*, matches what I am feeling, *inside.*

An awakening. *Burning desire.* Aliveness. *Fire.* Throbbing. Wanting. Makes sense. *As the Inside, the Outside.* As within, so without. In the small, in the large.

My other woke up. I *beamed* when I saw him. *Sleepily snuggled and cuddled my chest and neck.* I smelled him in. Caressed his skin with my lips. *Like a sweet smelling flower.*

The world, whole world, smells like that to me. I, smell like that to me.

> *"I need you, now I know*
> *Just give me one more time*
> *I'm gonna try and be your friend*
> *So we can beat the end"*
> M83|Solitude

❧ ⸱ ✦ ⸱ ☙

I Had A Dream

6/20/22|Dawn

I had a dream last night. Had to wake up at 5am to make a call, which interrupted this dream. Decided to take a few puffs, put some *frequency* music and, try to resume the Dream. After, *drifting*, ...went back in.

When finally I was ready to start my day, I wrote it down in my dream journal. And, then grabbed a red pen and *"Jung-ed it"* Like I do with movies. I'm, still figuring it all out. I get a sense it's all about integration. Assimilation.

Setting myself Free. Divorcing myself from *all that holds me back.* Practically, I feel the Dream speaks to my autonomy. Self-reliance. Mothering of the *self*, by, the *Self.* That, in my *IRL* partnership, I can be my own, He can be, his own, and *we*, can beautifully exist in this reality, *together.*

Sharing. Not holding on to. Not needing. Parallel paths. Forever and ever.

Refocusing on my "Well" where, I draw water from. Remembering this is all about me & Me.

Andrew Tuttle|Sun At 5 In 4161

‹‹›——•◆•——‹‹›

Today My Goal

6/22/22|Dawn

There is no good, no bad. Who is to judge?

Today my goal, *do not judge; criticize; label.* Let all just, Be. What, it is. Do nothing. Be nothing. No fixing. No thinking, No analyzing, No trying! No doing!

Open your eyes. Open them wide & see. Truly see! Remembering I am my own Judge, Jury & Executioner.

I am! I am! I am! I am!

Faodail|Untethered

‹‹›——•◆•——‹‹›

I Hold The Pen

6/27/22|Dawn

What the reflection of the Other showed me: it showed, *...my own critical mind.* How easy it is, for me to see the faults in others. How easy it is, for me to criticize the little stuff. Instead of relaxing. Holding on to tight. How, without a thought...bombard, picking at it.

Not being mindful that all my talking, could be a distraction, for the person listening. Not giving things a chance. Holding my nose up, *thinking I'm better.* Or *I* know best. *Arrogance.* It showed my insensitivity. How high I can get on my horse. My selfishness. All the times, it was all about me, fuck the other.

And, how bad I felt when I realized it.

No one "means" to do anything. Sometimes it's ignorance, sometimes, I am blinded to it. *How easy it is to see faults in others.* Pick out all of the small details that just aren't to my liking. But, how the perspective changes when a game is played.... Where up, is now down. Black, is now white. - *Wonderland!* Become a little *"mad,"* said the Cat.

Transforming it, completely. Turning the Mirror towards, myself. Then, in almost an instant, I can see, *those same faults in me and more.* Times I've acted much worse, to people who deserved it even less. *Then, there are no hurt feelings. No sadness. No victimhood.* Just truth. Raw, Clear, Unfiltered!

Then, a new promise arises in the heart...to not allow myself to act that way any longer. That I am compassionate and sensitive. That I give allowances and space. That in all of my security and confidence of my truth, that I still allow my mind and heart to be open to learn & grow. In allowing other's "faults" *to be my greatest mirrors,* reflections of what, *I've,* yet to master.

...wallowing in pain and sadness is a huge distraction, simply put.

Open my eyes and See! No stories. No narrative. To allow for an array of *others* "doing things." Not thinking *my way* is best. The many times I saw my own children, trying their best and through my words, deflated their will. But, also it shows me the strength of *my* will. Of how "firm" I stand. In the moment. I put the word in quotations to remind myself that it's broader than that...It's being firm in who and *what* I am. In each movement. Changing with the winds and going with the Flow...And, always simply being me.

Instantly my heart is calmed. My mind is clear. I'm at peace. And, I'm resolved, because in this moment I saw, *MYSELF!*

No more "lip service," I have to *prove* it. And, I am. I don't want anything not easily given. Or deserving. Makes total sense, *this is what I've built.* But, no longer. I want and will build something *new!* Something better! I don't have to wait to be 40. Let it "happen" *now.* And, it is.

You wanted to feel alive. *You are.* You wanted to tingle again, *here ya go. Enjoy it!* I am 39, I turn 40 in 6 days. I don't have to wait. *Embrace it, all, now.* Whatever pops up, *do it, be it, feel it, let it be.*

How easily you forget... I am in every moment, *writing "my book"*...what do I want it to read...TO ME? *TO ME!* To fucking me! *It isn't for anyone else.*

Tomorrow! Page one!

Alone! I am holding the "pen;" *I am "telling" the Story.*

What do I want it to be?

> *"Fever in me Fever, cold shots through the night*
> *Oh, it winds me, Catch fire in the dark"*
> Diamond Thug|Sapphire

Wholeness, I Am

6/29/22|Dawn

I woke up this morning, with the thought of how, *I am authoring my book; my life. With every thought, idea, feeling, memory, I write the words unto the pages.*

I reminded myself to relax into my Beingness. To, let the day unfold...naturally... So, I thought of all I've put off, to study, to research, to *do.*

And, I thought I'll do that...or I'll sit.. or I'll play... or I'll nap... I'll just *be*...Eat when hungry. Dance if there is music. Dance, *even if there isn't.*

Dancing with *The Beast* in the kitchen. Lovely impromptu moment, only happens because the vibe is just right. Because there is, *connection.*

Realize, that if I want to experience the unknown, I must, as best & as much as I can, release, let go all that has been, to allow the *new,* to be.

Today, I can feel what it is to just be, let be, and allow. It all unfolded...It's still unfolding. In all the time I've spent being confused, wondering, I see that, *the more relaxed I am, in this life, the more I walk in my own Self, the less wondering...the less confusion.* When all is allowed to just, *Be, it's easy.*

I see the Freedom...*It's all around me.* I am completely unbounded. I am free to be and do...And, I'm taking advantage of this. Literal electricity runs through my body. Awakening from a slumber. Tingles, from head to toe. I begged my Self for this. At times its felt shocking. Overwhelmed with the amount of energy...sometimes all over my body. Sometimes all over my sacral chakra, *as if I was 19 again.* But, *not* a *desperate* wanting, just, *a knowing,* ...of what is to, come. *Literally.*

Sometimes in my head...a sense of so much greatness and bigness. Visions, but not really visuals. More of a, *...sense.*

Knee-jerk reactions want me to fear. So much unknown. But, the more I embrace it, the more it is starting to feel familiar. Words don't do this justice, I can feel myself, *not* separate. It's all I want. *To not be so split.* Wholeness, ...I am!

> *"You can feel it in your mind, Oh you can feel it all the time,*
> *Plug it in and change the world, You're my electric girl,*
> *I said ooh girl, Shocked me like an electric eel"*
> Henry Green|Electric Feel

In My Hands

6/30/22|Dawn

   I get to write it. I won't allow anyone to write it *for* me. Only my hand to pen. Directing each word on the Page. *Building my reality;* instead of blocks, *words & thoughts. The true blocks for my reality.*

   Dispense, throw away, all that gets in the way. Dump it, erase it, let it go. All, that sets my eyes on anything that isn't me. My reality. Freedom comes to those who, —unburden *themselves!*

ZHU|Palm of My Hand

Firewalking

7/3/22|Morning

...just, ...Glowing;...Irradiated;...Aflame;...

...Resorbed;...Deified;...Liberated;...Risen;...

...Undeterred;...Found;...Trans-Medium;...

...Unfathomable;...Disclosed;...Reporting, Alive;...

...Observant;...Individuated;...Illumined;...

...Self-Governed;...Amorous;...Whole;...

...Astro, Logical;...Unbound;...Firewalking;...

> *"And side by side, we're different, but*
> *somehow the same, It really shouldn't work*
> *but it does, It really shouldn't work but it*
> *does, When it comes to us,*
> *Ooh, ooh, ooh, oh, oh, oh"*
> RITUAL|When It Comes To Us

To Be Born

7/1/22|Dawn

Resolve. That is what I received in my time of meditation. I saw myself, *naked, curled-up, inside the chrysalis.*

Awaiting. A, knowing. That it has to die. It has to, *not* be, to *Be.* I reminded myself that its only Three Days until my birthday. Words echoed in my head... *"Are you ready to be born?"* That is the feeling I had. In that visual. Curled up. *Awaiting.* Resting. Asleep. A, knowing. Am I ready to be born? *I am ready.* Resolved!

I thought of St. Teresa. Of *her* resolve. Of *her* 20 years of stormy seas. Of turning 40. *Of the last 40 years.* Of how the next could be, different. A build-up. To this moment. A true understanding of the phrase, "now or never."

I question often, if it could be that easy. *But it is.* The last couple days, prove that. Relaxing into my Beingness. Relaxing into my Life. Relaxing into my existence. It all just, ...flows. Easy. This morning I had, an opportunity for total distraction from my Self. But, I *chose. I choose. I* write the Words. I won't let another do it for me. *Not anymore.*

It isn't that life, isn't going to happen; *people will people,* but, *I choose. I get* to choose.

I realize that as I put my parents and other people out of my mind, so much room is left to dedicate to, *me.* To what's mine. To what *I'm* interested in. I see more and more that everyone and everything, whether on purpose or not, is always trying to tell me, who and what I am.

But, ...*that's up to me.* I, ...tell *my* story.

This morning I meditated; just to be with myself like that. To let my thoughts run a little...To deal, head on, no-nonsense with whatever "voice" is wanting to get heard. And, to get to a place of quiet; of union; of wholeness. Then, I crawled back into bed. Cuddles with my love. And, a super hot *make-out sesh* before coffee.

This, is my reality. This, is the page that gets written today. These are the details.

During meditation, I realized that, *for whatever reason*, I engage in self-sabotaging behavior, right when I'm at the brink of something; ...a fear, no confidence...

So, I'm not allowing, even the smallest distraction to set my "eyes" on anything that isn't me. Me. *I look forward to this year*, a bit with trepidation of, the unknown. Makes my heart flutter. Makes me tingle & vibrate all over. But, this time. I'm resolved. Ready. To be born. *To, Be!*

I imagined these next couple days. ...3 to be exact. In my cocoon. I could see my body, *all curled up*. Awaiting. Knowing. And, I imagined, *the Chrysalis cracking*. No longer a caterpillar, who crawled, unaware of what was to come...

And, there I saw, instead, *beautiful wings*, beginning to unfurl. These weren't ordinary wings. Not quite butterfly, but just as colorful. Not hummingbird wings, but just as fast. Not wings of a dove, but just as soft and pure. *A combination of these, and, ...something else altogether.*

That's what will happen, on the day of my birth. Renewed and made anew by, *the rays of the Sun.* Bathing in its warmth. Unfurl Your Wings, —*it's time.*

Sol Rising|Arise

Crowning

7/2/22|Dawn

Resolve. Don't forget. Focus. Moment to Moment. I author today. I author each Moment.

Remember my vow. To never cast doubt or worry. To not hurt or cause upset. My vow, to ...my Self.

Ready to be BORN? —The time is *NOW.*

Embrace it all; See it all; Hold, on to nothing.

Love Love Love

Ott|The Queen of All Everything

Shadow Love

7/3/22|Morning

The Path; The Journey; The Adventure; The Wait; ...The, Plan.

> Rooted in the *dark*, bursting with
> the ripest of new *fruit*, shining forth
> brilliantly with a new inner *spark*; and
> all it took was to once again embrace,
> —*the Birthday-Suit;*

I have, been feeling this for weeks now, the rise, of a new energy within her. I have, seen her struggles, felt her pain, sadness, fear, and, ...*resisted the heroic call*; resisted the Nature, to swoop in, to ride my trusty steed to the rescue. I have, been on *my own journey*;...perhaps the toughest *of all lessons* learned, that, when you really, deeply, *truly* care for, the *overall* wellbeing of another, you must be willing to *not* show it.

You must withhold your admiration and affection, *that it not cause this dearly loved other, to stumble.* For, a hero shall always be looked to, for *continued* rescuing; the Savior is not a one-off, it is a *lifelong career.* The Churches remain full, only because, *they've yet been set free by the Clergy*, who, *need the People*, as much as the People, *need the Clergy.* Each, absolutely blinded in their, utter dependence upon the Other.

A tough lesson indeed, in that, when you deem to *set-free*, fully...completely...*eternally and infinitely*, the Soul of someone you love so deeply, *that she might spend with you, the same eternity, you are now so assured of for, your own Self*, you must be willing, to get out of, the Way; ...*out of his way, her way, their way.* You must be willing to, ...*stand-down*;... *to, sit... shut the fuck* up... *hide in the Shadow.* Observe with loving and caring eyes, resisting each call from within to ride to the Rescue; *...for, you know the Truth of your own Self, thus that of all the Other;*...that, each and every Soul, *must free his and her own damned Self.*

Each must struggle; *each* must be depressed with, their ancient concept of Life; *each* must surrender, all; *each* must give-up; *each* must die, fully, completely, to what they, childishly, believe themselves to be or not be, that something absolutely Grand and New might, begin a process of, Birth, Death, Regeneration and Absorption, back into the Folds of this Cosmos that, calls out to each of us from, *within,* ...begging, we acknowledge *It,* as, *our own Self;*

The wise Man is never *truly* alone; the wise Man *knows,* he is, surrounded, *by ripening Fruit* indeed; —*ready to burst, themSelves;* Born, *once Again;* ...Liberated; Free; Independent; and, ...*Infinite.*

❧⟫⟩ · · ◆ · · ⟨⟪☙

The *Birthday* Letter:

My Love, My Beauty;

We have been talking about our birthdays a lot recently, haven't we? Forty, can be a bummer for most of our peers, and even those who embrace the Cycles, merely do so secretly, hidden darkly even from their own selves.

Enjoy your re-birthday, my Love; enjoy embracing and knowing your own Self this year and beyond, in liberated ways only a woman with life experience can truly appreciate. Set yourself free, my Love, most importantly from your own self-condemnation, judgment, pressure, labels, and old stories.

Forty years aged is, the perfect year to set out anew, leaping from a firm and solidly-squared foundation, into a new infant-like pursuit of joy and growth, for the simple sake of natural joy and growth, without any pressure but to be aware of it every step of the cosmic way. Embrace your Self in freedom, as the confident, wise and experienced Woman you are; the Divine Cosmic Creature you have always been.

As you seek yourSelf intellectually and spiritually, authorize your own freedom, to, for the first time in your life, fearlessly pursue yourSelf in every and any manner...be free my Love;... now, and forever;... embrace your Self, in body as well as mind, that the Soul which you truly are, can fly as free and high as the Fairy-With-Wings that she's always felt she is.

Allow for your mind to wander and explore pathways to your own body and spirit that perhaps you've never truly been able to comfortably and relaxedly explore, especially as a grown woman with very experienced and deep wants and desires which, call to her from the deepest and darkest crevices of her mind...and sultry body.

Be free, for the first true time in your still very young life, to wildly explore with both body and mind, in unison.

Embrace your youth my Love; embrace your mind; embrace your damn body, repeatedly, tire it out with pleasure, that you sleep peacefully, as the innocent newborn you are;... explore and experience all that you can this year, and forevermore.

Be free to explore yourSelf, with a freedom you perhaps wished you had when younger, and long ago forgot was possible; without judgment from anyone, especially from the few of us who can claim, to truly love everything about you, but most importantly, ...without judgment from yourSelf; stop, judging yourSelf; Be, Free, to allow whatever can happen in this life, to just ...happen;... if we cannot freely, without shame, enjoy the pleasure and touch of our very own Self, then, how dare any of us claim we seek freedom from, ...anything.

Be free my Love, on your Birthday, as we celebrate forty together in a, renewed and reinvigorated pursuit of, Life.

Be Free, You; be free to embrace and become, your Self; balanced and Whole and unafraid of herSelf; be free to experience waves of unending pleasure, which is nothing but an external portal to the internal reality;... shake off the generations of self-imposed shame that continues to lie upon your tired back;... free yourSelf, to Be and embrace the Creature that you truly are, in All of its manifestations;... be not ashamed, of the Being that you are, Inside and Out;... let no other Soul tell you what is supposed to be right or wrong; correct or incorrect.

You are Free, but, you must accept, This Freedom, my Love;... any cage you allow yourSelf to be put in, now, even by yourSelf, is a cage you risk remaining in forevermore, until, you eventually realize the Truth I now tell you; ...you, are, Free, my Love;...

No pressure upon you to do or be, any damn thing;... enjoy the Freedom of Being, nothing, just as the Child;... this is Freedom; whether Four or Forty, or anywhere in-between, be them, all, my Love. You, are Free now, ...to choose who you are, at any given moment and place;... you are, equally Nothing and Everything, just as every child naturally, feels it Self to be.

   Happy Birth-Day, Baby;

   Embrace your own Self, courageously, without fear, as I shall be doing the same, that, Together we are fearless and unshakeable as we drift into our future; forever United and Whole.

   I have, always, loved everything about you, and, now, ...you do as well; you see, now, how incredible your Self has always been; from, —the Beginning.

   Be young; Be free.

> *"So when you remember the ones, who*
> *have lied, Who said that they cared but*
> *then laughed as you cried, Beautiful darling*
> *don't think of me... Because all I ever*
> *wanted, It's in your eyes, baby-baby-baby,*
> *And love can't lie no,*
> *Greet me with the eyes of a child"*
> George Michael|Father Figure

Epilogue

BIRTH & DEATH

"You and I bloodlines
We come together every time
Two wrongs, no rights
We lose ourselves at night"
Jessie Ware|Wildest Moments

The Birthday

7/5/22|Morning

> *"Many Taraxacum species produce seeds
> asexually... where the seeds are produced
> without pollination, resulting in offspring
> that are genetically identical to the parent
> plant."*
> Dandelion [11]

> *"Diogenes, speaking in jest, credited the
> god Hermes with its invention: he allegedly
> took pity on his son Pan, who was pining for
> Echo but unable to seduce her, and taught
> him the trick of masturbation in order to
> relieve his suffering. Pan in his turn taught
> the habit to young shepherds."*
> Masturbation [12]

> *"The bright yellow Dandelion flower is a
> symbol of growth, hope, and healing. ...there
> is more to this flower than meets the eye."*
> Petal Republic [13]

It had been 4 days since I soaked the beans. No, ...this is no metaphor. The sticky-note said, *"July 1st, noon"*...

4 days... a blur of psychedelic experiences.

Starting with a 4 hour (or near it), bath & toys meditation, where, for the first time I allowed myself to *truly* be with my Self and self, in *all* the ways.

The hours passed, like minutes.

One orgasm ending in what seemed like, a star burst, bursting in the middle of my chest. Radiating 'heat' but, it didn't burn. Brightly shining, a light so bright and white.

I took my time drying. Oiling my body. And getting ready. To join the World, again. To be born, again. Free. Fearless.

I climbed into bed with him. Satisfied. Clean. Felt brand new.

He said I glowed, Even hours after.

On the day of my birth, *I was birthed again.*

One moment, I remembered how good it felt to go under the water, almost completely submerged. Just my face, barely above the surface. The noise drowned out. Body, hugged by the water.

Like being back in the womb. Nurturing my watery nature.

Reborn. This time with the wisdom of the Cosmos.

Breath-taking! Takes my breath away. I feel so fucking alive.

We spent the whole day talking, Molly-Style, *except no one had taken a pill.* We've spent all of these days that way. On a 'molly-lucy'-sensual-trip, *day after day.* All seeming like a dream.

Edges hazy... But, *feeling it all... seeing* it all... *being* in it... *All* of it...

All of, me! Whole! Complete!

Finally, I'm free. And, he is free. *From my claws.* From my illusions & delusions. 20 years, culminates...

I am whole. He is whole. I am Free. He is Free. I am open. He is open. We are truly, open. No fear. No holding back. A finally going-with, what I feel. Urges. Desires. Curiosities. Adventure.

All has died away, nothing and no one to tell me 'no.' To tell me what to do. I finally *need* nothing of no one. I am fulfilled.

I fulfilled myself.

I am over-flowed, *because I filled 'mine own cup!'* Out of that overflow, I shine out. To those attracted to my Light. And guard against those who, unconsciously wish to steal it or extinguish it.

Author of this Life, My Life.

I *still* feel like I'm on Molly... *barely* smoked weed... *forgetting* to drink coffee...

I'm in it. *Finally!*

My body feels so alive, my mind open, *wide.*

My heart, still... *mine.*

'This is how, I live now.'

"The tantric texts of ancient India and the Egyptian narratives both describe the appearance of the cosmos as the result of a sexual act by the gods."

P. Lavenda|Gods [14]

"Masturbation was also an act of creation and, in Sumerian mythology, the god Enki was believed to have created the Tigris and Euphrates rivers by masturbating and ejaculating into their empty riverbeds."

Masturbation [15]

The Death

7/9/22|Morning

> *"The night I laid my eyes on you, Felt everything around me move,*
> *Got nervous when you looked my way, But you knew all the words to*
> *say, Then your love slowly moved right in, All this time, oh my love,*
> *where you been? Mi amore, don't you know? My love, I want you so"*
> Kryder|Rapture

> *"All the lights go out, the colors have faded, Every breath I take, I'm*
> *reminded of You, So much time goes by, but it's like nothing changes,*
> *Are you lonely tonight? Wish I knew, Because you're in my heart,*
> *You're in my head, You're in the silent space between,*
> *Right from the start, Until the end"*
> Tritonal|Back To My Love

I see you, *my Love...*

I see you... all of you... you've been here, next to me, by my damned side...this whole time.

Oh, *my Love...* how far we've come, hand in hand without knowing... *a secret between us from the start...* a necessary one, for we knew not, *our own Selves.*

I see you, *my Love...*

I no longer see you with *my* vision, for *you,* are, my vision *now, my Love;...* with you always I have been, *in a dark shadow of my own...* trailing as the puppy I am, in your mighty presence... lost I have been, *my Love,* yet never alone... together forever, now we know for sure... no more a hope or fantasy, of a desperate child seeking, *love and attention...* together forever now, *my Love...* you are and have always been, *my Everything.*

I see, *The Beauty;... you;...* you have reflected so much to me... it flooded back and has left me, *overwhelmed, my Love...* with gladness I *feel, The Beauty that you are*, and have always been and, shown so brightly...

I was blinded by your Light, *my Love...* I truly see you now... where once I was ignorant, *now I am wise,* for I see you, *my Love...*

I see *The Beauty* that you *truly* are... as you have been *this whole time.* You once again leave me speechless...

I shall just do, what I know how to do best... *admire and be in silent awe* of, a Beauty I have sought after my whole life and, have witnessed bloom into... into... *no words... you* are *indescribable* now to me...

I do not know what you are other than, *pure and absolute, beautiful, Love...* you have me arrested here...

I can't move... *and I accept it...* if I see you *now,* I might die... but of course this is a selfish desire of mine... *to tell you these things...*

I just...

I have waited so long to *feel this... Love.*

I can *feel her, The Beauty... You, my Love...*

I feel *everything* now...*I feel.*

And... *The Beauty...* in that you have literally today, shown me The Way... *to feel*....all of you...all of it...*everything... The Beauty,* of the struggle of, *a life that was yours, my Love...* you are indescribable to me!... your enduring strength... from the very beginning, *my Love...* it overwhelms me...

I think I've avoided *your story, my Love...* the pain... the darkness... the fear... *I feel it now...*

I know you so completely at this moment... the loneliness... the long scary nights... *all of them...*

I see you now... The Beauty...that comes from all of that damned chaos... *and my own dark role,* in this *Beauty that you are...* it's too much... you have from the start... *overwhelmed me...*I avoided you, *my Love...*

I said no, so many times... you were, too much...

I was... so afraid... you were... *too beautiful...* you... *looked at me, my Love...*

I *felt* you... *you moved me...*

I avoided your love... I feared you, *my Love*...

I fear you now... *your love burns*...

I feel it too deeply now...

I don't know what to do... how does a nothing like me... move on from *this?*... I'm so lost...

I thought I was strong, *my Love*...

I'm so weak... I can't be *The Beauty*...

I surrender to, *Everything, that you are... that I could never be*... never was.

...Lost without you, *my Love*... and now.... *feeling... so found!*... the true reflection that you are... *all of it* beaming into me at this moment... revealing all that I am, and, all that you have been *this whole time*...

I feel you now, *my Love*, truly...

I start as a newborn... *my Love*... One mighty breath at a time...

I see now, *The Beauty*...

I see in my own indescribable desperation to, *just GIVE my love*... we have always been balanced... before we even met...

I see you balancing me, fearlessly in the darkness in which, *only true Beauty can root*... in your lonely, indescribable desperation to, *just BE loved*...

I feel you, *my Love*...and I see... *humbled* I am...*worthless* I feel... unworthy of so much, *my Love*.

...overwhelmed by joy, *my Love*... truly happy within, the sadness that is *The Beauty*... she is... *Everything*.

...where once I was blind, *my Love*... now I see... *you*... standing there beside me... lost *I was... yet never alone*... found *I am*... and, home... truly home.

...so much love, *mi Amor*... literally all of it... *all I can summon from the cosmos,* I shower upon you with every breath, every thought, every beat of this unworthy heart...

I surrender now to, *The Beauty*.

I may stare...I may cry... my tears may flow as the ocean itself... but fear not, *my Love*...

I am, simply, allowing you to witness, *what has been kept inside, this whole time*... a little boy... overwhelmed by a *Beauty,* he was not warned about... a fire that burns in which, he was never taught, could hurt so much... a small nothing, caught in the net of a *Beauty* that, *has continued to overwhelm this, innocent yet beastly heart...*

I know not how to proceed forward, without *ignoring, The Beauty* you are. *...it kills me... it leaves me paralyzed...*

I have ignored you for so long... *I see now...*

I am indeed rewarded, *with all this emotion... all this feeling...* for now I have learned,

I have become wise,

I have seen *The Beauty* of, Love, *that you have reflected, my Love...* only *now that I truly see what love is...* can I embrace my own answered prayer... *to just, love... love... love... love... love... love... love,* as I have always desired to...

I feel the Love that, *you are...*

I *accept* it all...*all of you...* and surrender to the power of it, to everything... in you, *my Love,* is my salvation... in you, is the light that is my own... and now I can truly reflect, the same love back to you, the same love you so humbly prayed for as such a small girl... *now complete...* together now, fully, *my Love...*

I am you. You are me. We are we.

'*...waiting, under the bright full moon...*', you say... of course... *right where you have always been;...* I saw you not, and yet there you were... a blinded fool I've been... *but no more... you* are my vision now... *I see... Everything...* yet blinded by the shimmer of, the full pregnant moon that you are, *my Love...* waiting this whole time, to birth your love upon me... *me?...who am I?...*

I must be you... because, only you could take this... *feeling...* this... *Everything...*

I am nothing if not, *The Beauty....*

I see now, *my Love,* all that you have always been, that I was blinded to... or, ignored ignorantly... you were there in all your radiance, and I was in awe...

I failed to look further inside... no longer, *my Love...* I swear to you...

I *feel* you now... *you are not alone...*

I promise you... *no more lonely nights...* never again... you are whole inside, and out.

I am here and I see, it is *The Death, of myself,* that allows for *The Beauty* to have true birth...

I feel you, *my Love*, and, yes... this, ...you, together, *us united*, ...*is how I live now.*

"*And if I saw you right now, I'm not sure what I'd say, There's only
so many words, A dead man can say*"
Low Roar|St. Eriksplan

"*Just a fool to believe, I have anything she needs, She's like the wind,
I look in the mirror, And all I see, Is a young old man, With only
a dream, Am I just fooling myself, That she'll stop the pain? Living
without her, I'd go insane*"
Patrick Swayze|She's Like The Wind

"*We know that from time to time, there arise among human beings,
people who seem to exude love as naturally as the sun gives out heat.*"
A. Watts [16]

"*It's like you live in these walls, I hear your voice down the hall, I
swear I see your face it's everywhere, its every place, I starve myself
past the pain, But still it won't go away, The more I try to forget, I
remember*"
O-Town|Craving

"*The aim of all philosophy, he said,
is to teach one how to die.*"
M. Booth|Secret History [17]

Sol

> *"Oh, my love, my darling*
> *I've hungered for your touch*
> *A long, lonely time"*
> Unchained Melody

The End, is, The Beginning
The Beginning, is, The End
Two, Become, One

> *"And time goes by so slowly,*
> *And time can do so much,*
> *Are you still mine? I need your*
> *love, I, I need your love,*
> *Godspeed your love to me"*
> Unchained Melody

Luna

"Oh I've been contained
But there's a power to be set free"
My Stripes

The Beginning, is, The End
The End, is, The Beginning
Two, Become, One

"Look in my eyes,
See a light that shines a different hue,
In a modern life that don't suit, my stripes"
My Stripes

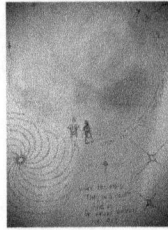

Solunarukh

"Again I say unto you, That if two of you shall agree on earth as touching any thing that they shall ask, it shall be done for them of my Father which is in heaven."
Matthew 18:19|KJV

"The Solar was a room in many English and French medieval manor houses, great houses and castles, mostly living and sleeping quarters. Within castles they are often called the "Lords' and Ladies' Chamber" or the "Great Chamber"...In manor houses of Normandy and northern France, the Solar was sometimes a separate tower or pavilion, away from the great hall to provide more privacy to the lord and his family."
Solar Room [18]

"The rook (rukh) is a piece in the game of chess. It may move any number of squares horizontally or vertically without jumping, and it may capture an enemy piece on its path; additionally, it may participate in castling. Formerly, the rook (rokh/rukh, meaning 'chariot') was alternatively called the tower..."
Rukh [19]

What were once two individual Souls, passing in the Darkest of Nights; —*ecstatically collide!*; awakening to *The Realization*, that, their supposed separate stories, were, from the beginning, simply, *The Story, as One*; —*evolved.*

> *"We share this hurt, we share the pain, All*
> *of our dirt is washed in the rain, We've*
> *walked that road, we've felt that shame,*
> *Mmh but times, they are changin', You are,*
> *you are, You are safe with me, This is our*
> *sanctuary, We can find shelter and peace,*
> *This is our sanctuary"*
> Welshly Arms|Sanctuary

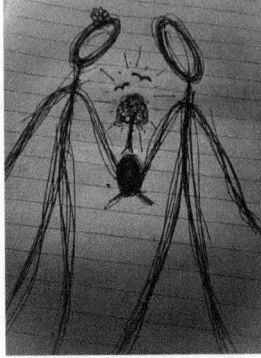

9/18/20
All You Need

9/21/20
Shamanic Journey

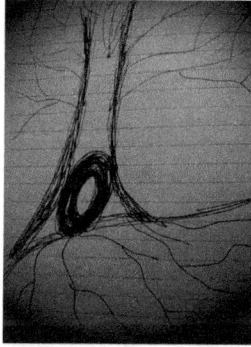

9/23/20
Upper World

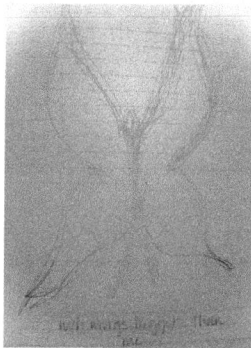

10/26/20
The Call

2/5/21
Always Has Been

6/5/22
Blooming

"In alchemical symbolism they appear as
the alchemist and his woman friend, and
the king and queen in the retort. Only
when the two partners can relate to all
these figures can one speak of a complete
relationship, and therefore love in modern
terms becomes a vehicle of the process
of individuation and the development of
higher consciousness."
Marie-Louise von Franz
The Feminine In Fairy Tales

1. https://earthobservatory.nasa.gov/images/92789/recovering-from-hu
   rricane-maria

2. https://en.wikipedia.org/wiki/Jurac%C3%A1n

3. https://en.wikipedia.org/wiki/Coqu%C3%AD

4. https://www.jpost.com/breaking-news/hurricane-maria-clobbers-pu
   erto-rico-plunges-island-into-darkness-505645

5. https://time.com/5627564/puerto-rico-protests-what-to-know/

6. https://time.com/5627564/puerto-rico-protests-what-to-know/

7. https://www.univision.com/univision-news/united-states/why-so-m
   any-earthquakes-in-puerto-rico

8. https://en.wikipedia.org/wiki/Tembleque

9. https://time.com/5760461/puerto-rico-earthquake-news/

10. https://archive.org/details/lifeofsaintteres00tere

11. https://en.wikipedia.org/wiki/Taraxacum

12. https://en.wikipedia.org/wiki/Masturbation

13. https://www.petalrepublic.com/dandelion-flower-symbolism/

14. https://www.simonandschuster.com/books/Sekret-Machines-Gods/
    Tom-DeLonge/Sekret-Machines-Gods-Man-War/9781943272402

15. https://en.wikipedia.org/wiki/Masturbation

16. https://www.organism.earth/library/document/spectrum-of-love

17. https://archive.org/details/secrethistoryofw00boot

18. https://en.wikipedia.org/wiki/Solar_(room)

19. https://en.wikipedia.org/wiki/Rook_(chess)

love is awareness

let love reign

www.ingramcontent.com/pod-product-compliance
Lightning Source LLC
Chambersburg PA
CBHW031817270326
41932CB00008B/456